A collection of ponderings full of wit and wisdom from the pen
of a mountain preacher living in the Town of Pittman Center,
in the Great Smoky Mountains of East Tennessee

THE PASTOR'S
PONDERINGS

Pastor Alta Chase-Raper
With Foreword by Mayor Glenn Cardwell

WESTBOW
PRESS
A DIVISION OF THOMAS NELSON

All scriptures quoted in this manuscript are from the following five versions and will be identified as either: KJV, NKJV, NIV, NLT, or NJB

KING JAMES VERSION, 1987 printing. The KJV is public domain in the United States. (No Limit)

NEW KING JAMES VERSION *. Copyright © 1982 by Thomas Nelson, Inc. Used by permission. All rights reserved. (Up to 250 verses)

THE HOLY BIBLE, NEW INTERNATIONAL VERSION®, NIV® Copyright © 1973, 1978, 1984, 2011 by Biblica, Inc.® Used by permission. All rights reserved worldwide. (Up to 500 verses)

Scripture quotations marked (NLT) are taken from the Holy Bible, NEW LIVING TRANSLATION, copyright © 1996, 2004, 2007 by Tyndale House Foundation. Used by permission of Tyndale House Publishers, Inc., Carol Stream, Illinois 60188. All rights reserved. (Up to 500 verses)

THE NEW JERUSALEM BIBLE, Copyright © 1985 by Darton, Longman & Todd, Ltd. and Doubleday, a division of Bantam Doubleday Dell Publishing Group, Inc.

WestBow Press books may be ordered through booksellers or by contacting:

WestBow Press
A Division of Thomas Nelson
1663 Liberty Drive
Bloomington, IN 47403
www.westbowpress.com
1 (866) 928-1240

Because of the dynamic nature of the Internet, any web addresses or links contained in this book may have changed since publication and may no longer be valid. The views expressed in this work are solely those of the author and do not necessarily reflect the views of the publisher, and the publisher hereby disclaims any responsibility for them.

Any people depicted in stock imagery provided by Thinkstock are models, and such images are being used for illustrative purposes only. Certain stock imagery © Thinkstock.

ISBN: 978-1-4908-0495-8 (sc)
ISBN: 978-1-4908-0496-5 (hc)
ISBN: 978-1-4908-0492-7 (e)

Library of Congress Control Number: 2013914906

Printed in the United States of America.

WestBow Press rev. date: 09/27/2013

To

My Mother
Frances Alta (Musgrove) Chase

The Memory of
My Husband and my Daughter
Clyde Vernon Raper (1944-2009)
Rev. Maria Luise Parham-Newman (1965-2010)

My Sons
Samuel Chase Blair
John Ralph Parham
Victor L. Loveday, Jr.

and to
The People of Pittman Center, Sevier County, TN

Foreword

After several years of raising a family and being employed in the business world, Alta Raper surrendered to the call of the ministry in the United Methodist Church. Her surrender to that call in 2000 required her to return to school, at age sixty, taking special courses of study for her assignment. Her first and only appointment was to become pastor of three small churches in the Pittman Center Circuit—Burnett Memorial, Webb's Creek, and Shults Grove United Methodist Churches. She spoke once to me laughingly that she would probably be the only pastor still in school when it came time to retire. She finished these course requirements in 2007. With her fulfilling the role of pastor-minister, Pastor Alta is faithful to visit members who are sick, shut-in, or hospitalized. She truly has a pastor's heart.

Pastor Alta Raper of the Methodist Pittman Center Circuit for the past thirteen years has continually emphasized a positive philosophy each Sunday morning when she emailed her ponderings to her readers. These emails went out entitled "The Pastor's Ponderings" and covered informational, inspirational and challenging values. She lives this philosophy, so it is easy for her to impart such in words, written or spoken. Pastor Alta is an artist with words rather than a brush. Her readers feel they can visually see and feel the circumstances of which she writes. Her ponderings include a reflective look remembering good old days and recent events, scenes and places, seasons and weather, family and people who have entered her life. Pastor Alta has the gift of writing, and works magic with words in ways that pull you forward to read the last line of the thoughts she wants to convey. Many were selected by *The Mountain Press,* a local Sevier County newspaper, and were published in their Sunday edition.

Many ponderings describe scenes of the present in picture words that make one feel they are on the journey with her, or at least wish they were. Some of the topics which she writes seem almost sacred emphasizing that each day is a gift from God. The reader quickly notes Pastor Alta loves this wonderful world created and given by our Great Creator to each of us, but we do not own it. We are merely passing tenants and responsible stewards of nature. She says she does not sing, but along with the many hymns she knows so well, I think the song "What a Wonderful World" would be one of her favorites. A poet once wrote "beauty is in the eye of the beholder." Yes, while the landscape belongs to the owner, it is also possessed by those whose eyes are open with appreciation of the landscape, and who take the time to wake up to wonder and ponder. This is a daily venture, or adventure with Pastor Alta.

Her community and home is in Pittman Center which is located in the southeastern section of Sevier County bordering the Great Smoky Mountains National Park. I feel sure many of her readers far removed from this area possess a desire to live here, or at least to vacation here. Pastor Alta has expressed she would like to remain here forever. Locals for years have called the Town of Pittman Center "God's Vacation Home."

Pastor Alta has been encouraged to combine these weekly articles into a book since the newspaper editions become yellow with age, frayed, or lost. She has brought forth some selected "ponderings" from the last ten years or so into a bound volume. She continues to write her life to her congregations and friends, but we now have a written document she has shared with her message of love and the gospel of Christ to read and be read again and again. May you be blessed as you read each 'pondering.' They will help you "Keep on the Sunny Side of Life," a song made famous by the Carter Family.

Glenn Cardwell,
Mayor, Town of Pittman Center

Acknowledgements

The author wishes to acknowledge and thank all those who have been a part of encouraging her to publish her ponderings. Many thanks to the folks who have been, and still are, a special part of her life and who have been the subject of many of her stories.

Special thanks to her dear friend and award-winning photographer, **Jane Brewer**, for providing expertise behind the lens of the camera revealed in the cover photo and other photographs in this book.

If you are reading along and you think the words are familiar or that you have read them before, you probably did. Remember, these ponderings were written over a period of ten years or more and sometimes the author may have become repetitive and used similar or same stories. Read on, dear friend, and the next pondering will likely be something quite new and different.

About the Author

Pastor Alta Chase Raper
Pittman Center Circuit—United Methodist Churches

Born July 23, 1940 in Cleveland, TN, Alta was appointed Pastor of the Pittman Center United Methodist Churches in 2001 at sixty years of age and serves the same three churches today. Before entering the ministry, Alta had a varied background, not only in religion but in law and insurance as well. She served as Deputy Clerk for Circuit, Sessions, Criminal, Juvenile and Probate Courts in both Bradley and McMinn Counties. Named "Outstanding Young Woman of the
Year" for McMinn County in 1974, Alta was included in "Personalities of the South" honoring her many civic and professional contributions. For 22 years she was a licensed insurance agent and Executive Vice President of Blackwood Insurance Agency in Maryville, TN. A Certified Lay Speaker for three years before her call into full time ministry, she enjoyed speaking in many Methodist pulpits; drawing from each a sense of *"being in the right place, at the right time, doing the right thing. It just felt good!"*

About the Book

A collection of ponderings full of wit and wisdom to inspire you, make you smile, and even laugh out loud. Sit down, relax and take a moment to stroll down a sun-dappled roadway, climb the steps to an old country church, wade in a clear mountain stream, listen to the rushing water as it pours over river rocks, smell the fresh air after a rain and soak in the beauty and grandeur of God's masterpiece found in the ever changing panorama of the Great Smoky Mountains. You will enjoy a bit of history as well as introductions to many interesting folks who call this mountain paradise 'home.' You won't want to miss the story of burning palm fronds entitled "Don't Sneeze on the Ashes" . . . they sure smelled sweet, a bit like marijuana . . . and "If Those Old Steps Could Talk" among many others, to keep you reading. Each one, a feel good story, intertwined with God's own word.

Table of Contents

MARCH PONDERINGS

APRIL PONDERINGS

MAY PONDERINGS

JUNE PONDERINGS

JULY PONDERINGS

AUGUST PONDERINGS

SEPTEMBER PONDERINGS

OCTOBER PONDERINGS

NOVEMBER PONDERINGS

DECEMBER PONDERINGS

JANUARY
PONDERINGS

A Beautiful Day
January 27, 2013

The golden rays of the sun shown down and enveloped the mountains like a warm cloak under a sky of azure blue. It has been a while since we have seen such a beautiful day as yesterday. It was a day that just made you feel good, a day to do something you've been putting off as you just didn't have that spring in your step.

Little peepers have already begun their spring peeping, daffodils, jonquils, buttercups, and hyacinths are breaking the soft earth where they have been napping since last fall and the yellow forsythia bush was in full bloom in Mom's back yard. Gorgeous signs of spring bringing back that special oomph to your life. Most likely there will be more cold days ahead but I believe in enjoying each day as it comes.

This past Friday brought an icy blast to the mountains and most of this area. It was a special day bringing to me, its' own pleasure. It was a time to stay inside and sit by the fire as I studied from J Vernon McGhee's Commentary preparing for today's sermon. In the evening as it grew dark, icy crystals on the tree branches shone like tiny diamonds in the light from across the street. Snuggled down in my chair by the warmth of the burning logs, Kitty climbed up on my lap and took a nap while I continued reading into the night.

Today will be another awesome day, a day of sunshine, and one filled with smiles and laughter as I go about my day as the pastor of three small churches. Each church has a wonderful feel of its own and each one is alive with God's sweet presence and good Christian people who love God and love each other.

Not a Sunday has gone by in the past thirteen years that I haven't thanked God, before I ever get out of bed, for allowing me to serve Him in this beautiful piece of heaven on earth. They have truly been the happiest years of my life. I get excited knowing for the first time in my life, I am doing exactly what I have been called to do. Folks, I really do have all the finer things of life right here. The clear mountain streams, beautiful flowers and trees, the ever changing colors of the mountains and the people. Ah, the people, they are among the nicest I have ever known. I love them all, each and every one.

"Shout with joy to the Lord, all the earth! Worship the Lord with gladness. Come before him, singing with joy. Acknowledge that the Lord is God! He made us, and we are his. We are his people, the sheep of his pasture. Enter his gates with thanksgiving; go into his courts with praise. Give thanks to him and praise his name. For the Lord is good. His unfailing love continues forever, and his faithfulness continues to each generation." Psalms 100:1-5 (NLT)

The Baptism of Jesus
January 13, 2013

The day was hot and the air filled with tiny clouds of dust rising up from the dry land on the riverbank. He was standing out about waist deep in the shallow waters of the river Jordan; this man with the wild hair and unkempt beard. Sweat from his brow was dripping down and mingling with the water droplets on his body that gleamed in the sun. He could be heard ranting loudly to anyone who would listen, "Repent, and be saved! I baptize you will water, but there is one coming after me, the straps of his sandals I am not worthy to untie. He will baptize you with the Holy Spirit and with fire." Oh, he was recognized by many in the crowd. He was Elizabeth and Zechariah's boy. They called him John, yes, John, now known as 'the baptist.'

As he looked up, he lifted his hand to shade his eyes from the glare of the sun on the water and saw the figure of a man coming toward him. Who was it? He looked familiar. Oh my Lord! It is Jesus, the one I have preached about for so long! I am in the presence of the Savior, the Messiah! It can't be him. Surely he doesn't want to be baptized! He should be baptizing me! Why, he is stepping into the water coming to meet me. What should I say? What shall I do?

When Jesus neared John in the water, John seemed to be rooted to the spot where he was when he first saw Jesus walking toward him. With hands outstretched, Jesus reached for John who lifted his own hands out of the water and they clasped them together and drew each other near. John seemed to protest, but Jesus seemed determined. John placed his hands on the body of Jesus and gently lowered Him back into the water. When he was completely covered, John lifted Him up. With the water still dripping down his face, Jesus remained in the water and immediately bowed His head in prayer. As He was praying, the Holy Spirit descended upon Him bodily in the form of a dove and a voice from heaven could be heard, "This is my Son, in whom I am well pleased."

Baptism, whether it happens as an infant, a young person, or an adult, should always signify the grace of God and a new way of life. Are we living that new way which baptism demands or are we merely Sunday morning Christians who leave our worship services and, once out the door, once again, we belong to the world. When you can't tell the difference between God's people and all the rest, something is wrong! Are we truly living as born-again Christians or are we just playing a game? When are we going to take our salvation and our baptism seriously and become God's people, easily recognized by all whom we meet?

Yesteryear Memories
January 6, 2013

The old man sat in his rocking chair by the warmth of the blazing fire as it roared up the chimney and knocked off the chill in the drafty room. Slowly he stood, reached up on the mantle and with hands aged and gnarled from working on the farm all his life; he picked up the precious old Book with the worn leather binding. He sat back down in his chair. His wife of over fifty years drew her own chair closer to his and their two grandchildren who were visiting, gathered around them, each in their own child-sized chair. Opening the Book, he gently and reverently turned the fragile pages to the back of the Book, which he said was the "New Testament." Finding the Second Chapter of the Gospel of Matthew, he cleared his throat and in his cracking voice, began to read, slowly and determinedly:

Now when Jesus was born in Bethlehem of Judaea in the days of Herod the king, behold, there came wise men from the east to Jerusalem, 2 Saying, Where is he that is born King of the Jews? for we have seen his star in the east, and are come to worship him. 3 When Herod the king had heard these things, he was troubled, and all Jerusalem with him. 4 And when he had gathered all the chief priests and scribes of the people together, he demanded of them where Christ should be born. 5 And they said unto him, In Bethlehem of Judaea: for thus it is written by the prophet, 6 And thou Bethlehem, in the land of Juda, art not the least among the princes of Juda: for out of thee shall come a Governor, that shall rule my people Israel . . . 7 Then Herod, when he had privily called the wise men, enquired of them diligently what time the star appeared. 8 And he sent them to Bethlehem, and said, Go and search diligently for the young child; and when ye have found him, bring me word again, that I may come and worship him also. 9 When they had heard the king, they departed; and, lo, the star, which they saw in the east, went before them, till it came and stood over where the young child was. 10 When they saw the star, they rejoiced with exceeding great joy. 11 And when they were come into the house, they saw the young child with Mary his mother, and fell down, and worshipped him: and when they had opened their treasures, they presented unto him gifts; gold, and frankincense and myrrh. 12 And being warned of God in a dream that they should not return to Herod, they departed into their own country another way. Matthew 2: 1-12 (KJV)

As he finished reading, he yawned, put the Book back on the mantel and said to the old woman whom he loved with all his heart and to his grandchildren that he adored, *"it's time fer bed now young'uns. God's going to take care of us just as he always has and He will always guide us and keep us from stumblin'; along the way. We had our black-eyed peas and hog 'jaw' on New Year's Day. Remember, God's our hope! G'night Norie (Nora), g'night Ralph, g'night Aldie" (Alta). "Now close yore eyes so the sandman will come."*

New Year's memories flood my mind as I think back to the many New Years spent in the old farmhouse with my maternal grandparents, the **Musgroves**. Good, obedient, salt-of-the-earth folks who loved God and their neighbors. I never heard a cross word pass their lips, no profanity, no sense of futility; just good honest, hard-working people who knew if they lived right, God would take care of them. They taught their family by example.

Keep God and His promises in your New Year too, and remember, sometimes he tells us to find another way when he senses we are on a path that will lead to danger. *"²And being warned of God in a dream that they should not return to Herod, they departed into their own country another way." Matthew 2:12 (KJV)*

Shalom!

A History Lesson
January 14. 2012

Are you ready for a history lesson? This past week, I enjoyed my second tour of the new Pittman Center Elementary School in preparation for our Open House on May 5th of the Pittman Center Museum located inside the school sponsored by the Museum Board and the members of the Historical Preservation Committee. As I marveled at the great architectural design of the building (thanks to Jim Coykendall), I savored each and every exhibit of the early days of Pittman Center.

My mind kept going back to the year 1919 when **Dr. John Sevier Burnett** had a dream of a Christian Community Center which would benefit the mountain folks of East Tennessee. Dr. Burnett was himself born and raised in the neighboring North Carolina Mountains and knew the hardships these folks faced in getting an education. He worked tirelessly until at last his dream became a reality.

One of the persons he convinced to help him was **Dr. Eli Pittman**, Superintendent of the Elmira District of the Central New York Conference of the Methodist Episcopal Church who then enlisted eight other District Superintendents, all of whom came to these mountains to find just the right spot to begin this new community. As Dr. Burnett and Dr. Pittman were tramping through the hills and valleys, they stopped on a knoll overlooking several acres and knew at that very moment, this was the place! Dr. Pittman became the person responsible for raising the funds which led Dr. Burnett to name this mountain project in honor of him.

The school opened on August 15, 1921 with an enrollment of 100. Folks read the headlines in ***Montgomery's Vindicator*** on September 7, 1921, *"The Pittman Community School at Emert's Cove will be dedicated Sunday Sept. 18, Monday, Sept. 19, and Tuesday Sept 20, 1921."* "Two school wagons, pulled by horses, ran to and from the school each day for students living too far away to walk. It was the best equipped school building in Sevier County, with electric lighting, steam heat, its own water system and toilets, drinking fountains on each floor, and a shower bath for the teachers. There was a large auditorium, six large class rooms, lockers for the students and teachers and book cases; a manual training room, domestic science kitchen, and a large sunny sewing room. A *Teachers Cottage* was to the right of the school and *Janitor's Cottage* to the left."

In 1939, one **Knoxville News-Sentinel** reporter made the following statement: *"It is the only school in Tennessee supported by a county (Sevier), the state (Tennessee), and a church (Methodist Episcopal Church). It is set on 1,500 acres of forest and farm land, containing 15 buildings, and cost approximately $9,000 to operate in 1938. Out of a faculty of ten, there are five ordained ministers."* Pittman Community Center continued to minister to the various needs of the people, until the last graduating class of 1963.

Except for the happy laughter of schoolchildren at play, very little of the original settlement remains. However, a dream that is born never dies; it lives on in the memory of those who care. I am so blessed to be just a tiny part of this very special place and to carry on the legacy of those who have gone before.

A Brand New Year
January 1, 2012

Here we are on the first morning of a New Year!!! Can you believe it? Where has the year 2011 gone? It really is true that time flies when you're having fun. Through all the years of my life, the last eleven years spent in these beautiful mountains have been the happiest and most rewarding of all. God has blessed me at every breaking of the dawn, every sunrise and sunset, with blessings I never dreamed possible.

There is a lot of difference in waking up dreading to go to work and waking up excited to begin the day. Most of my work experiences have been good ones with only two exceptions. One of my first jobs was political and therein I found my greatest disappointment. I began working as a deputy clerk in the Circuit Court Clerk's office of Bradley County in the early 60s. I fell in love with the job, but after four years my very good boss, Clay King, was not re-elected. Being young and naïve, especially in the field of politics, when I was asked by the newly elected Clerk (who had no experience in the court system) to stay and train his girls, I thought it was an honor and an affirmation of my worth. Wrong! After only a few months when he and all the girls were fully trained I was told that (*his political party*) had said he had to get rid of me. They said he just couldn't have a (*the other party*) working for him, *it was bad for his image.* It was then I realized truth and politics do not always go together.

Years, later, a rival insurance agency lured me away from the agency where I had worked for twenty-two years and had become Vice President. Promises were made regarding my future if I joined their agency. I accepted the offer and immediately knew it was a mistake. I was miserable in their fine establishment when I discovered they cared nothing for the *people* who brought them their business, only the amount of money they had.

All things worked together to bring me to where I am today! God allowed me to accept His calling on my life after nineteen long years of denial! He was there all along waiting for me to get my priorities in order. And I'm so thankful I did.

Let me tell you about my Boss. He is perfect in every way. He keeps His promises, is good, kind, loving, understanding, sympathetic, compassionate, forgiving, and He wants only the best for me. He provides all the life insurance and fire insurance I could ever need and it is free! The rewards and bonuses are the best ever and my benefits are out of this world!

"And we know that God causes everything to work together for the good of those who love God and are called according to his purpose for them." Romans 8:28 (NLT)

May you and yours experience great joy, perfect peace, good health, and love beyond measure in the coming New Year!

The Greatest Love
January 16, 2011

It's dark and early and I can't see the morning sky, but I'm really praying for a bit of sunshine today. The snow-gates of heaven have been wide-open in the mountains for the past several weeks. Pondering on the *Twenty-Third Psalm:* "He maketh me to lie down in green pastures . . ." I sit and imagine how green the pastures will become in springtime and how delightful it will be to walk barefoot through the soft grass on a warm sunny day. The air will be filled with the delicate fragrance of new blooms and blossoms as they burst forth from their long winter's nap! Oh yes, I can still dream on a cold winter morning, of the joys of spring.

I've been pondering a lot lately on the simply awesome thing called *love* and how just the thought of it can bring warmth to your body and soul. Somehow, if we know we are loved, the world is a little brighter, and life's troubles and trials don't seem so bad after all. I'll bet we can all remember our *first love*, the one who could make our heart skip a beat, the precious love of our husband or wife, the love that exists between us and our children, or the "I care about you" love between friends. If we never knew what it was like to love or to be loved we would miss all the joy that makes life worth living.

It is also because of love that we all found we would suffer heartaches as well. The ache you thought would rip your heart out and would never end. You were certain you would never be able to love again . . . only to find another love that filled the void. Throughout our lives we will experience love in many forms and love will wear many faces. Sometimes even lost loves will repeat themselves.

And yet, the greatest love of all is THE LOVE OF GOD; the forever love that has no end and resists the ravages of time. We find personal delight in both giving and receiving love. In *knowing* love, we find untold blessings as we allow ourselves to be enveloped in the warmth of contentment, peace of mind, and sweet, sweet solace for our soul. There is pleasure in knowing we are special and thought of every moment of every day with a very special love that knows no bounds and, best of all, it is unconditional. Nothing can separate us from the love of God. My friend, if you have never experienced that kind of love, let me introduce you to Jesus Christ, the Savior of the World. He is the totality and embodiment of all that is good; He *is* Love.

"I am not writing you a new command but one we have had from the beginning. I ask that we love one another. And this is love: that we walk in obedience to his commands. As you have heard from the beginning, his command is that you walk in love." 2 John 1:5-6 (NIV)

The Tolling of the Bell

January 2, 2011

One of my desires is to keep alive the traditions and stories of this area that have come to mean as much to me as they do to the folks who have lived here all their lives. I write about them to keep them fresh in our memories that we might tell them to the children as they grow up here and to new folks moving into the area who will eventually call this home; just as I do now. Let's visit again the tradition of the tolling of the church bell at Shults Grove United Methodist Church on Rocky Flats Road in Cosby.

In the quiet and still of the darkness, the old bell tolled at midnight. It rang out, loud and clear, for at least three minutes, signaling the beginning of a New Year to all the residents of the sleepy little community known as Rocky Flats. Nestled in a little valley abundant with rocky soil and giant hemlocks, many of the folks living along the narrow, winding road were wide awake, counting down to the stroke of twelve when they knew the old bell would ring. Others were awakened from their slumber to turn and whisper "Happy New Year" to the one lying beside them. Children stared wide-eyed into the darkness of their room as they listened to the distant clanging of the bell in the steeple on the little church sitting high on the hill; known as Shults Grove United Methodist Church.

This ancient old bell is like a friend or maybe even like a Paul Revere who rode through the night shouting "the British are coming!" It has rung out many times throughout the years since the church was built in1914. It has rung out announcing Sunday Worship services, the death of loved ones, and every New Year. The tradition is still carried on today by **Theresa Moore**, a dedicated Christian and daughter of the **Shults** and **McAlister families**. She remains true to her heritage. The land on which the church is built was given by her mother's family, the Shults, and the building and grounds have long been maintained by the McAlisters, her father's family.

Many folks may remember a few years back when the old bell rang out on a warm December afternoon in 2001. The tolling of the bell that day announced the death of **Paul McAlister**, a kind, generous, and gentle man who had spent the last several years of his life dedicated to the little church on the hill within walking distance of his home. The church had just welcomed a new preacher lady who had come to know and love the community and this precious family during the six months she had been there. She spent many hours with Paul during the last weeks and months of his life. Cancer had taken its awful toll on his frail body but his eyes were still bright and alert as he spoke words of wisdom to her from a voice grown soft and low with the advancing of the disease that would claim him. When the preacher came to pay her last respects to the family after Paul had passed on into Glory, she drove by the little church on her way home. The church Paul had loved; probably the one thing he held dearest in life except for his family.

As I passed the church, I felt compelled to stop and climb those long steps up to the church at the top of the hill; the same steps that Paul had built not so many years ago. It wasn't my own thinking that caused me to stop but as a thought from somewhere in heaven where God looked down.

And I did as I was compelled . . . walking up to the front door, I went in and looked up at the cord hanging down from the old bell. Taking it in my hand for the first time in my life, I rang that old bell and after the first loud clang, I rang it again and again. Somehow I was saying to all those who could hear *"praise God for the life of Paul McAlister"* while at the same time the tolling declared his passing. When I finally let go of the cord and fastened it back on the wall hook of that precious old church, shivers ran over me. Like the Spirit of God had just passed through and for a time rested on me . . . and it felt good.

I'm pondering now on the words of a song I heard **Clyde** sing so many times, *"What a day that will be, when my Savior I shall see, and I look upon his face, the one who saved me by his grace. And forever I shall be with the one who died for me. What a day, glorious day that will be!"* And so shall it ever be!

A Winter Wonderland
January 31, 2010

Whoooo-eeeee, I stepped outside a minute ago and it is nippy! I sure am awake now, not just pondering, but really skipping along. That was better than jumping into an icy shower after forgetting to turn on the warm water. The layer of snow and ice looks as if God has cleansed the earth and covered it with a blanket of pure white. If you're still inside and just waking up . . . go ahead and yawn. Open wide and take in all that much needed air to get you going. Take another sip of nice warm coffee or if you're like me, open up an ice cold Diet Dr. Pepper. The caffeine is the same . . . even if the temperature isn't.

The scenery along the roadside this past week has been just breathtaking. A virtual winter wonderland of icicles jutting from the mountainsides frozen in long slender needles and plump spikes immobilized in time; water cut off in the midst of its journey. Which reminds me of how our own lives can have a certain destination, but somehow we are stopped in the middle of it all by unforeseen circumstances. We find that we must wait a while until the thawing begins before we can take up where we left off.

Gazing out over the dull brown of the fields, few cattle ventured out onto the frozen earth; their breath making steamy tendrils of vapor in the cold air. Even the streams, usually flowing effortlessly and gurgling along, seem to be struggling as they make their slow familiar journey while the frigid air forms icy patches and clumps along its way.

The skies have been overcast for much of the week and I have had to stop and remind myself that the sun *is* still shining. Far above the clouds out of our sight; it is there. That sun will shine again and bring warmth and light in God's own time. Our lives have cloudy days but they don't last, for soon the sun comes shining through and we marvel that we were ever afraid, or lonely, or lost. The path is made straight again and we take up our journey once more, guided by that unseen hand. (Which I wish had been there this morning when I stumped my toe on a stool in the kitchen!!!)

"*. . . Let us draw near to the house of God, with a sincere heart in full assurance of faith, having our hearts sprinkled to cleanse us from a guilty conscience and having our bodies washed with pure water. Let us hold unswervingly to the hope we profess, for he who promised is faithful.*" *Hebrews 10:22-23 (NIV)*

The Mailman
January 27, 2008

Years ago when I was a child, the highlight of our day was when the mailman came bringing our mail. It was our window on the world and held great importance as there was no TV, mostly static on the radio, and we rarely saw a newspaper on the day it was printed. We knew our mailman by name and he was considered a friend that was often invited to come, sit, and rest a spell. Of course he was always offered a cool drink of water from the pail on the porch or from the dipper beside the spring running clear and cold just on the other side of the road. If it happened to be a cold winter day, he might come in for a cup of the strong black Luzianne coffee with chicory that was always hot on the back burner of the old wood stove in the kitchen.

Grandmother used to get real excited when the ***Sears-Roebuck*** catalog was in our mailbox. She was a seamstress and always turned to the pages of patterns and material, picking out pretty pieces to make our dresses and plaids for the men's shirts. Now, Granddad got excited when the ***Progressive Farmer*** magazine came. Being a farmer and sharecropper, he read it from cover to cover getting tips on farming. Both my grandparents loved to get the seed catalogs in early spring. During this time, in the early 1940s, my mom, my brother, and I were living with my grandparents as my Dad was 'overseas' in WWII. Mom really looked forward to receiving letters from Dad who was stationed in the South Pacific.

Even today, we still look forward to receiving mail . . . yes, it still has its intrigue and when we open up the mailbox door, we still find catalogues and other surprises. Have you ever received one of those prayer cloths in the mail? I did; one day last week. I opened up the envelope expecting to see a cloth of some substance but it was only a heavy piece of paper imprinted with the face of Jesus with his eyes closed which I was to spread out on my knees or I could put in on the floor and kneel on it. Now I knew right away it wasn't going on the floor. It would be too hard for me to get up again.

While it was pressed on my knees the instructions were that I should stare at the face of Jesus and his eyes would suddenly open up and I was to tell him my heart's desire: money, fame, fortune, etc. Then I was to return the prayer cloth to the address on the envelope (along with my little "seed gift") so they could pass it on to someone else to have their prayers answered as well. What a pathetic way to make money. Now if I am wrong and these folks are sincere, I pray for God to bless them with the knowledge that neither cloth nor paper is needed to "have a little talk with Jesus." All God wants is a sincere heart, one that is filled with gratitude and love, has accepted Christ as Savior and the Holy Spirit has been granted a dwelling place therein.

Christ taught his disciples to pray: *"Our Father which art in heaven, hallowed be thy name. Thy kingdom come, Thy will be done in earth, as it is in heaven . . ." Matthew 8:9b-10 (KJV)*

Let's follow HIS example.

Lord, Don't . . .

January 13, 2008

Have you ever sat in your pew in church or in Sunday School silently praying *"Lord, don't let them call on me to pray!"* There was an old man by the name of **Jim** who was called on by the preacher to pray one Sunday morning at Midway Baptist Church in Maryville. The old man stood up and said *"Can't do it preacher. Just can't do it."* He then sat back down. There are some folks who simply do not, will not, or cannot, pray out loud. It makes them quite uncomfortable. They have no problem talking/praying silently with God. To them, it is something so personal they want only God to hear their supplications.

When I was a child I heard someone say we had to pray out loud so the devil would hear us and run away! I would go out in the woods and pray real loud as the devil always had hold of my dress-tail. The truth is that God hears us no matter *how* we pray. The Scriptures teach us that He hears even those prayers which we find too deep for words and can only groan and sigh from the depths of our very being. *(Romans 8:26)* The Scriptures also say we should pray without ceasing but can you imagine the chaos if we all prayed out loud all the time? Of course, there are times when we should pray quietly alone in our own 'prayer closet.' I make many visits there myself, pouring out my heart to my Heavenly Father who never fails to hear and understand.

Have you heard someone pray that was really open and truly honest with God? They might say something like *"I'm at my wit's end"* or *"Lord, you're going to have to help me out of this mess,"* or *"I'm so mad I could explode!"* Some may think this is being irreverent but I don't think God is shocked at all. He already knows our feelings long before we confess them before Him. He knows us better than we know ourselves and we must not forget that. He can't be fooled!

In *Psalm 142:2 (NKJV)* David says *"I pour out my complaint before Him; I declare before Him my trouble."* And then Jonah was so depressed that he told God he wanted to die. *Jonah* said in *4:8(NKJV) "And it happened, when the sun arose, that God prepared a vehement east wind; and the sun beat on Jonah's head, so that he grew faint. Then he wished death for himself, and said, "It is better for me to die than to live."* No matter what, we should always be honest with God sharing the way we truly feel. If we try to be any other way He sees right through us. Every prayer should show proper respect to God. He cares about our struggles and He wants to share with us our joys. *"Let us have a little talk with Jesus . . ."*

The Secret of a Good Sermon
January 28, 2007

Typical of East Tennessee, the weather can change in an instant and so can our spirits. Much of the week was cloudy and dreary which left me fighting the blues. Yesterday was a gorgeous sunny day and I felt like turning cartwheels. (I know I know . . . stop laughing, I said I *felt* like it, not that I *could*!) As I have had to work to keep from feeling low several times, I have purposely looked for things to focus on that were either funny or filled with beauty.

I laughed as I remembered some one-liners about preachers: The only people who like change in churches are wet babies. Many folks would agree with George Burns, *"The secret of a good sermon is to have a good beginning and a good ending; and to have the two as close together as possible."* Some preachers have an open mind and a mouth to match. Our Bibles have more side-notes than written text. Our job description requires a three-ring binder. At least we know which of these do not belong: KJV, RSV, NIV, TLB, CEV, NAS, FBI, NKJV, and CIA. We might be asked to lead in silent prayer! Ah, just joking; but, maybe you smiled . . . which was my intention.

I have a dear friend who loves rainy days; I think if we could spend them together, I would learn to like them too. Driving along the valley roads and looking up toward the mountains, you can see clouds nestled and entwined in the outstretched arms of the trees. Such a beautiful sight! These misty formations look so much like smoke you can barely tell the difference! At times, you can see snow-capped mountain peaks and trees bending under a thick white blanket while you are enjoying warm sunshine below.

Bright frosty mornings make the fields sparkle like glass; a virtual winter wonderland. Young bucks with beautiful racks strut alongside the fence rows as you drive along, or wade in the cold mountain streams with heads held high. Their glistening coats exuding elegance and power. Your heart is literally filled to over-flowing with their incredible beauty. Golden rays of the setting sun filter through bare branches of huge oak and fir trees, dappling every path with rays of glorious light. These are my focus!

Don't ever let yourself get to the point where you do not thrill to feel blood surging through your veins. Live each day with excitement and vitality and know this is truly "Our Father's World." *"I am still confident of this: I will see the goodness of the Lord in the land of the living." (Psalm 27:13) NIV*

Interesting People
January 21, 2007

One of the greatest joys of my ministry is the many interesting and colorful people I get to meet on a daily basis. Every week I find that I have received a blessing from conversations with these fascinating people. Folks who are genuine, honest, salt-of-the earth people who have experienced life and lived it to the fullest.

'**Miss Cora**', is the widow of **Conley Huskey** who served many political positions in Sevier County and Pittman Center as mayor, councilman, justice of the peace, landowner, and gentleman farmer. Cora celebrated her 93rd birthday on January 2nd and still plays the organ every Sunday morning at Burnett Memorial. She is always upbeat, with a ready laugh. We were having lunch together a couple of days ago and we both commented on the absolutely delicious slaw we had been served. To which Miss Cora piped up "I've already told them not to bring flowers to my grave just bring a bowl of slaw!" The laughter that followed was indeed good medicine!

I also enjoyed visiting with **Lucinda Ogle's** daughter, **Billie Nolan**, last week. You may remember Lucinda from the Heartland Series, known for her lovely wildflowers and being the daughter of Wiley Oakley. Lucinda passed away some time ago and **Bill Landry** gave the eulogy at her funeral. Lucinda's daughter, Billie, told me about a time when her mother was in the hospital and was waiting for her paper work to be completed so she could go home. It had been a long wait and Lucinda was getting anxious. She go up slowly, pulled her walker in front of her and slowly walked to her door and looked up and down the hall for some sign they were coming to release her. When she saw the silent and empty hallway, she turned around quickly, picked up her walker and carrying it in front of her, she walked back over to her chair with a loud "humph!" "Anybody can be slow!"

Another precious lady is **Zeltha Williams**. Zeltha is in her 80's and is now at home, the result of a stroke a few years back. Even though her speech is slower now than it was, her smile is as radiant as sunshine! This lady was always among the most faithful at Shults Grove UMC and never missed a Sunday. She may not be among the most talkative, but she is the epitome of gentleness, and kindness. You can't be in her presence very long without feeling good. What a blessing to know her.

There are many others I hold dear in my heart. Time and space dictates I must wait for another time to tell you about them. *"As iron sharpens iron, so one man sharpens another." Proverbs 27:17 (NIV)*

Stop the World from Spinning
January 14, 2007

Another fantastic Sunday morning! I can't wait for the day to begin! I've had so much fun this past week. There were so many things to do, folks to visit, and lots of year-end reports to complete. It's hard to believe another year has come and gone. Sometimes I want to say "Lord, stop this world from spinning so fast and let me just sit and savor the sweet joy of living."

I guess many of you are already struggling trying to keep New Year's resolutions. I never could keep them, so I quit making them years ago! But this year, I did make *one*—to become more organized! It will probably take me all year to do it but this is one time I really hope to succeed. Would you believe we have boxes that haven't been unpacked since we moved here six years ago!!! There's just too much 'stuff' around here. I've told my children I'm cleaning up and tossing out and if they want something, they better come and get it!

Speaking of 'stuff,' I remember several years ago when our District Superintendent **Carol Wilson** was my pastor. One Sunday morning she preached a great sermon entitled 'Stuff.' She talked about how we refer to so many different things as 'stuff" and how hard it is to define exactly what 'stuff' is! When we try to explain what's in a drawer, a storage box, our refrigerator, our overflowing closet, our pockets, or purse . . . we cover it all with 'stuff.'

If we aren't careful, our lives can get cluttered with so much 'stuff' we find it impossible to give our best to any *one* thing. Life becomes so fragmented; we must stop and prioritize if we are to do justice to any of our tasks. Prioritizing is often difficult as we try to determine what is most important and what we should do first. If it is *people* vying for our time, we can create hurt feelings. When it is a task or job, determining rank according to importance is never easy. I still remember what my mother taught me and what I have tried to instill in my own children; two things: (1) *"If it is worth doing at all, it is worth doing well."* (2) *"If you always put God first, everything else will fall into place."* That may seem an oversimplification, but it works!

"Commit to the Lord whatever you do, and your plans will succeed. In his heart a man plans his course, but the Lord determines his steps." Proverbs 16:3, 9 (NIV)

He Was Only Seven
January 7, 2007

As I ponder this morning, I have a myriad of thoughts running around in my head and with each one I have had to stop and say "thank you God for yet another blessing."

Last Sunday afternoon, a little seven year old boy lost his life in a tragic accident involving a four-wheeler. He was a second grade student at Pittman Elementary School which is just across the road from the parsonage where we live. The principal of the school, **Susan Carr**, invited me to speak to their assembly on Wednesday morning and try to help the children understand a little more about the death of their friend. I struggled mightily with what I would say and still pray that something I said made a difference in a positive way. I tell you this only to say that I was not hindered from reading the Bible, using God's name, and in leading a prayer to Almighty God. This great school still holds to the values of God and Country. What a blessing!

One of the little boy's classmates, **Courtney** with long blonde curls, asked her mother if she could come talk with me as she was having a hard time with her sorrow. We had our talk and I think she felt better. The next day, she sent me a hand-written note in her second grade lettering and I share it with you . . . word for word. *"Dear Alta, I love you with all my heart you are incredible and you are very very old but thank you for all you have done. I love you."* And she drew big hearts all over the page. Will I keep this? You bet!! Another blessing!

Our mayor, **Glenn Cardwell**, was at our table Wednesday for lunch and he related the following story: A few years back, one of the students' assignments was to write a paper on "Why I Like Pittman Center School." Two of the papers stuck in his memory. The first one said "because I love to hear the sound of the water surrounding the school and not the sound of an eighteen-wheeler." This young lad had obviously moved here from a big city. The next one said "because everyone here seems like your mother." What greater compliment could a school receive!

Friday morning, a bus took the second and third grade classes to the funeral of their beloved classmate and friend. Anyone who attended the funeral was not counted absent. When I was telling my mother about this, she said she remembered that was a tradition when she went to school so many, many years ago. She was surprised that it still happened. We both agreed that it happens now *only* in a small community school such as Pittman. You will never hear of such leniency and compassion in our big city schools. What a blessing to be part of this community!

Jesus was asked, "Who is the greatest in the kingdom of heaven?" Matthew records His response: *"He called a little child and had him stand among them. And He said; "I tell you the truth, unless you change and become like little children, you will never enter the kingdom of heaven. Therefore, whoever humbles himself like this child is the greatest in the kingdom of heaven. And whoever welcomes a little child like this in my name welcomes me." Matthew 18:2-5 (NIV)*

We grown-ups need to learn to become more childlike.

Amen? Amen!

Follow the Recipe
January 18, 2004

I've been pondering on the importance of recipes! Have you ever tried to make a pound cake? Let me tell you a short story. Two years ago at Shults Grove's Homecoming, **Uncle Bill Matthews**, brought a lemon pound cake. That was the most delicious cake I have ever tasted . . . makes my mouth water just thinking about it. I asked Uncle Bill if I could have his recipe and about a week later, it was in the mail. I couldn't wait to try it.

Here goes . . . the first line said *"have all ingredients at room temperature."* So, out comes the butter (margarine), eggs, and milk from the refrigerator and I put them on the cabinet along with the other ingredients: Crisco, granulated sugar, 3 cups *plain* flour (didn't have any so I used *self-rising*, flour is flour, right?), vanilla, lemon *extract* (didn't have any so I used *lemon juice*, that should be better anyway) and baking powder. I greased and floured my pan, let the oven preheat (uh oh, the recipe said a *cold* oven); waited about five minutes and decided to go ahead and stir up my cake . . . what difference would "room temperature" make in eggs, butter, and milk? The recipe said to leave oven door closed until cake was ¾ baked. It was hard to wait but I did and then sneaked a peek . . . funny, it didn't look like it should but I felt sure the last 15 minutes would take care of that.

As soon as it came out of the oven, I started looking for a hiding place!!! Instead of a pound cake I had a *ton* cake! I couldn't let Clyde see it, he would never let me live it down, so I put it out in the woods at the far end of the parsonage thinking the animals would devour the evidence!! Two weeks later it was still there!!! Needless to say, I found out how important a recipe really is and how much more important it is to follow directions!!

God has directions for us if we want to receive salvation and desire to be called Children of God. We can't use any substitutions in His recipe.

The Bible gives us these very simple instructions: *"Yet to all who received him, to those who believed in his name, he gave the right to become children of God." John 1:12 (NIV)*

"That if you confess with your mouth, 'Jesus is Lord,' and believe in your heart that God raised him from the dead, you will be saved."... for, "Everyone who calls on the name of the Lord will be saved." Romans 10:9,13 (NIV)

"For it is by grace you have been saved, through faith-and this not from yourselves, it is the gift of God-not by works, so that no one can boast." Ephesians 2:8-9 (NIV)

FEBRUARY
PONDERINGS

Rose Glen Literary Festival
February 24, 2013

Oh my, it is early and still dark outside but soon the sun will be peeking over the mountain on this bright new day! I have had a very interesting, and exciting week. Now that I look back on it, it makes me a little tired just thinking about all that has transpired. Oh, but I would do it over again in a heartbeat; I have learned so much!

The first part of the week was spent at Minister's Convocation in Lake Junaluska, NC. Our worship leader and speaker was **Leonard Sweet**; a deep and provocative thinker who grabs and holds your attention from beginning to end. Let me say, no one nodded off, not for a second. He is the author of tons of books, articles, sermons, etc. and was voted by his peers "One of the 50 Most Influential Christians in America" by *Church Report Magazine*. We were blessed to have him for those four days of intense learning and fellowship.

Returning home late Thursday evening and being behind already; I quickly checked to see if there were folks I needed to check on or pray for. Then I began researching my sermon, and preparing and delivering bulletins to the churches.

Moving right along to Saturday; it was another good day. **Carroll McMahan** had invited me to be a participant in the *Rose Glen Literary Festival* as both an author and to give the invocation. I first told him I would have to check my calendar but when he said **Dr. William Bass** would be the keynote speaker, I *immediately* said *"I've thought it over, if there is anything on my calendar, I will move it. I don't want to miss meeting Dr. Bass."* Religion and forensic anthropology may seem a strange combination of subjects of interest to a mountain preacher and a woman at that. Let me say, I have long been fascinated by the *Body Farm* and I have read all of Dr. Bass's books. He certainly is an interesting speaker and kept us in rapt attention as well as giving us some good laughs. He was most gracious to autograph the big stack of books I had with me and even posed for a picture. What a wonderful event and gathering of many local authors held at Walters State Community College in Sevierville.

I will have to tell you something funny. A sweet lady stopped by the table where I sat with fellow author, **Teri Pizza**, of *"The Joy of Growing Old*

With God." When I introduced myself to the lady, she looked blank for a moment, then confused, then surprised, then amused, and with laughter she said *"I have been reading your articles, how long now, well, for the past ten years I guess, and I have always thought you were a **man**!"* Ah, what can I say? How about *"Laughter is good medicine"* from the book of Proverbs? May the blessings of the good Lord be upon you this day and every day!

The Ladybug
February 17, 2013

Some of the funniest things seem to happen to us in times when we are supposed to be serious. Such was last Sunday . . . I had just finished my sermon and was preparing to give the benediction when I felt something drop into my hair. I knew right away it had nothing to do with a Holy Anointing but with that fat little ladybug that had been having such a joyful time soaring just above my head all morning. It was simply a natural instinct to want to reach up there and get that bug out; any red blooded woman doesn't want anything in her hair, much less if it is alive and kicking! You start itching all over, and your whole body tenses up from the top of your head to the tip of your toes. It actually does feel like your skin is crawling. Woe is me! Here, when I wanted to let the Word of God sink in and give the blessing before they were to leave; I needed to be serious. I just had to. I was wondering how I could possibly stand still while this thing was playing in my hair!

In my mind I was thinking, I must get this service over in the quickest way possible before I lose it altogether. I decided I would give the shortest benediction possible, delivered in much haste. I was even on my tiptoes by this time trying to remain calm as that ladybug started crawling down through my hair seeking to sit a spell on my scalp. I barely got the "amen" out when I reached up and shook that thing out of my hair. I had my hair in a "fro" in a second flat. I don't know quite what the members of the congregation thought at first; maybe they thought I was in the Spirit.

If you laughed as you pictured this . . . try to remember the time years ago in the summer when we had the door and all the windows open at Shults Grove. I was right in the middle of my sermon when a wasp flew in, made a bee line to the vee neck of my shirt and stung me . . . really hard, in a very tender place. I thought I had been shot in the chest. I could see the headlines . . . 'woman preacher succumbs to gunshot in the pulpit.' Oh my, you can readily see that my life is anything but dull here in the mountains. Me and the Lord have some mighty good times here!

We are now in the Season of Lent, the forty days between Ash Wednesday and Easter Sunday, when we look into our own lives and see those places that need to be given to the Lord for forgiveness and cleansing.

It is also a time when we remember Jesus' forty days in the wilderness as He prepared to give His own life for our sins.

"My command is this: Love each other as I have loved you. Greater love has no one that this, that he lay down his life for his friends. You are my friends if you do what I command." John 15:12-14 (NIV)

My friends, come walk with me in the light of His love.

Bread and Kool-Aid

February 5, 2012

I've been pondering on the one thing in all churches that seems to be the same. Everyone loves the children's sermon! One reason could be that we all understand it since the preacher doesn't use any of those big words with the children. Another is we love to hear the sweet, innocent things that children say. There are always huge smiles all over the congregation as we listen with rapt attention to these little ones. However, it can be a trying time for some parents as they wonder what their child is going to say next. Having raised four of my own, I was always one of those fearful parents.

I remember one time when I actually asked our pastor at Pleasant Hill UMC Maryville (where I was a member for 26 years) to please not ask my youngest son, **Vic**, any more questions for I never knew what he might say! This is the child that used to chase me around the house with a live frog in his hand when he was only three. I have always been scared to death of frogs, though I dearly love their little legs, fried up all golden brown. On my twelfth birthday, I remember my Dad frying frog legs just for me because he knew they were my favorite. Yummee, were they ever good.

If my memory serves me correctly, **Ron Fisher** was pastor at the time of this story. It was Communion Sunday and in the children's sermon, Ron began by asking questions to see just how much these little ones understood about Communion. The first question was "Does anyone know what we have under the cloth on the table." Immediately, and without hesitation, my son, **Vic**, raised his hand and yelled "I know, I know . . . bread and kool-aid!!"

I remember another little boy whose last name was **Marcus** being asked during the children's sermon how he knew his puppy loved him and he replied "because he runs up to me, wiggles all over and pees on the sidewalk." What a laugh that one got!!

Is it OK to laugh a little in church? Of course!!! Being a Christian doesn't mean we need a long face and sad expression. Christians should be the happiest people in the world. Jesus loved the little children, he gathered them up in his arms, and I know there were many times when he smiled and even laughed out loud at some of the things they said and did.

"He called a little child and had him stand among them. And he said: "I tell you the truth, unless you change and become like little children, you will never enter the kingdom of heaven. Therefore, whoever humbles himself like this child is the greatest in the kingdom of heaven. And whoever welcomes a little child like this in my name welcomes me." Matthew 18:3-5 (NIV)

Store Britches

February 19, 2012

Last night, for the third time this week, I attended the Gatlinburg Garden Club's presentation of **Lula Mae Ogle's** play *"Store Britches."* What a delightful way to pass an evening watching the story unfold of love and marriage in the days "way back yanner." The **Olde Harp Singers** lent an air of "ole timey" entertainment to the evening. The cast was superb and kept us smiling and laughing. What "good medicine" that was and we left feeling happy, with a spring to our step and a smile on our faces.

"Give the world a smile each day . . . helping someone along life's way. From the paths of sin, bring the wanderer in, to the Master's fold today." I can still hear the **Blackwood Brothers** singing that lovely old song! There is so much that can be done with a smile. Ladies, it's the best face lift you will ever find, and it can happen in an instant. Smiles have a miraculous way of lighting up your whole face like no make-up can do. And what it does to your eyes! It brings a sparkle like nothing else. We can't leave you men out either. Want to catch a lady's eye? Just flash her a beautiful smile that comes straight from your heart, and you will have her attention.

I remember when my children were little. My daughter, **Mia**, loved mustard sandwiches (yuk!) and I would always draw a smiley face on the bread with the mustard and she thought that was delightful. **John** and **Vic** loved *smileys* on their toast made from butter and jelly and **Chase**, the oldest, wanted a smiley on his pancakes drawn with syrup. Of course, every hamburger had to have a smiley face with ketchup. Throughout all the years of their growing up, we found more and more ways to use *smileys*. We drew *smileys* on notes written to each other, put them on cookies and cakes with the icing, drew them with finger paint, and all the while, found our own faces smiling as we worked and played. Those little smiley faces were a wonderful way to convey our love for each other even without words.

It is amazing how your spirits are lifted when we walk into a room lit up by the smiles of happy people. Smiles can preach a sermon and they can speak volumes. *"Nothing in all creation is hidden from God's sight. Everything is uncovered and laid bare before the eyes of him to whom we must give account." Hebrews 4:13. (NIV)*

Like a tray of smiley faced cookies waiting to be devoured, God sees how we look and how we treat each other. He wants us to hold each other gently and savor friendship as a treasure. He wants us to love each other and to offer a smile with the same care and love we receive from Him. He commands us to love the way He loves. *"For the eyes of the Lord range throughout the earth to strengthen those whose hearts are fully committed to Him." 2nd Chronicles 16:9a (NIV)*

Humility
February 6, 2011

I'm pondering on humility this morning. Have you ever been just totally humbled by something or someone's actions toward you?

Things have happened this past week that have certainly humbled me. I received a sweet note from my daughter-in-law **Becky** noting the anniversary of my daughter **Mia's** death and wishing me a cheerful day in spite of the circumstances. I enjoyed having my family around for a bittersweet birthday party for my grandson, **BJ**, who was sixteen yesterday on the first anniversary of his Mother's passing. There was a phone call asking me to perform the wedding of a couple from Ohio who had visited one of our churches and I was able to tell them *"yes, I will be glad to do that for you;"* being informed quickly when a church member's father was sick and hospitalized so that I could begin praying and involving others in that prayer process; being asked to assist in preaching the funeral of a dear friend from Maryville, **Phyllis Stephens**, who was a long-time member of Pleasant Hill UMC where I was a member for many years; visiting another precious friend **Bernice Headrick**, in Morning View Rehab Center who broke her hip on Tuesday; getting disturbing news that one of my high school friends, **Charlyne**, is facing a forced retirement because of health issues; and in knowing that every member of my flock care so much for each other. I see them suffering as they share each other's pain and I see them praising God as they share their joy. I am humbled.

Very quickly, I will tell you that any good I do as God's servant is possible only through His grace and mercy. The ability given me through the Holy Spirit of God is for His praise, honor and glory. I am totally committed to this love affair with my Lord, and the Pittman Center Parish . . . the flock that I serve and shepherd. No way would I exchange what I have right now for the biggest salary in the most prestigious church in the world (not that I would even be asked . . .). I did not enter the ministry for any reason other than *a profound calling to serve the Lord and His people.* What I have is a wonderful and blessed gift from God, freely given and freely received. The most wonderful gift anyone could ever imagine . . . complete joy and peace as I go about my work in this place at this time. Yes, I am truly humbled that I have been given such blessings. Excuse me while I go outside and shout toward heaven "Hallelujah!"

"The Lord is my strength and my shield: my heart trusts in him, and I am helped. My heart leaps for joy and I will give thanks to him in song." Psalm 28:7 (NIV)

Noises in the Night
February 27, 2011

Last night I went to bed early as I was unusually tired. I needed a good night's rest so my mind would be fresh and clear on this fine Sunday morning. I was in a deep sleep when sometime in the wee hours of the morning I heard a cacophony of loud noises. I was instantly awake as Miss Kitty let out a bloodcurdling meow. She zoomed down the hall and into my bedroom like her tail was on fire. My heart was beating ninety miles a minute as I sat straight up in bed, my mind racing. What was happening? Had a bear broken through the window in my dining room just waiting to pounce on me or maybe even a two legged intruder dressed in black with arms raised holding a hatchet ready to chop off my head? Oh Lord, I hadn't said my goodbyes . . . who would find me . . . could they identify me after he was through chopping up my body? I began shivering.

Sitting quietly, listening, praying, finally willing my legs to move, I put my feet on the floor and began slowly tiptoeing up the dark hallway toward the dining room. *Lord, hold my hand, if I've ever needed you, I sure do need you now!* Holding my breath, I peeked around the corner and looked toward the big plate glass window facing the mountain barely three feet away and where my bird feeders are hanging. As I looked toward the window two pair of the greenest eyes I have ever seen were swaying to and fro in the feeders as they filled their cheeks with birdseed.

Venturing another few feet into the dark kitchen area, I saw something big and black partially concealed under my dining room table. It had to be the varmint that caused Miss Kitty to become so frightened! Something strange was in my house! It wasn't moving and didn't make a sound. Miss Kitty is a pretty big cat but she could never tangle with a bear even if it was a cub!!! Oh my . . .

The moonlight shining through the windows onto the floor provided only dim patches of light and shadowy figures. I had to get to the light switch. Slowly making my way to the far wall, I flipped on the light. It took a minute for me to focus (I had not thought to put on my glasses in my haste and fear). The dining room was one big mess! As I stood there in amazement, I suddenly knew what had happened. Miss Kitty had been on her perch on the window sill watching the raccoons feeding. One of them must have frightened her causing her to jump straight down into a forty pound bag of sunflower seeds. She was inside the bag fighting to get out when it overturned spilling the seed onto the floor and underneath the dining room table.

Have you ever tried to clean up 40 pounds of black oiled sunflower seeds in the middle of the night? You can do one of two things, you can get real angry, or you can have a good laugh while you are cleaning it up. I grabbed my new broom from **Mr. Ogle's Broom Shop** and began sweeping away. When I finished I let out a 'whew," went back to bed for another couple of hours, and here I am.

Why am I writing such drivel this beautiful Sunday morning? I can't think of anything else! I tried to think of something serious but my mind would not cooperate.

Now what scripture comes to mind this morning in my befuddled state? Something from *Psalms 56: 3-4a (NIV) "When I am afraid, I will trust in you. In God, whose word I praise, in God I trust, I will not be afraid."*

Praise and Song
February 28, 2010

I awoke this morning with the words of a song permeating my thoughts and dancing through my mind . . . *"I feel the touch of hands soft and tender, They're leading me in the paths that I must go, I have no fear for Jesus walks beside me, And I'm sheltered in the arms of God."* Wow, that sends cold chills up my spine . . . just pondering on being sheltered in the arms of God. *"He walks with me and <u>naught of earth can harm me</u> . . ."*

How can we not be glad for this beautiful day before us? The awesomeness of God's great goodness is never more present than on Sundays. The day we take some time out from the drudgery of work and everyday worries and cares to spend time in God's house; basking in the peace of His presence, learning from His word, and singing those great hymns of the church. Can you even imagine a worship service without singing? I don't care how good your preacher is, we still need to lift our voices in song to receive the full blessing.

We began a new service at Burnett Memorial UMC a couple of months ago called "Praise and Song." We meet every third Sunday at 5:30PM. You lift your praise to God and then call out your favorite hymn and we all sing it together. This has quickly caught on and the joy that flows in these services is something to behold. Testimonies are given and praises lifted from folks that may have never spoken aloud in a church service before. We usually end up singing much longer than we had planned as no one wants to leave. The blessings flow as we all share and sing together. Everyone leaves with a smile on their face and a powerful sense of having been in the very presence of God. We leave anticipating the next time we will come together as brothers and sisters in Christ lifting praises and voices to the Lord our God.

To me, there is nothing like the sound of a good old southern gospel all-male quartet. Remember *The Statesmen, The Blackwood Brothers, JD Sumner and The Stamps, The Rebels* and *The Prophets?* What about the *Kingsmen,* and *the Cathedrals.* Now that was singing at its best. My favorite quartet was, and is, the original *"Oak Ridge Quartet"* when Willie Wynn was the tenor. Wow, what a fantastic voice . . . he could knock the top off those high notes! I can just hear him now!

Guess I better stop pondering on things of the past, step into the present, and my 'Sunday-go-to-meetin' clothes! Yep, it's going to be another great day! I can feel it in my bones!

Love Letters
February 8, 2009

Ah, February is here and brings with it Valentine's Day when a young man's fancy lightly turns to love. And his thoughts are on valentine cards and candy for his sweetie. I will admit my favorite Valentine was a handmade card with a poem written just for me. Some of you may even write love letters on Valentine's Day. There's something exciting about receiving a letter, especially a "love letter." Go ahead and admit it! I'll bet you can remember the first one you ever received. Was it a note slipped to you in class when the teacher wasn't looking, or in the hallway at school; or maybe it was from a boy who was away in the military, a girl back home, or a sweetheart away at college? Some of you may still have them from years past; hidden away in an old shoebox and tied with a faded red ribbon.

When I was a teenager, way back in the Fifties, I used to get sweet love letters from a boy named **James** who was away at National Guard camp, and **Larry** who was in the Navy and there were two boys in college, **Bud** and **Randall**. No, not all at the same time!! Oh, how I loved to get those letters. I couldn't wait for the postman every day! Well, OK . . . so maybe you never got that excited about letters, but I sure did. Actually, I still enjoy getting love letters from my sweet hubby of course!! He wrote me lots of letters when he was in California singing with **Heaven's Avenue Quartet.** Not only did he write me, he called me!! Our phone bill was $600 for the six weeks he was touring. Ah, what can I say . . . it was good to be missed! He loved me!

I'm pondering today on another kind of love letter. Letters written by Paul to his churches throughout the many cities he visited. All of Paul's letters were love letters; written with the love of Christ in his heart.

In *1 Corinthians 13*, the apostle Paul, under the inspiration of the Holy Spirit, penned the world's most beautiful Ode to Love. Paul tells us that love suffers a long time. Then he says love does not envy and goes on to tell us the unselfish love that God calls us to is not puffed up. Every time I think of being "puffed up" I think of the little bantam rooster we used to have on our farm when I was a child. He would parade around the chicken yard with his chest all puffed up, just like he owned the place.

A common word for love in the Greek language is *eros*, suggesting physical sexual desire and not much else. Another word, *philos*, suggests the affection in a casual friendship. Neither of these words came anywhere close to describing the kind of love Paul wanted to communicate, so he chose another Greek word for his passage on love. This word, *agape*, describes a love based on the deliberate choice of the one who loves rather than the worthiness of the one who is loved. It is a giving, selfless, expect-nothing-in-return kind of love. Paul's description of love is short but it sure is powerful.

"Love suffers long and is kind; love does not envy; love does not behave rudely, does not seek its own, is not provoked, thinks no evil, does not rejoice in iniquity, but rejoices in the truth; bears all things, believes all things, hopes all things, endures all things" I Corinthians 13:4-7 (NKJV)

This is the kind of love that God has for us. He never gives up on us and He never stops loving us, even though it must be terribly hard the way we sometimes act.

Memories

February 22, 2009

I began this morning as I do most mornings; opened my eyes and jumped out of bed. Well okay, I *crawled* out of bed . . . but it wasn't long before I had an extra spring in my step as I realized . . . this is Sunday, the Lord's Day. Yea!!!

I sat down in my favorite chair and turned on the TV for the weather report. Snow flurries! How can that be? Well of course, this is East Tennessee and you never know what nature has in store. Yesterday was such a beautiful day; a might chilly but filled with bright sunshine and brilliant blue sky. While making my daily drive down Pittman Center Road I enjoyed some of the most beautiful pastoral scenery you could find anywhere and imagined how those brown fields would soon be green and growing, the barren branches of the trees would be bursting with tiny leaves in the tender shade of spring green and forsythia bushes would be in full bloom sporting yellow flowers on graceful branches. They have always reminded me of a ballet dancer pirouetting with arms and hands gracefully extended up and out. In my mind's eye, I painted that beautiful landscape in all the gorgeous shades of spring signifying growth and newness of life. Oh yes, I even put in a few pale orchid crocuses in the front lawn of the old farm house barely visible until you almost step on them and then I added in a splash of brilliant yellow jonquils dotting the fencerows and pastures.

Looking over to the right was the crystal clear and very cold water of the river as it meandered beside the roadway. I have always loved being near water, the feeling, the gentle massage of its ebb and flow. Creeks and streams always bring back so many memories. My favorite pastime as a child was going down to the creek which ran through the pasture and gathering tadpoles in the spring to take them back home in a fruit jar. There they would stay until they turned into little frogs and back to the creek I would go to let them loose. That is if I could catch them before they hopped out into our house causing my mother to scream and run. I can remember walking down the path to the creek like it was yesterday, taking my shoes off and dipping my feet into the shallow water running through the rocks in the creek bed. Our old dog was usually at my heels and lay in the sun waiting for me as contented as a purring kitten. The cattle used to scare me when they came down to drink and I tried to get back over the fence as soon as I heard them coming. They seemed enormous and I felt like a tiny ant in their presence, especially the gentlemen cows.

I can remember what those hot summer days smelled like and hear the banter of the neighbor kids wafting across the breeze. Memories from the past remind me how powerful and important remembering can be. Memory can be good or bad, friend or foe, but the absence of memory is a horror we all fear.

Faith has much to do with memory. Embedded in my memory are the many times and places that were special. Intentionally, I remember good times and good things. Just as intentionally, I push bad memories back to the reservoirs of my mind only to bring them out when absolutely necessary. Memory is one of the greatest gifts God has given the human race.

Memory is powerful. Let's use it to the glory of God in our lives as we remember His life and hear that gentle voice echoing down through the centuries, *"This is My body which is given for you; do this in remembrance of Me" Luke 22:19b (NIV).*

Yes, memory is a powerful gift! Let's not lose it or take it lightly.

An Ounce of Love
February 10, 2008

Yesterday was such a beautiful day with rays of golden sunshine beaming down from a bright blue sky. In a few days, we will celebrate Valentine's Day when young and old alike will be thinking or dreaming of love, the greatest gift of all. **John Wesley** declared the preeminence of love as he expounded *"Beware you be not swallowed up in books! An ounce of love is worth a pound of knowledge."* Though he was a great advocate of books and learning, he knew the strength that comes from love.

This past week I received an email that so touched me and was so genuine, I asked for, and received, permission to share it with you. It was written by **Leroy Rogers** of Maryville. He is in his 70s and he and I worked together for over twenty years in the insurance business. His sweet wife, Fay, is an invalid and Leroy cares for her daily.

"Having had a good rain yesterday, over an inch, and Fay not having been out for a few days, I suggested we go to Cades Cove and drive the loop! Of course she said, yes. We counted 15 streams with water running across the road, under bridges, or culverts. We only saw a couple of deer but several people were out.

We only use the wheel chair when we think it is a must! Today, we chose not to take it. After the hour-long drive around the loop, Fay said she needed to use the rest room which is quite a walk. When I opened the door to let her inside the ladies room, I asked her to stay close to the wall to keep from falling.

After several minutes, I became concerned, opened the door and asked if she needed help and she said yes!!!! So, in I went and locked the handicapped stall. {Naturally other females came in, but for a change, I kept my big mouth shut!} As we were leaving and I was trying to help her keep her balance, while holding the big belt around her waist. A kind lady opened the door and held it open for us. Fay said "thank you" and I added "have a nice day," which is common for me to say.

Now here is the "bone chiller!" As we started the long walk to the car someone behind me starting "patting me on the sides" as we ambled along. It was the kind lady! As she passed, she never looked back, or spoke, and neither did I. I was spell bound! Never in my life have I ever heard of this before!

Fay said "I think, in silence, the dear lady was wanting to just thank you, in a different way, for seeing to my needs at the time." This I shall never forget!

We know life is a day at a time for all of us, however, this is one time the "salesmanship" of Rogers failed him! Another example of, silence being golden, I think.

Thank you dear lady, where ever you are and where you live. May God send many more like you as we journey down the pathway of what's left of our lives."

If you have ever loved someone enough to share your life with them, this story will have to humble you while it tugs at your heart strings. Love will sometimes require us to go that extra mile. God is that love that shines in us, around us, and through us. It is *love* that allows a man to care for his wife in such a special way. I wish you, my friends, much shalom with love!

Broken Pieces
February 26, 2006

All morning, my mind has been whirling with the words "broken pieces."
That happens quite often as I get something on my mind that simply will not
let go until I address it. As I try to analyze my ponderings today, my mind
strays to the mantle above our fireplace and a very special earthenware vessel.

On Sunday morning March 14, 2002, I preached a sermon entitled
Broken Pieces with the text from *John 6:12 (NIV): ". . . Gather the pieces
that are left over. Let nothing be wasted."* Within that sermon I had shared
a very personal story of how my own life, some years ago, had been
shattered and how God had strengthened me to pick up the pieces. And
even though the scars will always remain, I was mended and made whole
by God's own hand.

Something within this sermon touched another person's heart and that
afternoon, my doorbell rang. There on my doorstep, being offered to me in
the outstretched hands of **Chris Gray**, was this incredibly beautiful vase
that bore the scars of having been broken and mended.

For all the years I have remaining on this good earth, this precious
piece of pottery will always hold a special place in my heart. It fills me
with joy and assurance that God truly is the Miracle Worker. He can take
a million pieces, gather them together, and fashion them into something
beautiful. He can take clay dirt and mold it into a masterpiece, and a
repentant sinner can be made into a child of God; pure, clean and whole,
fit for the Kingdom.

This week we will be celebrating Ash Wednesday and again I will be
burning the palm fronds from last year's Palm Sunday Service to make
the ashes. These pieces of ash combined with a drop or two of olive oil,
will come together to form the cross on our foreheads. I am humbled to
be God's servant as I impose the ashes. It is on Ash Wednesday that we
confront our own mortality and confess our sin before God within our
own community of faith. We will focus on sin and death in the *light of
God's redeeming love in Jesus Christ.*

My First Run-in with the Law
February 19, 2006

The year was 1954, and I was fourteen years old. It was a hot Saturday afternoon when **Dad, Mom**, and I left our home on Fairway Drive, in Cleveland, TN to drive to the car sale in Georgia. I remember it well . . . it was a long night and the first time in my life I was so hungry, I ate a hotdog with kraut on it! I did not like it! I was anxious for the sale to be over so we could get back home. But, Dad who was a car dealer, bought a car that night. The problem being, there was no one to drive it home. Except me! Even with no drivers license, I was excited to get behind the wheel (in fact I couldn't wait) and with Mom in the passenger's seat, we began the long drive home, following Dad so I wouldn't get lost.

We hadn't been on the road very long before I saw blue lights behind me. With heart beating so fast I thought it would jump out of my chest, I pulled over to the side of the road and rolled down the window. The officer told me to get out and open the trunk. I couldn't imagine why, but I did as I was told. Mom was squeezed up in the front seat like she wished she could disappear and I was getting really worried as Dad had driven on, oblivious that I had been stopped.

When I opened the trunk, I could see it was filled with huge bags of sand!!! Back then, if you wanted to have a cool car, the rear end had to be lowered and the best (and cheapest) way to do that was to load it down with something heavy. The officer burst out laughing which I took as an opportunity to finally let out my breath which I had been holding for at least five minutes. I'm sure my face was turning blue. It seems there had been a report of a load of moonshine being hauled along this very road and when he saw my car, looking like it was heavy with 'shine,' he quite naturally thought it was me. After apologizing for stopping me, he told me to be on my way! Whew!!!! What a relief!!!

I tell you this story to say that things are not always the way they seem. The most expensive clothes and the brightest smile can hide a sinful heart from everyone *except God*. We should be aware of that which lies beneath the surface, or façade, and not be fooled. Sand is not always moonshine!

"Do not deceive yourselves. If any one of you thinks he is wise by the standards of this age, he should become a "fool" so that he may become wise. For the wisdom of this world is foolishness in God's sight. As it is written: "He catches the wise in their craftiness . . ." I Corinthians 3:18-19 (NIV)

A Marshmallow World
February 12, 2006

"It's a marshmallow world in the winter, when the snow comes to cover the ground. It's a time for play; it's a whipped cream day. In winter, it's a marshmallow world!" Remember that old song from the 50s? I can't even remember who sang it but I think it may have been Perry Como. Those words have been whirling around in my mind all morning just like the snowflakes that have been falling quite steadily for the past couple of days here in the mountains. Have you noticed that those who enjoy the snow really have no age as we all become like little children; wide-eyed and smiling with glee as we survey the surreal beauty of the earth, covered in a snow white blanket masking all the imperfections and leaving behind something clean and pure.

There is an awesome scene outside our bedroom window this Sunday morning which would rival the most beautiful postcard you have ever seen. Peering through snow covered branches my eyes come to rest on the stately steeple rising from the snowy roofline of **Burnett Memorial Church** across the road from the parsonage. Therein is the belfry which provides shelter from the elements for the old church bell that has rung out almost every Sunday morning since 1951 when the church was built. The bell will be silent this cold morning as there will be no church today. The roads are icy and dangerous.

The glistening white branches of the leafless young trees on the side of the mountain beyond the church look like dancers mid-leap, frozen in time and space. The silence of the early morn is broken only by the scrape of the snow-plow on the pavement of the roadway below. Our birdfeeder is filled to over-flowing with sun-flower seeds for the beautiful cardinals that will soon come to feast. Freddy the fat-cheeked squirrel is still around and sees that he gets his share. Life is good.

I feel like I'm playing hooky today, or maybe even sinning . . . well, just a little! Nothing seems right! What is a preacher supposed to do if she can't preach on Sunday? After all . . . I've heard that is *all* preachers do anyway!!! You'll never know what a great sermon I had prepared for you today . . . will you? We were also going to welcome four new members into our church family this morning. Now we will have to wait another week. Plans are made to be changed; we adapt to the change and know the future is going to be better than the past, or even the present! *"And we know that in all things God works for the good of those who love him, who have been called according to his purpose."* Romans 8:28 (NIV)

Bumps in the Road of Life
February 20, 2005

I awoke this morning burdened to share a story of my own with you. We are so aware of Jesus' suffering during the season of Lent and I've been pondering on *our own suffering* and how it is often the *only way* God can get our attention.

If there are no bumps in our road of life, the thought of Jesus' great sacrifice on the cross never seems to enter our mind. When troubles come, how quickly we turn our faces back to God. Our lives are like a big bunch of *broken pieces* and we long for God to scoop them all up and make us whole again.

Some years ago, I was a broken person. A relationship which I had thought would last forever was ending and in the chaos of my life, I began to feel that everything was my fault and I deserved the things I was going through. I made a bad choice and it was up to me to live with the consequences. I endured each day much like a clown; putting on a happy face for the world to see and told no one of my profound unhappiness. At night, I would cry myself to sleep with the words on my lips "Lord, I am so sorry for not listening and for trying to make my will Your will. Please give me strength to come back to You."

God heard my cry and as I picked myself up from the floor with blood streaming down my face for the last time, I left and never looked back. All this time I kept thinking that God had turned his back on me because this was not the way it was supposed to end. Now I know if I had not left, I would not only have lost my dignity but my life as well. Survival set in.

When the miraculous gift of time had healed a portion of my wounds, I was sitting in church as the pastor read scripture from the New Testament. The only words I heard were Jesus saying "Gather up the broken pieces that remain, so that nothing is lost." I have no idea what the rest of the sermon was about as that verse kept going over and over in my mind. I stayed after the service for a word with the pastor and told her of my hearing about the "broken pieces." Looking puzzled, she looked again at the scripture she had read "Gather up the fragments that remain, so that nothing is lost."

The words "broken pieces" were never spoken aloud, but that is what *I* heard; God speaking directly to me. No piece was too small and no hurt too big that He couldn't fix. I knew he could take those broken pieces and make them into something pure and whole. He did just that! And he can do it for you . . . Just remind yourself that His eye is always on the sparrow, and I know he watches me!

Live, Love, and Laugh!
February 6, 2005

There is joy in my heart this morning!!! There is nothing like having pneumonia in both lungs to appreciate how good you feel when you get well. I really had a horrible experience last week, folks. That's why there were no 'ponderings.' I woke up one morning and found out that I was no longer superwoman!!! Horror of horrors! What a ghastly revelation!!! Something had crept in during the night, stole my cape, and left me powerless!!! I felt like someone had driven a Mack truck up my body, jammed on the brake, and left it parked on my chest. The rest of my body felt like Mohammed Ali had used me for a punching bag!

Have mercy!!! I am never sick!!! I hate being sick!!! I can't stand not being able to go and do whatever I want!!! My calling is to take care of others, not have them taking care of and worrying about me. Oh Lord, what a humbling situation I have been in. Now all together say . . . "oh, poor thing," and "bless her heart!" Are you feeling sufficiently sorry for me . . . are you sure? Now I'll tell you, I am sooooooo much better and if I were younger, I would dance a jig or turn a cartwheel. Picture that!!! Well, I did used to, could!!!

I'm also thinking on three little words that we see a lot of lately: "Live, love, and laugh!" Think about that! These words have been like a short and simple credo for me. In fact, I have a necklace with those three words engraved on it, a gift from my daughter Mia, many years ago. It is my favorite necklace for its words make me feel *just right* and that's *much better* than feeling *just fine*. If I choose not to remember any of the bad times . . . I've been living, loving, and laughing for almost 65 years now. There is no greater joy than living life to the fullest, loving God and your neighbor, and being able to laugh at your mistakes. When we get to the point in our life that we don't worry too much about what *other people say* we've got it made!!! If we are pleasing God, then we are doing everything right. So find a bit of joy and happiness in each day.

Elvis Presley once explained where he found happiness: "Having some place to be, something to do, and someone to love." By Jove, I do believe he was on to something!! The joy *of* living is finding joy *in* living!!! We never have to look far before we can find someone who is a little worse off than we are and in comparison to many, we are actually sitting on top of the world.

"You have loved righteousness and hated wickedness; therefore God, your God, has set you above your companions by anointing you with the oil of joy." Hebrews 1:9 (NIV)

May God anoint you with the oil of joy today and everyday!!!

Don't Sneeze on the Ashes

February 29, 2004

I started laughing before I got out of bed this morning as I was pondering *sneezes*. Yep, *sneezes*. Sometimes they can be so funny; especially when they are unexpected.

This past Wednesday morning, the time was at hand for me to burn the dried palm fronds from last year's Palm Sunday Service for use in the Ash Wednesday Service that evening. Now, I have no idea how this is *really* supposed to be done as 'burning palm fronds' has not been included in any of my Courses of Study . . . so far!

First, I got out the snow shovel, covered the big flat scoop with aluminum foil and put it on top of the rock wall outside the carport. The fire began burning easily using a small piece of loosely folded newspaper on top of the foil and next, came the dried fronds. They literally went *'up in smoke'* before I could blink my eyes and *'smoke got in my eyes'*.

Did you know that burning palm fronds smell a lot like burning 'pot.' (*Remember, I worked in the court system for twelve years.*) As I smelled that smoke and my clothing became saturated with the smell, as well as the air, I was praying that the **Pittman Center Police**, who make frequent trips by the parsonage, didn't drive by with their windows down! I was already envisioning the headlines "Preacher Burns Pot on Parsonage Premises!" My imagination began running wild and what great fun I was having, especially creating my alibi as I would meekly explain *"but officer, it was only palm fronds."*

Now here is 'the rest of the story.' Taking the cooled ashes from the scoop, I put them atop the dryer in the laundry room so I would have a nice space to work. This is where the fun comes in . . . keep reading . . . I began sifting the ashes so they would be all nice and smooth for the paste which would be placed in the mark of the cross on each forehead that night. The sifted ashes were all ready in their little bowl, waiting for the dab of olive oil to form the paste, when suddenly . . . hold on . . . *I sneezed* . . . and ashes went everywhere . . . which necessitated a thorough cleaning of the laundry room!

I laugh every time I think how much God *really is* in control of my life. Thank goodness! As you all know, cleaning house is not one of my favorite pastimes and I had been putting off cleaning that laundry room for so long! God tickled my nose with those ashes and '*a sneeze* made me do it.'

During the days of Lent, we meditate and reflect on our own lives and realize that we, too, need cleaning up. Sin has dirtied our lives just as those black ashes did my laundry room. Let's ponder the Psalmist David's need for cleansing and *his* prayer. Perhaps we will find that it is still appropriate today: *"Purify me from my sins, and I will be clean; wash me, and I will be whiter than snow. Oh, give me back my joy again; you have broken me—now let me rejoice. Don't keep looking at my sins. Remove the stain of my guilt. Create in me a clean heart, O God. Renew a loyal spirit within me." Psalm 51: 7-10 (NLT)*

MARCH
PONDERINGS

Trains and Palm Branches
March 24, 2013

Last week, while sleeping on the sofa in my Mom's home, I was awakened by a familiar sound in the night; one I had not heard in a very long time. It was the sound of a train passing in the night, its whistle blowing that same old lonesome hobo sound I remembered from so long ago. It took me back to the 1940s when I was a small child living on a farm in the Michigan Avenue Community of Cleveland, TN.

These were the years when there wasn't much to do except find pleasure in each day as it came and find something new to learn and look forward to. I loved to watch my mother and grandmother prepare our meals on the old wood stove. There was my special place, on a big cushion, on the bench at our long wooden table. I loved the afternoons when Granddad and I would sit in the swing on our front porch and he would identify all the bird sounds and other sounds that were in the fields all around us.

It was in the evenings when I would beg Granddaddy to take me to the field in back of the old farmhouse and let me watch for the train. We would take off, hand in hand, and he would lift high the barb wire of the fence so I could crawl through without getting scratched. I learned to count by the number of boxcars of the train and was so excited to see the little red caboose and imagining that the man in the caboose could see me and was waving to me. I would wave back at him as long as the train was in sight. What a grand time; so much innocence, so much trust, so much love; that of a child.

Today is Palm Sunday and I think that those who gathered to see Jesus that day were experiencing the same joy I did as a small child, watching and waiting for the train. Something unusual was about to happen. The Messiah was coming to Jerusalem! They didn't really expect him to make His entry in such a meek and lowly manner, riding on a donkey, but soon their excitement ran to new heights as He came into view. They hadn't a clue what would transpire over the next few days. For this moment only, they could not contain their joy as they began waving palm branches and shouting 'Hosanna!' over and over. Many took their palm branches, as well as the cloaks they wore, and laid them on the dusty road for the donkey to tread. This kept the dust from rising up and choking the crowd as well as the One riding the donkey. Only He knew where this journey and the week ahead would take Him. Now they were cheering Him, but soon, He would be ridiculed and put to death. Jesus was riding into Jerusalem to face the hardest week of His life.

"Hosanna to the Son of David!" "Blessed is he who comes in the name of the Lord!" Hosanna in the highest!" When Jesus entered Jerusalem, the whole city was stirred and asked, "Who is this?" The crowds answered, "This is Jesus, the prophet from Nazareth in Galilee." Matthew 21:9-11 (NIV)

Oh, and He was so much more!

Possums and Paradise

March 17, 2013

Last night, the light from the dining room window was shining out onto my two birdfeeders which are just about a foot from the window sill. As I looked out, I saw something strange in one of the feeders and it sure was not the cute raccoons and squirrels that I am used to. It was an opossum (more commonly known as a possum) with a long pale snout, and little beady blue eyes; it was not very cute at all. I walked over to the window and was within inches of the critter and it refused to move. Sat right there and ate every single sunflower seed. Oh well, I guess it found my little feeders provided a nice hand out and it wasn't going to let a good thing pass by.

These critters are famous for "playing possum." When threatened, they flop onto their sides and lie on the ground with their eyes closed or staring fixedly into space. They stick out their tongues and appear to be dead. This ploy might put a predator off its guard and allow the opossum an opportunity to make its escape. As I studied this little creature, I thought about God and how He must have had quite a sense of humor as well as creativity. You have to admit, some of His creations are quite humorous: redworms, centipedes, turtles, owls, armadillos, and a fat and happy hippopotamus!

The most unique of all God's creations, after the animals, is the human creature, you and me. Made from the dust of the earth to live and journey through our allotted time on earth and then return to the dust from which we came. This was **not** God's original intention but he went to Plan B once SIN became a reality in the garden. The Bible tells us that the man Adam, named his wife Eve which meant "the life-giving one." *"And to the man he said, "Since you listened to your wife and ate from the tree whose fruit I commanded you not to eat, the ground is cursed because of you. All your life you will struggle to scratch a living from it. It will grow thorns and thistles for you, though you will eat of its grains. By the sweat of your brow will you have food to eat until you return to the ground from which you were made. For you were made from dust, and to dust you will return." Genesis 3:17-19 (NLT)*

Have you ever wondered what our lives would be like if God's original plan could have lasted forever? If the serpent hadn't tempted Eve and

Eve hadn't tempted Adam and sin had not forced God's hand to deal with humanity in a much different way than he intended? It is merely food for thought for reality is ours. We are as we are. God has, however, provided a way through His Son Jesus for us to be able to enjoy the original paradise when we reach our home in heaven where all our questions will be answered and we shall meet Him face to face. Have faith, trust in Him. He is our everything!

Why a Donkey?
March 10, 2013

Good Sunday morning! Today is going to be a beautiful day I can just feel it. Even if it rains, it's still going to be a beautiful day. Why? Because I choose to make it so! Each one of us controls our own mood and feelings and we can choose to be happy or sad. Today I'm choosing to be happy. I'm not letting anyone rain on my parade! Repeat after me . . . "This is the day that the Lord has made. I will rejoice and be glad in it!" Now, don't you feel better already? Ah, I thought you would.

In my preparations for Holy Week services and the many sermons which must be written and the different aspects of Lent and Easter that I want to be sure to cover, my thoughts have run merrily to donkeys! I wondered why Jesus chose a donkey over other means of 'transportation' and my research began. I've learned a lot about donkeys this week. They're not really stubborn but merely cautious. They don't like cold weather, snow or rain, as their coats are not waterproof, and the water soaks through to their bodies and makes them uncomfortable. They are gentle and bond easily. Donkeys are also used as a calming agent for other animals.

Back to Jesus who chose a donkey to ride into Jerusalem . . . He chose this unbroken donkey colt so there would be no doubt that He was Israel's Messiah. If we remember reading in *Zechariah 9:9 (NIV)* it is foretold: *"Rejoice greatly, O Daughter of Zion! Shout, Daughter of Jerusalem! See, your king comes to you, righteous and having salvation, gentle and riding on a donkey, on a colt, the foal of a donkey."* As he rode into Jerusalem on this unbroken donkey colt what better sign could he have given them, and it's one of the reasons when they refused to acknowledge Him, He pronounced judgment upon the city of Jerusalem in Luke 19:41-44.

A donkey is important to the story of Abraham's offering up of Isaac, a sign of obedience to the Lord. King Solomon rode to his messianic crowning on a mule that had once belonged to David (*1ˢᵗ Kings 1:33-44*). In *2ⁿᵈ Kings 9:11-10:28*, we learn of King Jehu who rode into Samaria over the garments of his supporters to destroy the temple of the false god Baal. One of the first things Christ does upon entering the city of Jerusalem is to bring judgment to the Temple which had become a den of thieves. Like King Jehu, Christ, too, came as a judge over ceremonial regulations.

The Pastor's Ponderings

Shults Grove UMC, my Sunday afternoon service, boasts its own donkey(s). When the church bell rings at 2PM signally the start of service, the donkeys across the road belonging to **Deborah Williams**, begin braying loudly. The bell seems to be their maestro raising his baton for them to sing! It brings joy and laughter and reminds us of the important part that donkeys have played throughout the Scriptures; especially on Palm Sunday when Jesus rode into the City to the waving of palm branches!

A Taste of Elixir
March 4, 2012

Ah, March is finally here and the earth is coming alive! Spring is on its way and already we taste that great elixir which makes us want to get up, get out, and get going. Sitting here in my study I hear the happy twitter of birds preparing to nest. There is a scuffle in the leaves on my front lawn as they seek their breakfast of fat lazy worms who mistakenly thought they were hidden. One morning last week, I counted eight young robins having a delightful time hopping in the leaves and feasting on the busy bugs and insects. What gorgeous creatures those robins were; some with their beaks in the air, their bodies strong and straight as they seemed to preen toward heaven.

The birds suddenly flew to the lower branches of the small cedar tree in the corner of the yard; something had frightened them. Looking back I saw more activity in the same place where the robins had been. Three gray squirrels, their eyes bright and alert, bushy tails twitching in motion as they played happily, jumping and scampering in the soft new grass and warm sunlight. And I praise the joy of earth and its creatures!

Running through my mind are the words of the beautiful hymn we sing in our churches this time of year, "Hymn of Promise." *"In the bulb there is a flower; in the seed, an apple tree; in cocoons, a hidden promise: butterflies will soon be free! In the cold and snow of winter there's a spring that waits to be, unrevealed until its season, something God alone can see."*

Then suddenly, *"He sends his command to the earth; his word runs swiftly. He spreads the snow like wool and scatters the frost like ashes. He hurls down his hail like pebbles. Who can withstand his icy blast? He sends his word and melts them; he stirs up his breezes, and the waters flow." Psalm 147: 15-18 (NIV)*

We are blessed as each new season approaches. Spring is unique as it reminds us of the newness of life and provides the fresh earthy smells that set our senses on fire. We can't wait to shrug off the confines of winter and put on the newness of spring. So much to be done . . . cleaning the house from top to bottom, planting flowers, tidying up the yard . . . putting up the wool clothing and bringing out the light airy fabrics of spring. So much to be thankful for!

"Praise the Lord from the heavens, praise him in the heights above. Praise him, all his angels, praise him, sun and moon, praise him, all you shining stars. Praise him, you highest heavens, and you waters above the skies, Let them praise the name of the Lord for he commanded and they created. He set them in place forever and ever; he gave a decree that will never pass away."
Psalm 148:1-6 (NIV)

The Old Cantilevered Barn
March 11, 2012

An old cantilevered barn, belonging to the **Green family**, still sturdy and strong, sits far off the main highway at the end of the road leading back to the sprawling farm house. A crystal clear stream runs in front of the property between the front yard and the huge fenced pasture running along Pittman Center Road. In the spring and summer, this pasture is lush and green; yet even now, the horses and cattle that graze there have plenty to eat and are well tended. Huge bales of hay are abundant, from corner to corner of the pasture.

As I pass this beautiful scene almost every day, it has come to be the highlight of my morning as the sun's rays filter through the huge old hemlocks on the mountains surrounding the farm. The serenity that seems to exude from these fertile fields fills me with a sense of peace hard to describe. It is as if they are saying, "There is still goodness in this world, be still and *see*, be still and *hear*, be still and *know!*"

Taking a closer look, I see elegant Clydesdale horses nibbling away at the hay, languishing on the ground, or standing neck to neck facing opposite directions with their sleek heads close together. One wonders if they are whispering some kind of horse sense in each other's ear. Such extraordinary animals they are! Large powerful draft horses of a breed developed in the Clyde valley of Scotland, with white feathered hair on their fetlocks. But, wait, that's not all. Mixed in with the beautiful horses are Black Angus cattle, and if you look *more closely*, you will see a *goat* in their midst.

Now, that brings me to something I learned a few years back. I love talking with older folks who are so knowledgeable. Such is our Mayor of Pittman Center, **Glenn Cardwell**, who is a walking history book, encyclopedia, and memory bank. I have often wished we could clone him; he is so full of priceless information! Even the **National Park Service** comes to him for answers! It seems, according to Glenn, a goat is placed in a pasture with horses to keep them calm! I didn't know that!!! Did you?

And as I ponder this morning, I am filled with awe as I remember the *Twenty-third Psalm* of David who must have felt much as I do when viewing this scene of rare pastoral beauty. *"The Lord is my shepherd, I shall not want. He makes me lie down in green pastures, He leads me beside quiet waters, He restores my soul. He guides me in paths of righteousness for His name's sake. Even though I walk through the valley of the shadow of death, I will fear no evil, for You are with me; Your rod and Your staff, they comfort me. You prepare a table before me in the presence of my enemies, You anoint my head with oil, my cup overflows. Surely goodness and love will follow me all the days of my life, and I will dwell in the house of the Lord forever." (NIV)*

A Day Apart
March 25, 2012

It's another beautiful Sunday morning here in the mountains of East Tennessee and I can't wait to get going. Many of you wrote that you missed my "ponderings" last week. Thought I would explain I was honored to be the guest speaker at the **Cleveland District UMW Day Apart** at the **Soddy United Methodist Church** in Soddy Daisy, TN last Saturday. What a pleasant day it was, reconnecting with old friends and making new ones. **Kathy Farner** was in charge of the Day Apart and it turned out to be one of their best, I was told. The day began rainy and overcast but by noon the sun was shining brightly. We all enjoyed the time together and a most delicious lunch.

Being in the area, I spent a few days in Cleveland with my mom and slept in my old room. Mother's home is always warm and inviting. I was also privileged to spend some quality time with my brother and his wife. Funny, how much we love each other now; we used to fight like cats and dogs when we were growing up. Being a boy, he got to do so many more things than I did and I didn't like it. Therefore, I was a tomboy most of my childhood trying to be just like my hero, my brother, and wanting to best him at everything he did. Oh, but once those high school years began . . . well our years of quarreling were over as I found him an excellent big brother and he became my "ride" to all the places I enjoyed, movies, dances, and dates.

Have you ever thought about a world without love? What if . . . we never knew the love of our parents and grandparents, our siblings, pastors, teachers, friends, that very special *first love*, the one that made your heart race with joy, the precious love of your spouse, and inevitably because of love, we remember our first heart ache. The ache you thought had no end and you would never love again . . . only to find another love just around the corner. Throughout our lives we will experience love in many forms and love will wear many faces. Sometimes even lost loves will repeat themselves.

Yet, the greatest love of all is the precious love of God; the forever love that has no end and resists the ravages of time. We find delight in both giving and receiving love. In *knowing* love, we find untold blessings as we allow ourselves to be enveloped in the warmth of contentment, peace of mind, and sweet, sweet solace for our soul. There is pleasure in knowing we are special and thought of every moment of every day with a very special love that knows no bounds and, best of all, is unconditional. Nothing can separate us from the love of God. My friend, if you have never experienced that kind of love, let me introduce you to Jesus Christ, the Savior of the World. He is the totality and embodiment of all that is good; He *is* Love.

"I am not writing you a new command but one we have had from the beginning. I ask that we love one another. And this is love: that we walk in obedience to his commands. As you have heard from the beginning, his command is that you walk in love." 2 John 1:5-6 (NIV)

Spring is Here
March 20, 2011

Oops! Don't look now but spring is here in all its glory and I'm pondering on the new life that is all around us. The earth is warming up and awakening crocus and buttercups have already burst forth from their long winter's nap. Seeing their tender beauty brings a song to our hearts and a spring to our steps. I love the golden yellow gracefulness of the forsythia as their branches flow freely outward and upward in their silent dance toward the warmth of the sun. Too many folks are chopping them up to look like boxwoods and my heart hurts as they contain their beauty in a forced prison.

There's something special about this time of year! So much new birth; all of nature is growing, budding, and blooming. It makes me think of fresh new wallpaper on a winter weary world! And for a few moments, even old folks (like me) can look at the world through the wonder of a child's eyes. Anticipating, watching, and waiting for the next surprise with the new sunrise.

Birds are beginning to warble their morning songs, anxious to begin building their nests and preparing for the arrival of a new family. How happy they are, without a care in the world, completely dependent upon God to watch over them and provide their every need.

Our own sweet little ones are unutterably precious to God. As they come down for Children's Church each Sunday; I delight in how they are growing both physically and spiritually. Last Sunday, **Susan Carr** brought her little grandson, **Jax**, for a first visit. How sweet, pure, and innocent he is. Soon, when he begins walking, he will join the others in "my time with the children" which I look forward to every Sunday morning. Each child is claimed by God for training and nurture within the community of faith. They will have their time of growing and blooming as they bring joy and unimaginable love and laughter into the hearts and lives of parents, grandparents and all those around them.

So here we are, once again in the spring of new life . . . anxiously awaiting all that God has in store for us. New thoughts to think, new roads to travel, new paths to trod, new heights to climb, new friends to meet, new decisions to make.

What twists and turns are within the days ahead? I don't know about you, but I can't wait to find out!!! Why? Simply because . . . God is good . . . all the time! *"Godliness is profitable unto all things, having promise of the life that now is, and of that which is to come." I Timothy 4:8b (KJV)*

Wind Chimes

March 27, 2011

March winds have surely been kicking up their heels, or maybe I should say *hills*, this past week here in the mountains. I have awakened, almost every morning, to the beautiful sound of the wind chimes on my front stoop which were a gift from **Erma McAlister**, a precious saint from Shults Grove Church. What melodious music! It is good to be alive! I love mornings and I love this beautiful mountain home!

This past Thursday morning, I left home fairly early, around 7:35AM, to glean some knowledge and a bit of joy and laughter from the Golden Opportunities event at Fairview United Methodist Church in Maryville. My alarm failed to go off that morning (I had set it for 6:15PM instead of 6:15AM!) and I slept until 7:10AM. I surprised myself at how quickly I could get ready when I had to. Jumping in the car and heading out, I silently prayed for the "road law" to still be sleeping. Thank goodness I didn't see a single one and I got there at 8:59AM. I had one whole minute to spare.

It was still fairly dark as I pulled out and headed down Highway #416, and for the next hour I enjoyed *watching the day dawn* even as the morning mist enshrouded my car. It was like watching through a veil as the day dawned. The raindrops on the windshield soon faded away but the mist lingered on. I marveled at God's watering-can and how it provides the necessary moisture for the burgeoning soil to bring new life to every flower, bulb, bush, tree, and shrub. The green of the tender new leaves on the weeping willow down in front of the old school building is surreal in its beauty. I look forward to mornings when the eastern sky just over the mountaintop becomes brilliant red and the sun slowly climbs its way upward spreading its golden rays over the earth. Watching the day unfold is an awesome experience.

While driving along, I looked up and whispered "Good morning, Lord." It is refreshing to know that spring is here once again and a wonderful way to start the day is recognizing the Creator of all that is, and ever shall be. Surely better than waking up with a frown, a shrug, and a sigh.

I know today is going to be a good day as well. We have the assurance that we have a Friend who ever walks beside us as we journey through this life; how good it is to view each day as a new beginning. Who knows what God has in store! The day before us can be whatever we want it to be. We can make of it what we will. If we get it *started* right, the rest will fall into place. Let's make a determined effort to be a positive person; not an old negative Nell.

Acknowledge God, and ask him to guide our paths. What a friend we have in Jesus . . . and what other great friends we have in our brothers and sisters in Christ.

So, today, I'm thankful for morning, for Jesus in my life, and for precious friends! What are you thankful for?

"God saw all that he had made, and it was very good. And there was evening and there was morning . . ." Genesis 1:31 (NIV)

The Gray-Haired Soldier
March 14, 2010

My goodness it's early! Rise and shine! It's Sunday morning and I hope you set your clocks ahead before going to bed last night. Lots of 'stuff' has happened this past week and my head is awhirl with my mind's meanderings. May I share some of them with you?

Last Friday I conducted his friend's memorial service. My heart skipped a beat as I watched him; the gray-haired soldier, **Jimmy McAlister,** walking up the aisle of the old country church. Slowly, he approached the front of the church where the cremains of his friend from childhood were resting; the one who had also served a stint in the US Army. Standing tall and erect, he lifted his right hand in salute, a serious and far-off look on his face, clicked his heels, crisply turned and walked away. The ultimate respect, the last goodbye, understood by every soldier everywhere . . . and it touched my very soul.

Moving on to another thought and story I must share with you. Patience is not one of my virtues. My impatience gets me in trouble every once in a while . . . like the day I planned a trip to my **son-in-law, Curt's** home in Rutledge. I am probably the worlds' worst when it comes to directions; the only way I can get to Rutledge is with my Garmin GPS. (I am forever grateful to the dear friend who recognized my inability and gave me this gift which has become as much a part of my car as gas.) Being in a constant state of hurry here and hurry there, I drove to Newport (I knew how to get that far) and then turned on my GPS for final driving directions to Shiloh Church Road in Rutledge. The screen was blank!

My heart sank and I began to get nervous! I pulled over to the side of the road and tried to ascertain the problem with this precious little instrument. I unplugged it and plugged it back and still nothing happened. The screen was unresponsive to everything I tried. Panic took control! I knew I couldn't get to Rutledge on my own . . . so I did the only sensible thing I could do . . . I came back home.

Not willing to be defeated, I searched for the little instruction book that I had completely forgotten about. When I found it hiding in the box it came in, I began to peruse it from cover to cover. Ten minutes later I had my GPS fixed!!! Such a simple little thing! All I had to do was lift the cover (which I had no idea would even lift) and push the little black 'reset' button. Had I read the instruction book first, I could have saved myself lots of time and miles.

I am getting to the age that I am grateful for all that I have learned no matter what it has cost me. Years of experience have certainly taught me a thing or two. I know life is tough but I've found that I'm even tougher as I cling to the words "I can do all things with the strength God gives me." I have also learned that the instruction book should be read first, not later.

If we would read the greatest instruction book ever written, the Holy Bible, we would find the answers for all of life's problems. We would learn quickly how to find the fruits of the spirit that we need for virtuous living: those of love, joy, peace, patience, kindness, goodness, gentleness, and the one I have the most trouble with . . . self control.

Whew!! That was a bunch of jumbled thoughts to share. Perhaps you found some connection to it all. Life is good! I'm happy!! How about you?

Don't Litter
March 1, 2009

Wow! March! Finally! I have been anxiously waiting for spring, much more than usual. This past winter has seemed an especially gloomy one for me as there were so many days without sunshine; just sort of cold, dark, dreary days. (Beautiful snow days not included!)

Today is the first Sunday in Lent. During the next forty days we will be observe Lent and herald spring at the same time!!! I can't wait for spring's glorious beauty. To see the earth come alive with new growth; feel the crisp cool mornings and the warmth of sunny noondays; touch the warm moist earth and marvel at the tender shoots of each shrub and flower, taste the sweet nectar from the honeysuckle blossoms, and hear the birds singing as they flit about, happily calling to mates, building their nests and preparing for their own 'new life.' Ahhhh, spring . . .

There's an extra bounce to my footsteps as I walk along the streams and in the woods that I enjoy so much. I used to enjoy long, leisurely drives in the country but it seems that you just can't be leisurely driving anymore. Everyone is in such a hurry. Makes you feel like a stuck cog in the fast wheel of life.

Pondering on leisurely drives brings me to ponder on something I don't like to see along our beautiful mountain roads! LITTER! I wonder why so many people toss their garbage on the side of the road? When we first moved here, a little over eight years ago, I always marveled at how clean these beautiful mountain roads and highways were. Very seldom did you ever see any trash. Now, it's a different story. It seems folks can't find their litter bags anymore and they've all lost their way to the dumpsters. Remember the old TV ads about a laid back individual driving an old pickup, or was it a convertible, and tossing out trash. I think he was referred to as 'Tennessee Trash'! Guess what? He's baaaaack!

I just have to share a story about littering which was told me by a pharmacist friend, several years ago. You will probably get a good laugh, just as I did.

"When we had our Pharmacy in the Poconos of PA, someone emptied out their car trash right in front of the Pharmacy. Well, I saw it, picked up the trash, found an address, and packaged the trash neatly, with a note inside: "You

left this in the clean, pristine Poconos" and mailed it back to them. Then, I sent their address to the Fern Ridge State Police and told them to collect $300.00.

Another time, my wife saw someone drop a piece of paper out a car window, she stopped to retrieve it, then followed them clear to their house, into the driveway, and handed the surprised people their piece of paper. Then smiled, turned, and left." (Perhaps this is something we should all try . . . at least once.)

"While the earth remains, seedtime and harvest, cold and heat, summer and winter, day and night, shall not cease." Genesis 8:22 (NIV)

Feelin' Fine

March 31, 2008

Remember the lines of that old song: *"Well, I woke up this mornin' feelin' fine, I woke up with Heaven on my mind, I woke up this mornin', with Heaven on my mind, and now I'm feelin' mighty fine!"* And, that's just what I did! I can't wait to get this day started. It's Sunday and time for church! Hope you are up and have your 'Sunday go to meetin' clothes on. I'll see you there.

Oh, these beautiful spring mornings! The crispness of the cool morning air, the incredible blue of the sky, the gentle melody of the wind chimes, and the golden rays of the sun as it peeps over the mountaintop! God is once again bringing us into another season and another reason to rejoice in the ever changing landscape of life. Everything is in order. We must praise God and be *positively* thankful!

If we are to experience all the blessings that God has in store for us, we must "stop worrying and start living!" Don't worry about what is wrong and be thankful for what is right. Focus on the positives in our lives and by doing so, we will find there are even more than we ever imagined . . . and the negatives? . . . well, we won't have any time left for them because we are too busy rejoicing.

Live each moment with sincere thanksgiving in your heart and you'll find more and more good things to be thankful for. You might question if it is right to focus on the positive when there are so many problems in our world today. Absolutely! The best response we could ever have to the difficulties of life is not to wallow in them, and not to moan and groan in self pity and defeat; rather we are to be positive and move ever forward, away from them. There are too many good and valuable things in life to hold onto and let them take over our very being; thereby, increasing the abundance of our blessings, born of a positive attitude.

Begin each day with the realization that whether we enjoy life or not, is truly up to us. We are as we think! Our very life . . . the ability to see, hear, think, smell, taste and communicate . . . is a glorious gift from God! It is precious, valuable, and it just gets better!!! Experience the abundance of all that God has given you!

"In the beginning God created the heavens and the earth . . . God saw all that he had made, and it was very good." Genesis 1:1, 31 (NIV)

Pittman's People
March 2, 2008

One of the things I love most about living in Pittman Center is the wonderful people I am privileged to meet and call my friends. Last Tuesday, I was at the Senior Lunchroom in our City Hall and it was there I was introduced by **Mayor Glenn Cardwell** to **Dr. Robert W. Morris Jr.**, better known as **Wilford**. What an intelligent, interesting gentleman, now in his 80s, with a ready smile and hearty laugh!! Does he have stories to tell!!!! I sat there wishing I had a tape recorder so I wouldn't miss a word. But it wasn't to be, so I trust my memory not to fail me. Dr. Morris graduated from Pittman Center School in 1944, served time in World War II, returned to further his education at the University of Tennessee in Knoxville, and later graduated from the UT College of Medicine in Memphis. In addition to his general practice, Dr. Morris continued his medical training at the University of North Carolina and became recognized as one of the best surgeons in East Tennessee.

Everyone around this area knows or has heard of **Dr. Robert F. Thomas** who was one of the pioneers of Pittman Center arriving here in 1926. He was the renowned minister-physician who was commended by the President of the Untied States as a 'great humanitarian" in the early 1980s. Doc Morris (Wilford) holds the status of being the first baby he delivered in Pittman Center; although the most *famous* was probably **Dolly Parton**. After Wilford grew up and had his own surgical practice, he tells of a time when he got a call from Dr. Thomas. "Wilford" he says in his soft voice, "I've got a man here who has appendicitis. Will you see him?" "Well of course I will see him. Send him on down here!" Doc Thomas went on, "Now I want to tell you first of all, he has no insurance and no money!" Wilford told him "Send him on. I told you I'd take care of him." And he did! I tell this story as I can't imagine a doctor today, being that beneficent!

Wilford's grandmother lived to be 114 years old!! She had her first child when she was 18. On her 108th birthday, her family gave her a big birthday party. Her firstborn was on his way to the party when he was killed in an auto accident. The newspaper headlines read something like this *"90 Year Old Son Killed on way to Mother's Birthday Party!"* Wilford's grandmother lived another six years beyond that! God has certainly blessed the Morris family with longevity of their days. And yes . . . the town of **Morristown** was named after Doc Morris's family.

"My son, do not forget my teaching, but keep my commands in your heart, for they will prolong your life many years and bring you prosperity." Proverbs 3:1-2 (NIV)

And may God also bless you and yours with peace and longevity of life as you keep his commandments!

Daddy (Fred) Raper
March 21, 2010

Have you ever noticed that funny things often happen in places where you aren't supposed to laugh? I am pondering on one time specifically which happened at a funeral of all places. Heaven knows there is no more somber place to be when a giggle rises up from the very depths of your belly and you feel you are going to explode if you can't let it out.

My own Dad died when I was only twenty-three, so when I married **Clyde**, his father **Fred,** became like a second dad to me. We got along so well and I always enjoyed our many long and interesting talks. He had some great tales, some real and some 'tall' and I loved every one of them. Most of all we enjoyed laughing together. He had the finest garden anywhere around and he took great pride in teaching me just exactly how to grow the biggest, juiciest tomatoes and how to cut the okra in that special way that would keep it producing more and more of those delicious little green pods . . . fried up golden brown in a big iron skillet . . . uh oh, that's *another* story . . .

For the last year of his life, **Daddy Raper** was in a nursing home and it gave me the greatest joy to stop by each afternoon after work for a visit. I would help him with his evening meal then take him strolling in his wheelchair up and down the hallways and even outside if the weather was pretty and warm. As it drew time to leave each evening, he always wanted me to turn his bed down just a certain way. I cherish the memories with that big gentle man who allowed me to become a part of his family.

He died quietly and we were grateful that he didn't have to suffer too long. A great sadness came with his passing, as is usual when someone we love leaves us to make their entrance into Glory. We know we will sincerely miss them. If Daddy could have planned his funeral, I think in some way he would have planned it just exactly the way it happened . . .

The preacher, **Rev. A.J. Rowland**, being a long time friend of the family, delivered a beautiful message highlighting many special times in Daddy's life. He was extolling his faithfulness in the little Baptist church where the family had attended for so many years. Brother A.J. was telling about one Sunday morning worship service when a chirpy little bird flew straight into the church and perched on the beautiful painting behind the baptistery. He announced that the artist of that painting was *Willie Nelson*!!! What he had meant to say was *Willie Ferguson*, but by then . . . the damage had been done. About half of us who had gathered to mourn, had to use all the strength we could muster not to completely disrupt the funeral by exploding with pent up laughter. Even the preacher had a hard time finishing with a straight face. It was like Daddy was sending us a message that he had given us the last laugh. He would have loved it!

Even in laughter, the heart may ache. And joy may end in grief. Proverbs 14:13 (NIV)

An Ode to Clyde—My Husband
March 22, 2009

Many of you have told me you were disappointed that last week's ponderings were not about **Clyde**; that you had looked forward to it. So today I will ponder a bit on Clyde who would have been 65 years old tomorrow, March 23. This is a much longer pondering than usual so for those who are interested . . . read on . . .

Thank you to everyone who came to celebrate Clyde's life on Friday night, March 13! It was just what he wanted as he had left me specific instructions . . . truly a celebration of life and not a declaration of death. I wanted everyone to hear his beautiful voice and his solo tapes as well as his quartet tapes were played during the entire viewing. Clyde sang "The Lord's Prayer" acappella and then "Tears are a Language God Understands" during the service. **Rev. Carol Wilson**, Maryville District Superintendent of the United Methodist Church brought us words of comfort and assurance from the Scriptures.

Clyde and I were first introduced by **Bob Bean** who played the piano for the quartet Clyde was singing in and Bob was also the accountant for the insurance agency where I worked. It was not your typical love at first sight! It took a little time for us to warm up to each other as neither of us was anxious to get married again.

In one of his first phone calls to me, Clyde said he wanted to play me a song to see if I had ever heard it. I listened and said *"Sure. I've heard it lots of times. It's "Don't Worry 'Bout Me" by Marty Robbins."* He said *"Do you know who is singing it?"* and again I said *"I told you, it's Marty Robbins."* He said *"No that is me."* And I was speechless. I never did believe him until I heard him sing it in person. Then and there I fell in love with that wonderful voice and the man behind it.

We loved each other . . . for all the days we were together . . . we never failed to tell each other so, not once, but many times every single day.

Clyde was so funny . . . he could always make folks laugh! And, I learned early on how to make him laugh! I would sing to him!!! He could never understand why other people couldn't sing. It was so easy for him. I think he was born singing. I can't carry a tune in a bucket. So every time he got grumpy or down in the dumps I would sing *"You Are My Sunshine"* exaggerating the "you'll never know deeeeeear" which never failed to make him laugh and shake his head, covering his ears and begging me to stop.

Our early years together were spent going to southern gospel quartet singings almost every week-end. We loved Gold City and the Kingsmen and of course, JD Sumner and the Stamps, Hovie Lister and the Statesmen and James Blackwood and the Blackwood Brothers. They have all gone on to be with the Lord and I know that Clyde jumped on stage as soon as he got there. He and Hovie are probably having a grand old time taking turns at the piano. Clyde was multi-talented and could sing all the parts: tenor, lead, baritone, and even a little bass. When he listened to a southern gospel quartet he heard each voice individually and could always tell if someone was missing their part or . . . doing an exceptional job.

Clyde sang with so many groups as well as individuals . . . I wish I could name them all but for fear of leaving someone out, I won't even try. His last singing duo was with **Diandra Trotter** at Burnett Memorial UMC and their voices blessed us so beautifully many Sunday mornings. We will surely miss them singing together.

Ken Smith was owner and baritone singer of **Heaven's Avenue Quartet** out of Irvine, CA. This was the last quartet Clyde toured with; I think it was in 1995. Heaven's Avenue Quartet was the only group in which Clyde sang lead rather than the beautiful high notes of the tenor. Heaven's Avenue toured the western states performing thirty-six concerts in six weeks in nine different states. Ken told me *"when Clyde got off the plane, he did not know the program or the songs, and we taught them to him while riding to the first concert. It took him about 30 minutes to learn the entire program. My guys were amazed at him and his talent, but of course I wasn't surprised at all. He was the easiest guy in the world to sing with."*

Ken loves to tell this story as well: *"Clyde had a great sense of humor. When we were traveling, I remember one incident when we were ordering breakfast, and he ordered eggs, and the waitress said "How do you like your eggs?" (Meaning how do you want them cooked?) And he replied, "I really like them a lot"."* Clyde had the time of his life on this tour and brought back many memories to cherish and just as much to laugh about.

You always knew where you stood with Clyde. His personality was best described as raw honesty laced with humor. He acted up in church every once in a while to the delight of everyone. He was known to pull **Kat LeFever's** hair at Webb's Creek. I caught him smiling and sticking out his tongue at **Rylee Genseal** at Burnett Memorial and he always fell asleep at **Shults Grove** during my third service of the day. He said he had heard my sermon twice and already knew it by heart. And he always kidded **George Minnigh** and **Odis Chambers** about their singing abilities. Thank goodness they endured his humor. When we told him we were going to form a trio and sing one Sunday, he said to be sure to let him know so he wouldn't be there that Sunday!

Clyde was a good husband, a good stepfather, and he was a good man! He was a dedicated Christian all his life, loving, caring, compassionate, and funny. He knew the Bible front to back! Many were the times when I went to Clyde to help me find a particular scripture in the Bible . . . and more often than not . . . he knew exactly where it was.

Clyde and I enjoyed being together and we were best friends. We never had an argument that lasted longer than a few sentences; we both said I'm sorry at the same time and then promptly forgot all about it. He was a wonderful father figure to my children especially to **Vic** who was only eleven years old when we married. The other three were already grown and out of the home.

Clyde's passing was not easy and he suffered mightily the last few weeks of his life but that is all over now and he is resting from the struggle, at peace at last. It is time to say farewell on this earth to my husband and friend of seventeen years . . . with the calm assurance that . . . we shall say hello in Heaven.

Clyde . . . until then . . . with all my love . . .

My Bosses
March 19, 2006

Good morning! I trust that God has been good to you this week. My week has gone quite well. These warm sunny days have brought a renewed enthusiasm as I go about my "labor of love" in this mountain parish. One thing did happen that brought me sadness, and that was the death of a former employer and a true friend of more than 30 years, Leland Blackwood, Sr. I have mourned his passing.

So I am led to ponder this morning on 'bosses.' We all have those whose memory we cherish and those we would love to forget ever existed. I have had only one I would like to forget; jokingly, I refer to it as "The Judas Years" where I was extremely unhappy and I have learned they were necessary only to bring me to where I am today!

The 22 years I spent at the **Blackwood Insurance Agency** were the best! During much of the time I worked for **Mr. Blackwood**, I was supporting my children alone. He allowed me to become, not only the VP with a good salary and commission, but also the janitor (don't laugh) so I could make extra money. I remember when he and **Mrs. Blackwood** made a trip to visit some relatives in another state. They came home with some new business cards for me; a small package tied with a blue string. After I had thanked him, he said "aren't you going to read them?" To my surprise, underneath my name were the tiny words "Vice President and Janitor." I still have those cards and I still laugh when I see them. Later on, he hired me as property manager for the several apartments and duplexes he and Mrs. Blackwood owned. I wore many hats during those years and I made a very good living. I shall always be grateful for their generosity and the friendship of the entire Blackwood family. I cherish his memory. When the time came for the Blackwoods to sell their big home, it was purchased by Reggie White of football fame.

Oh, but my **Boss** now is beyond compare! Wow! He has put a song in my heart and laughter is the music of my soul. Blessings abound. Every day is a new day full of opportunity, excitement, anticipation, and wonder. Being His servant and doing His work provides me with everything I could ever want or need. My wages are beyond compare! He gives to me freely and abundantly and assures me I shall have a 'good work' to do for the rest of my life. My Master and my God! I am sated. And, it does feel so gooooood!

Truly, "The Lord is my Shepherd / I fear no evil / my cup overflows . . . and I shall dwell in the house of the Lord forever."

Tears a Flowin' Down
March 13, 2005

We can all quote the shortest verse in the Bible . . . *"Jesus wept."* But, have you ever really pondered the profound depth of sorrow Jesus must have felt as he shed tears over the death of his friend Lazarus and surely grieved right along with Mary and Martha. Tears come easy for some of us and harder for others. Tears are cleansing. However, many of us are loath to cry . . . because it makes us feel *vulnerable* and that's *not* a feeling we enjoy.

I've shed more than my share of tears but I must admit I don't like for anyone to see me cry. I'm *ugly* when I cry! I've always admired those who can weep gracefully, Scarlett style, with tears gently flowing down their cheeks while they dab them away with a delicate lace hanky. Me, I don't weep, I *bawl*, my face gets red and contorted and my nose runs and I snub and . . . well, I'm *not* a pretty sight!!! I would rather shed my tears in private if I have a choice!!

Pondering tears, I'm always reminded of a time long ago when my children were little; my oldest son, **Chase** was about seven and my daughter **Mia** was only three. Two other sons had not yet been born. Chase was always a good child and never caused any trouble. But, let me tell you about my little girl! Mia was a sweetheart . . . (she still is) and *an imp* if I ever saw one. Such a tiny little thing with blond curls and big blue-green eyes framed by long thick lashes. A real charmer she was; and she knew she could wrap me around her little finger with her tears. I can still remember when she didn't get her way . . . she would go stomping down our long hallway to her bedroom, little black patent-leather shoes tapping as loudly as possible and blond curls flying.

One evening I was standing at the kitchen sink preparing dinner when Mia came running in to ask permission to do something (can't remember what) but I do remember my answer was 'no.' She kept asking and I kept telling her 'no.' She finally left the room to go pout, and when she came back she began tugging on my dress-tail once again. As I looked down at her, she had managed to have tears running down her cheeks! With her lower lip pooched out, she whimpered "but Mommie, don't you see these little tears a' flowin' down?" I couldn't keep from laughing and that was the end of that 'no.'

Within the Christian life, there are also times of weeping and times of burden and sorrow; but, *insincere* tears cannot and do not fool God! Yet, for those who *genuinely* weep, Jesus has pronounced a special blessing *". . . weep now: for you will laugh." Luke 6:21b (NIV)*

Amen? Amen!!

APRIL
PONDERINGS

Wiley Oakley
April 28, 2013

I love books! In fact books are second only to my love for God and family and that's right up there. When I was at the Rose Glen Literary Festival a few months ago, I saw many books I wanted to purchase but I made myself a limit of seven, which seemed a pretty perfect number to me. Two of the books which I purchased were written by **Wiley Oakley**, a legend here in the Smoky Mountains and Gatlinburg. One of the books was published in 1940 in the year I was born and another in 1986. It has been a long time since I read such interesting books. They are published just as he wrote them, which makes them all the more real. I have come to the conclusion if we could all see the world through the eyes of Wiley Oakley, we would be most blessed. This man was truly a man in tune with God and nature. Everywhere he went, he saw beauty in God's world, trees, flowers, plants, old logs, bugs, and creatures. I want to share one of the paragraphs, just for your pleasure, and see if you don't agree with me.

"But as I slowly walked away, my mind wus wondering what a God that could make so many different mountains as I had been gazing on before dark shadows fell down among the butefull mountains. I only wished I could have had more time to gaze and dream of another world to come that is jest about to apeer in the east. Jest how long its not fer no one to no. But I leave my little whisper on a mountain top that is so high. Come see this mountain where you can sit or stand and see land below as dark shadows comes and goes from one of the highest in the Smoky Mountains, and you can study nature all around your feet. This mountain is not made by hand. I am not doing to much as time and money don't mean anything to me, and at this time I have meny good friends. I still want to sit on this mountain top and gaze and dream about its worth." *(Pg 39 "Rememberin' the Roamin' Man of the Mountains, Wiley Oakley.")*

Wiley was born on September 12, 1885 in a log cabin at the foot of Mt. LeConte. His mother died while he was just a small boy. He missed her so much, he began roaming the mountains thinking if he could get to the highest peak he would be closer to his mother in heaven. He said he thought the pretty white clouds in the sky might be his Mother's flowing white robes. He came to love the beauty of the mountains and all of God's creation which was the beginning of his lifelong journey by becoming a guide for the many who sought him out as a special guide and leader for their trek through the mountains. This is where he got the title of "The Roamin' Man of the Mountains."

If you would like to read the stories of a man who lived a life of joy and peace and simply enjoyed the pleasure of being alive in the wonderful world our Father created, finding beauty in everything, never in a hurry, and never seeming to worry too much about anything . . . go to Amazon, they have Wiley's books. He refers to his wife as the Golden Haired Girl from Scratch Britches Mountain and takes you on so many hikes and trails you might even feel your muscles tighten.

Pondering on Wiley Oakley, as well as my own love for the mountains and nature, I am reminded of this scripture: *"High on his holy mountain stands Jerusalem, the city of God, the city he loved more than any other. O city of God, what wondrous tales are told of you!"*

Mother
April 14, 2013

She sits still in the chair on the front porch of the home she has lived in most of her life. It is here where things are familiar, where she raised her children, and spent her days doing the chores of a housewife that she feels at peace. Her body is now bent with age and her hair has turned white. No longer is she the young woman who could work circles around everyone else and who kept her home clean and neat, in fact, it was spotless. The flower beds where she knelt on her knees planting flowers and pulling weeds are now gone and long since mown over so that they now blend with the rest of the lawn. Even the old hickory trees where she gathered nuts to put in cookies she baked for her children are also gone. Still things are familiar on the street where she has lived more than half her life.

She watches as the lady across the street dons her shorts and shirt and mows the lawn, rakes, sows grass seed in the bare spots, and finally hooks up the hose to water the seed allowing them to bury deep in the ground and shoot up tender green blades of new grass. A car goes by driven by a young mother, her children in the back seat. She wonders if they are going to a ball game or a dance recital. Someone else drives by holding a cigarette out the window and she thinks to herself, how distasteful and how glad she never smoked. She hears the singing of the birds and thinks how beautiful and wonders if they can understand each other. There are so many different warbles, tweets and twitters, a cacophony of sound like music to her ears. The Bradford pear trees in her front yard are full of dark green leaves and provide places of abode for many of the birds that gather there, and she is happy. She remembers that those mockingbirds can sometimes be a nuisance as their flight becomes more like a dive bomber toward lesser beings who get in their way.

Life is still good as she lives in the past, vicariously, from her front porch; her window on the world. No longer can she walk by herself without the aid of her walker and someone standing close by but she thanks God every day for life, for sight, sound, taste, smell and most of all for the joy of laughter. These are the most precious gifts! No longer does she dwell on material things but her thoughts are on making the most of each day as she enjoys the visits and care of her children and grandchildren, as well as her caregiver, **Nolena**, who sees to her every need during the times her own family can't be with her. Things are a lot different now, but she can still find joy in each day. Her memory is fading as she struggles to remember things that happened just moments ago. Memories of her childhood and younger days are still there but they are also fading. She knows God is readying her for the best which is yet to come. She doesn't worry because she has the blessed assurance of eternal life, a home in Heaven . . . whenever God is ready to call her name! **Mother**, we love you.

Getting Old Isn't Easy
April 29, 2012

How quickly the days are passing! The end of April is here and May will soon begin. This past week has been filled to overflowing with meetings, a Prayer Luncheon to kickoff the **National Day of Prayer**, the **Garden Club's Wildflower Luncheon**, a couple of weddings, preparation for Sunday's sermons, printing bulletins, several trips to Maryville to, among other things, pick up buckets that will be filled with food for Liberia. Every year at **Annual Conference in Lake Junaluska, NC**, as the big trucks blow their horns and leave out from Stuart Auditorium, our hearts quicken and a lump gets in our throats. We feel a sense of a job well done in knowing that we will be helping to feed hundreds of hungry men, women, and children who would otherwise have nothing.

I have come to the conclusion that getting older is not easy! I seem to get tired more often than I used to. Therefore, let's begin to pamper ourselves. What do you say? The first two thirds of our life was spent being good, minding our manners, minding our parents, eating what was good for us, going to school, studying to make good grades, getting a job, working hard, saying the right things (whether you meant them or not), and being a productive part of society. I'm getting a little weary now that I'm older and I think I will make a *few* changes. In this last third of my life, I will eat what tastes good (which means I will probably have my dessert first and my vegetables last), I will read a book for sheer pleasure, I will laugh out loud, I will fill my tub with mango scented bubbles and . . . I will allow myself to dream. Life is too precious to let it pass by and . . . who knows, this last third just may be the best part of all.

There are more years behind me than are now in front of me and I realize that all of life needs to be savored. Yesterday, as I sat alone in the swing in front of my house, I began thinking, pondering, and taking in the beauty of nature all around me. The spring rain had cleansed the air and everything smelled so fresh, the creek was gurgling along, leaves were moving gently in the breeze; it was cool and pleasant. I felt so blessed to be able to enjoy the simple (magnificent) things that God has provided!

Trials of life will still come. But, I am determined to think of those trials as "blessings in disguise" as that is when I am drawn even closer to the God of my salvation. My life takes on new meaning as I listen closely for the quiet whispers of His leading. He is the Rock I lean on, an ever present comfort and strength. *"I love the Lord because he heard my voice; he heard my cry for mercy." Because he turned his ear to me, I will call on him as long as I live. The Lord is gracious and righteous; our God is full of compassion." Psalm 116:1,5 (NIV)*

A Storm is Coming
April 17, 2011

Dark clouds loomed over the horizon and the air was still as death. Oppressive it was. The young mother's heart began beating a bit faster as she gathered her children together. The oldest, a son, came rushing in from hoeing in the garden next to the old farm house as he yelled, "Mama, Mama, a storm is coming; it's getting dark as pitch!"

"Come, children. Come quickly. We must get down into the storm cellar. We don't have a minute to waste." As she gathered her brood of four around her; they began descending the wooden steps; down into the dark earthen pit below the old farm house. She looked around at the barren shelves lining the walls. Earlier in the year they had been filled with hundreds of jars of canned fruit and vegetables from last year's crop. Meager now after all the months of use during the cold wintertime when nothing grew and fresh vegetables were scarce if nonexistent. It was now spring and storms came often this time of year.

Drawing together, mother and children waited anxiously for the roar of the wind and the driven rain to subside. Praying the dark ominous clouds would not form the dreaded funnel which would sweep away everything in its path. Mother and children sat huddled together and soon the sweet sound of her voice was heard singing softly, calming and soothing not only her children but herself as well. As the words of *"Blessed Assurance"* slipped from her lips, they felt protected by the mighty hand of God. Sometime later, they came up out of the darkness of the cellar and into the brightness of the kitchen as once again, the storm had passed.

We all must weather storms in our life and we draw together as children of God for his comfort and assurance. "Father, Father, help us," we pray. As we trust in him with faith in our hearts, he brings a new song to our lips, a song of solace and peace. We lift up our heads into the light of his 'blessed assurance' that 'all is well.'

And we remember on this Palm Sunday that a little over two thousand years ago Jesus rode into Jerusalem on a young donkey, to the waving of palm branches and the praises of the people. *"Hosanna to the Son of David!"* Five days later some of these same people would be yelling, *"Crucify Him! Crucify Him!"*

And Jesus prayed. *"My Father, if it is not possible for this cup to be taken away unless I drink it, may your will be done." Matthew 26:42 (NIV)*

Surprises at Easter

April 24, 2011

Happy Easter! Easter is full of surprises! Jesus certainly surprised many folks on this day over 2000 years ago. Not even *one* of His followers expected Him **not** to be in the tomb. When Mary Magdalene went to the sepulcher in the dark of the early morn on the first day of the week, that is Sunday, my friends . . . she found the stone rolled away and the body of our Lord . . . gone. Even when the angels spoke to her she was still focused on where was the body of her Lord. How could this be, how did it happen? Where was God? Where were the ten thousand angels? She was desolate. And it was then she saw someone she thought was the gardener and heard him speak her name, "Mary" and all of a sudden she realized *only Jesus* spoke her name in quite that way. It was Him!! He was alive!!! Surprised and oh, so happy, she couldn't wait to share the good news with Peter and John!!!

We have all received surprises at Easter but none of them quite as wonderful as Mary's. Like the time my youngest son, **Vic**, came home from an Easter Egg Hunt at Pleasant Hill UM Church in Maryville. His basket was overflowing with beautiful colored eggs, and all of them *real* . . . we didn't use *plastic* eggs back then. A few days later, as we were cracking and peeling the eggs to toss on the ground for our dog to have a snack . . . you can imagine the surprise when the first one we cracked, spewed out all over us . . . it was raw! Someone had forgotten to boil this one egg!! That egg smelled *so bad*, even our old dog turned up his nose, tucked his tail between his legs, and sauntered off to hide in the woods.

I remember another year when my three oldest children, **Chase, Mia, and John**, were attending an Easter Egg Hunt when we were members of Trinity United Methodist Church in Athens, TN. All the eggs had been hidden in a beautiful little city park very near our church. The children were having a grand time seeing who could find the most eggs and I, as one of the chaperones, was standing in the shade of a beautiful old tree watching them. Suddenly, I felt something drop in my hair. I knew it had come from the tree and . . . then, *another* something fell into my hair. Thinking it was just a twig or a leaf, I put my hand up to brush them off when what should my wondering fingers feel but a big wet pile of bird droppings in MY HAIR!!! Can you imagine how awful it was to have to drive all the way home with that stuff in my hair?? I will never forget that Easter surprise, it was *like no other*!!! Live, love, and laugh on this Happy Easter Day!

"Woman, he said, "why are you crying? Who is it you are looking for? Thinking he was the gardener, she said, "Sir if you have carried him away, tell me where you have put him, and I will get him." Jesus said to her, "Mary!" She turned toward him and cried out in Aramaic, "Rabboni!" John 20:15-16 (NIV)

They Made a Difference
April 25, 2010

Perhaps it's all in the aging process or maybe just a case of nostalgia that has me pondering this morning on the people who have made a real difference in my life. I am blessed to have had wonderful people who have nurtured, taught, challenged, corrected, guided, and influenced me throughout the years. Maybe you can say you are a "self-made" man or woman ~ but not me!! I know I could never have become the woman I am today without the help of the many folks who took time to teach and guide me along life's way. Some were in my life for only a short time, others much longer, and some for a lifetime but they all influenced me.

I always think first of my precious mother who taught me about God's love, how to behave, and to have a good work ethic. I can still hear her saying "if it's worth doing at all, it's worth doing right." My maternal grandparents were good, salt-of-the-earth people who worked hard, never owned a car, and stayed close to the farm where they lived throughout their lifetime. Their many friends traveled great distances to visit and knew they were always welcome in their home. My grandparents' table was always laden with delicious food; not steak . . . or shrimp cocktail . . . but fried chicken, scratch biscuits, skillet gravy, green beans or peas, mashed potatoes, sliced tomatoes, cucumbers, and onions fresh from their garden; and then for dessert, egg custard pie! My childhood was such a blessing.

I remember and am so grateful for my Sunday School teachers at Victory Baptist Church, elementary school teachers at Arnold Memorial, and those at Bradley High in Cleveland. Then came my mentors in the work world; **Kay Daniell** who first taught me to paint portraits long before color film came into being; **Clay King**, Circuit Court Clerk of Bradley County where I learned about our court system, and **Attorney Joe Goode** of Cleveland who taught me about wills and probate court; **Sam Feezell** and **Attorney Frank Bratton** in Athens; and **Leland Blackwood, Sr.** in Maryville. Now, I have great mentors and guides in my ministry; **Rev. Ray Robinson, Rev. Carol Wilson, Rev. Bob Bostick, Rev. John Trundle**, and **Rev. Eric Rieger**. And, I can't leave out the great intellectuals who taught in the United Methodist Course of Study: **Ellsworth Kalas, Brady**

Whitehead, George Morris, Dominic Nigrelli, Arthur Wainwright, and Winston Worrell.

God has been very gracious to me in giving me a loving husband and family, special friends, and colleagues; and the love and support of all my congregants. They have blessed me tremendously! Where would I be today had it not been for these folks? I don't even *want* to know.

"Remember your leaders who spoke the word of God to you. Consider the outcome of their way of life and imitate their faith." Hebrews 13:7 (NIV) And . . . if you have made it on your own . . . without any help or instruction for anyone . . . I want to meet you!

Spring's Garden of Color
April 11, 2010

Have you ever stopped to think what a dull place this world would be if there were no color? Color plays such an important part in our lives!! It brings us as much joy and beauty as sunshine brings warmth and contentment.

Spring's garden of color is in full bloom here in Pittman Center. You should see the yellow forsythia and the white Bradford pear trees in bloom! Magnificent! Morning always finds 'smoke' on the mountains as soft white clouds nestle themselves down into the misty green of the trees. The red buds, the soft pink and white of the dogwoods and other flowering trees gracing the landscape are now beginning to splash the mountainside with every shade of green imaginable, spring green, leaf green, apple green, lime green, brilliant and shimmering shades, glorious in their beauty. The early changing trees, especially the weeping willows by the creek, are already wearing new spring coats; awesome in the ever changing colors of the mountains.

I am doing my best to get out and enjoy these glorious brush strokes of color painted by the hand of God. I want them imprinted indelibly into my heart, mind, and soul; these colors warm me, brighten me, and lift me up as nothing else can. An important lesson is here in these changing colors; it doesn't matter how long your colors last in this world, but how brightly they shine while they are here.

Souls are beautiful, too, and just as each season has its own unique colors so does each soul possess colors of its own. We have the capacity to be bright, joyous and a pleasure to be around or dull, lifeless and dreary. I have known some truly beautiful souls and many are still with me today. The colors of their lives make me smile and my own life shines brighter because of their presence.

May we all live as beautifully as we can and let our colors shine as brightly as possible with boundless love, joy, peace, patience, kindness, goodness, and absolute delight!! And we shall live, love, and laugh . . . to the fullest!

"But blessed is the man who trusts in the Lord, whose confidence is in him. He will be like a tree planted by the water that sends out its roots by the stream. It does not fear when heat comes; its leaves are always green. It has no worries in a year of drought and never fails to bear fruit." Jeremiah 17:7-8 (NIV)

A Country Lane
April 4, 2010

Happy Easter to each of you today! I awoke this morning with an overwhelming feeling of blessedness; an awesome feeling of God's presence in a powerful way. This past week, I was blessed to participate in our Holy Week services as well as anticipating our Easter Sunrise service in just a little while. The past few days have been filled with so much joy as I sipped from the nectar of God's own cup.

If you need a real blessing today, just take a walk down a country lane with heightened awareness of your senses: sight, sound, smell, and touch as you take in all your beautiful surroundings. God will pour out his blessings on you, too many to count!! Many of you already walk, run, or jog as a part of your daily routine; but I mean a leisurely stroll, tuned in to nature, allowing yourself to be aware of God's presence.

Walking along **Emert's Cove Road**, my senses seemed to be honed to a new level of sharpness I have rarely felt. Perhaps it was because I had just left the home of a precious friend, **Cora Huskey,** who is ninety-six and mostly confined to her home. She sees God's glory from her huge window looking across the mountains. How blessed we are with mobility. I walked along being thankful as I experienced God's priceless gifts; the things we so often overlook and I indulged in them deeply and without shame.

The evening sun was shining brightly in a clear azure sky; its warmth as welcome as a lover's touch. I bent down to look more closely at a tender plant just breaking through the ground, and I thought of the miracle of *all* birth. The delicate sweet fragrance of tiny flowers, already in bloom, filled my nostrils and I felt wave after wave of sweet contentment. And I said, "Thank you God."

Walking that same path another late afternoon, a soft rain began to fall and the drops caressed my face, sprinkling me with a feeling of divine holiness. The clean smell of early spring rain and fresh mown grass was a fragrance so peaceful and satisfying it is impossible to describe. The sounds of the **Little Pigeon River** flowing past were ever changing, soft and gurgling in the shallow places and then a powerful crescendo as the waters deepened. Tiny whitecaps formed in the rapidly flowing and rippling waters, appearing as a miniature seascape in an unlikely place. Feeling the sunshine and the rain, smelling nature's sweet fragrance, listening to His silence and His rumblings; these things make me happy!

"For the earth is the Lords' and the fullness thereof." I Corinthians 10:26 (KJV)

His Mysterious Ways
April 26, 2009

As I sit here pondering, looking out my study window this dark, early morn, most of the world is still asleep. Well, except for that happy bird outside my window who seems to be chirping 24 hours a day! If a nest, some little eggs and a worm, can make for that much happiness . . . I think it is time for me to start digging worms! Seriously, I wonder as the day unfolds like a beautiful fragrant flower, what it has in store for me. Who will I meet? What will I do? Where will I go? How will I serve my Lord? Many amazing things have been happening in my life to bring me a constant source of awe and joy. I relate only one of them.

One afternoon I saw the Fed Ex truck coming slowly up our steep drive to the parsonage. Being a child at heart and always excited at what he might be bringing, I went out to meet the driver, pick up my package, and save him a few steps. To my surprise, it wasn't a *he* but a *she* who was substituting for the regular driver.

I believe God ordained our meeting that day. When she realized that I was "the pastor" it was like long-denied flood gates opened up and we talked for the next fifteen minutes as if we had known each other for *years*, not just *minutes*. She shared with me the many problems and concerns going on in her life . . . and, having been blessed by God with many difficult experiences in my own life, I was able to relate to her on a very personal basis. I could understand what she was going through . . . I could sympathize, and I could pray. I could allow God to use me as a filled vessel to be poured out for His good. This precious sister in Christ had a powerful witness of her own . . . the blessings we shared that day in a gravel drive, on the side of a mountain, was something neither of us would soon forget. We prayed together before she left. We asked God's blessings on each other and gave Him thanks for his powerful intervention in our lives that day!

Isn't it strange how God works in mysterious ways, his wonders to perform? Yes, strange, awesome, and wonderful! I can't wait to see what He has in store for today!

Remember these words from the book of Psalms. *"Look upon me and be merciful to me, As your custom is toward those who love Your name. Direct my steps by Your word, And let no iniquity have dominion over me. Redeem me from the oppression of man, That I may keep Your precepts. Make Your face shine upon Your servant, And teach me Your statutes." Psalm 119:132-135 (NKJV)*

Let this be your prayer today, as it is mine. God bless.

We are Easter People
April 12, 2009

Good Morning, and Happy Easter!! It's good to be alive because HE is alive! But, it sure is early!!! Easter Sunrise you know! *Early* . . . now that causes me to ponder . . . each morning this past week I have been awakened by the loud chirping of the 'happiest bird alive' who has come back to nest in the tree outside my bedroom window. This bird wakes me up long before I am ready. I may have introduced this little creature to you in my ponderings last spring! I don't know if it is male or female, or even what kind it is, but one thing I do know . . . it sure is happy! I have never heard anything like it. I believe this bird thinks it's a rooster!! I'll bet you there's not a rooster anywhere that can hold a candle to this bird, nor, wake you up any better!!! I know it must get *all* the worms because it sure is the earliest bird around! By the crack of dawn, it's out there chirping its little head off.

This morning as I sit at my desk pondering, I see a fat little squirrel, darting up and down the trunk of the spindly cedar in the front yard. All nature seems as if it can hardly contain itself wanting to burst forth from a long winter's sleep! The morning air here in the mountains is damp and pungent with an earthy smell as moisture gathers to invigorate the soil for birth. The warm fragrant days of spring are here. Familiar mountain roads present a new canvas as the hillsides come alive adorned in their pastel panorama of spring green, mauve, pink and white.

Today we celebrate Easter, the resurrection of our Lord and Savior, Jesus the Christ. We are Easter people, you know !!! *"He lives, he lives, Christ Jesus lives today! . . . He lives within my heart."* Oh, how I love that old song.

On that first Easter, more than 2000 years ago, Jesus' resurrection became our assurance of a new life, a life filled with meaning, a life eternal, bought and paid for by the precious blood of our Savior on a hill called Calvary. Every Easter since then, Christians everywhere look toward the eastern sky as each new day dawns . . . and *we remember.*

Christ arose on a day such as this. His resurrection signaled new life for all mankind . . . life filled with Good News! He said he came that we might have life, and have it more abundantly!

Judas

April 5, 2009

On this Palm Sunday, I'm pondering on Judas. Judas, the name that invokes loathing, the name we don't even like to think about much less dwell upon. But just for a minute . . . let's consider how important his part was in God's great plan of salvation. Judas, my friends, was the vehicle which put the whole process into motion. Without Judas, what would have happened? Would there have been someone else to betray Jesus?

Just as Judas was a very necessary part in the fulfillment of Jesus mission on earth . . . we can all identify our personal 'Judas.' Someone or something who has betrayed us, yet we have been able to use the consequence as a stepping stone to make our lives better! I certainly recognize my Judas! I made a decision to change jobs in 1997, lured by money of all things, the root of all evil!! I endured profound unhappiness for three years; but instead of letting the situation defeat me, I finally gave God complete control of my life. After all, He had a call on my life to say 'yes' to the ministry for 19 years!!! Without my Judas, I might never have received the blessings that God had in store for me!!!

Every day is the very best day of my life . . . and yours too, my friends! Why? Because God loves us!!! No matter how many bad decisions we make, what we have done, or how far we might have strayed, HE is always there! We are forever blessed to have a God who rejoices in our gladness yet also feels our pain and sorrow. We are His children and if we just think for a moment how much we love our own children . . . how much *more* must God love us. We are reconciled to our Father through his Son, God's own manifestation, into the realm of humanity.

If you have never *completely* surrendered your heart and life to God . . . today, the day we remember Jesus triumphant entrance into Jerusalem, would be an excellent time to do just that!

"Look, your King is approaching, humble and riding on a donkey and on a colt, the foal of a beast of burden." Matthew 21:5 (NJB) In describing the messianic king's humble mount in this way, the prophet had in mind the unpretentious, unwarlike nature of Jesus' rule.

Daddy's Little Girl
April 20, 2008

Many years ago, a young man left his home and family in Cleveland, TN to serve his country in the US Navy during WWII. When he left for boot camp, his son was six and his daughter was only three. He saw his family one time before being sent overseas to serve in the South Pacific. He was discharged in 1945, after the war was over, and came home to his wife and children.

The ensuing years saw his children grow into young adults but his daughter remained . . . 'daddy's little girl.' She cherished the pictures he brought home of the time he spent in the islands of the South Pacific and aboard ship. She asked a jillion questions about the natives who lived there and everything he had seen and done. Her dad died in 1964. When her Mother was going through her dad's belongings, she let her daughter choose the things she wanted to keep. She chose his white Navy cap and a pair of his navy blue wool pants with twin laces up the front. Life wasn't as easy as it should have been for his daughter and she lost all her personal belongings in a deliberate fire. Among the many items that were burned was her daddy's Navy cap. Sad and broken-hearted to lose the cap she cherished, she turned to her memories even more. They were all she had left.

Until . . . her mother delivered a precious gift which now has a special place on her daughter's night stand beside her bed. She picks it up each night and as she reads she remembers. As she runs her hands over the worn cover and turns the thin yellowed pages, she thinks of daddy and the war and how he must have felt lonely during those long days and nights aboard ship with only the rocking of the waves and the sound of the ocean for his night song . . . and he read *these same pages*. It has been over 60 years since her father held this book in his hands seeking solace and assurance and hope for the future; even in the midst of war.

Written on the front are the words "New Testament" printed in gold on a background of black. The symbol of the US Armed Forces is in the lower right hand corner. One of these was given to every man entering his country's service during WWII. It begins with the Gospel of Matthew and ends with the addition of the Psalms just after the Revelation of St.

John the Divine. In the back of this Holy Book there are words to many beautiful songs: *Onward Christian Soldiers, Faith of our Fathers, Rock of Ages, America the Beautiful, The National Anthem,* as well as several prayers and scripture references.

Thy word is a lamp unto my feet, and a light unto my path . . . and so shall it ever be. Shalom to you my friends . . .

A Glorious Panorama
April 13, 2008

Yesterday morning found me driving down the highway toward Maryville just as the sun was first peeking through the trees. The scene that unfolded before me was breathtaking. The golden rays of the sun intermingled with the colors of spring presented a glorious panorama of striking beauty. The tender green of the early spring leaves as they burst forth from once barren branches; graceful red bud trees filling in here and there with their delicate mauve and every field sporting a different shade of green. God is creating yet another magnificent masterpiece!

Last week, I walked along the creek bank below the parsonage and then traipsed back into the woods for a closer look at the bountiful display of plant life peeking from the dark, moist earth, just begging for attention.

So many interesting things inhabit this beautiful place in the mountains. Loudly chirping birds shout happiness from every tree. Squirrels nibble outside the dining room window without a care in the world. Their big brown eyes belie their intelligence as they are ever alert to any movement and quickly scamper away to hide when they sense the slightest intrusion.

There is so much 'God stuff' here!!! I marvel every day at His handiwork! No wonder so many folks make annual treks to the mountains. There are never enough hours in the day to enjoy it all. Living here is so different than anything I have known before. The pace is relaxed and the folks are genuine. A far cry from the business world I was used to for so many years. Always in a hurry, always worrying about 'business' decisions; and time and money were big priorities, *back then*. Business attire was all I had in my closet . . . high heels (ouch), tailored suits, and everything else that goes along with the trappings of a career-woman on the move. I was really quite successful, but I had no peace! Thank goodness, God changed all that! He has given me peace I never dreamed possible.

Oh, there's still lots of little society things to do if you so desire; and it's fun to 'dress up' . . . every once in a while. But, the *focus* is not on what you have, or what you wear, but on living LIFE and enjoying it. It is good here in Pittman Center! Church doors are always open and welcoming, not only to our own but to the many vacationers who visit often and soon become a part of our church family as they return year after year. There is joy in knowing that I am living out my calling as one of God's faithful servants.

"Consider the lilies, how they grow; they neither toil nor spin; and yet I say to you, even Solomon in all his glory was not arrayed like one of these." Luke 12:27 (NKJV)

Baptizin in the River

April 30, 2006

The young Methodist preacher, **Johnny** by name, was not much more than a boy back in the early 1990s. In fact, he was still a seminary student and had been sent to the little churches of Pittman Center as their pastor. He was to attend school on weekdays but weekends were to be spent ministering to the people. It wasn't very long before it became common knowledge that this little preacher was deathly afraid of snakes. Now, that presents something of a problem when you live smack-dab in the middle of the Great Smoky Mountains of East Tennessee.

As time went on, there came a need for a baptizing . . . not the sprinkling kind that we Methodists are noted for . . . but a full-fledged 'dunkin' in the creek. (If you don't already know, Methodism allows you to choose your form of baptism . . . immersion, pouring, or sprinkling). Well, the morning came and the church folk had all gathered along the creek bank to watch. They watched with rapt attention as the preacher stepped gingerly into the water with the candidate in tow.

When they reached the proper level of water for the dunking and were about to begin, the silence of the people was *not* out of reverence *only*! Each one had seen the big long black snake slithering silently not too far below the surface of the water . . . headed straight toward their preacher and the young man he was about to baptize. Each one kept their silence, their breathing barely audible, hearts beating so fast they felt the thumping could be heard a mile away . . . as they silently prayed, "Lord, don't let the preacher see that snake! Because, Lord, if he does . . . we're going to be watchin' a drownin' instead of a baptizin'!" God must have heard their prayers as the snake swam on by unnoticed, close enough for the preacher to reach out and touch it. When he stepped out of the water and heard the story, he fell immediately to his knees. Some thought he was praying . . . but he wasn't. His knees just refused to hold him up.

We all have something we are afraid of; a phobia, a dread, some kind of anxiety. What is it that troubles you today my friend? Do you know how many times the words "Fear not" or "Be not afraid" are mentioned in the Bible? Would you guess three hundred and sixty-five times . . . one for each day of the year!

The disciples also had times of doubt and fear. *"Why are you troubled, and why do doubts rise in your minds? Look at my hands and my feet. It is I myself!" Luke 24:38-39a (NIV)*

Mary Magdalene and the First Sunrise Service

April 16, 2006

It's 4:30 in the morning!!! What on earth am I doing up so early? Good grief, it seems I just went to bed and it was time to get up. Well, I guess I can do this . . . once a year . . . how about you? After all, it is Easter and we have a Sunrise Service at 7AM!! Will I see you there . . . what if I promise breakfast as well??? I thought that would change your mind!

Yesterday, three-fourths of my children and grandchildren were here for Easter dinner. Twelve of us gathered round the table. It was good to have the house alive once again with children talking and laughing. When you raise a big family you sure do miss them when they are gone from the nest. Having my Mother here visiting made it even more special as everyone loves "Granny Chase" who will be 88 her next birthday. My son Chase and his family live in Cleveland and spent Easter at home. They will be here later in the summer.

Most of the day was spent cooking and I enjoyed every minute of it; reminded me of years ago. I miss those noisy, happy times around the family table. Somehow, I've never got used to preparing 'dinner for two.'

As we were all sitting around reminiscing after stuffing ourselves, my youngest son asked if we remembered the Easter when 'someone' forgot to boil their Easter eggs before coloring them so beautifully. And . . . brought them to the children's egg hunt at church!! Some strange things happen at Easter!

On that Easter morning so long ago, Mary Magdalene was going to the first sunrise service . . . only she didn't know it. The Son of God had already risen. The grave clothes He had been wrapped him only a short time before had been lain aside and Jesus was gone. When Mary saw the empty tomb, she was frightened and wondered who had stolen His body and where had they taken him.

Mary came at dawn and dawn became a special time. A time of awakening, a time of disbelief, a time for weeping, a time of discovery, a time of wonder, a time of recognition, a time of running and telling. He's alive! He's alive! Hallelujah!

"Mary Magdalene came and told the disciples that she had seen the Lord, and that He had spoken these things to her." John 20:18a (NKJV)

MAY
PONDERINGS

A Bible Study
May 19, 2013

Traveling up Ski Mountain Road yesterday morning, I was thinking what a beautiful day for a Bible Study. A light spring rain was falling giving thirsty trees and flowers a drink from God's own fountain; their lush foliage and blooms taking on a lustrous shimmer. Arriving at Chalet #5, I barely had my car parked when I was greeted by **Kathy Wolfe** and a group of ladies from the Lutheran Church in Gatlinburg. They had invited me to come and lead a Bible Study while they were on a weekend retreat. What an honor for me and what a grand time we had. I had given them the choice of a topic for this study and they chose *The Bad Girls of the Bible*. I took it a step further and used Liz Curtis Higgs second book *The Really Bad Girls of the Bible*. The preparation for this study was a great learning time for me and one that I thoroughly enjoyed.

As we came together, we prayed, studied, learned, laughed, sang, ate delicious food and studied some more. It was a delightful day and I made new friends as we shared some of our own stories along with those of the *Medium of Endor, Bathsheba, Athaliah, Jael,* and ended with *Tamar.* The story related by one of the women in the group whose husband had been murdered in her presence and in her children's presence, right here in Gatlinburg some 25-30 years ago, held me spellbound. Our session closed with a prayer for others as we symbolically reached out with our arms, drew them close, prayed for them, lifted them to God and left them there. Our arms fell back to our sides as we let go and let God take our worries, our fears, and our cares.

That was yesterday! Today is Pentecost; that great and glorious day when the disciples were gathered together in one place and the Holy Spirit came down like divided tongues of fire which seemed to touch and linger on each of the disciples. This empowerment made it possible for them to begin the work that Jesus was leaving with them. It gave them the power to become teachers, and preachers, to make disciples of Jesus Christ for the transformation of the world. Jesus fulfilled his promise to send them a Comforter, a helper, and a guide, so they would never be alone. This power from on high was the same then as it is today. When the Holy Spirit comes into your heart and life you are changed from the old person you once were to a totally new life in Christ. That big hole that has been in your hearts for so long is now filled with the Spirit of God; we are His people, empowered to continue the work His disciples began.

"And it shall come to pass in the last days, saith God, I will pour out of my Spirit upon all flesh: and your sons and your daughters shall prophesy, and your young men shall see visions, and your old men shall dream dreams: And on my servants and on my handmaidens I will pour out in those days of my Spirit, and they shall prophesy." Acts 2:17-18 (KJV)

Oh my, did he say women too?

The Card Class
May 13, 2012

Happy Mother's Day! Once again we have that Special Day when we honor our mothers, those living and those now walking the streets of Glory. I am so blessed to still have my Mother with me. Most of you know her as she visits these mountains often and loves the people and places as much as I do. I spent a few days with her a couple of weeks ago and we had a great time together. We are not only mother and daughter, we are best friends. My own daughter and I shared the same kind of relationship. I miss Mia a lot on Mother's Day.

When I'm with my Mother, I usually try to help out in any way I can and this time was no different. I had found some small chore that sent me looking for a pair of pliers. Mom told me which drawer to look in and as soon as I opened up the drawer, I knew I had found a treasure! I couldn't believe my eyes. I quickly grabbed the small stack of old cards that were secured with a worn rubber band. Running quickly to Mother with the cards in my hand, I begged her," Mom, may I please have these!!!" She replied, "I don't see why not, those things are so old! I can't believe you want them."

In my hands I held Sunday School cards which had been given to my mother when she attended her "card class" as a small child in church. Many times, in my conversations with the older generation, they have mentioned attending a "card class" on Sunday mornings at church. I had no idea at the time what they were talking about but took the time to dig into its meaning. It was simply a Sunday School Class where each one attending was given a card with a colored picture of a scene out of the Bible, a Bible verse, and the scripture lesson on the front. On the back was printed a short story as well as questions and answers relative to the picture and the lesson for the day. These questions were used to promote a discussion of the lesson by the class members.

The dates on the cards I have go back to May 3, 1914 (which must have belonged to Mom's older brother as she was not born until 1918) to 1923,1924, 1925, 1926 and the latest ones are dated 1927. The color in the pictures is only slightly faded and the cards themselves are in excellent condition to be almost ninety years old. There is the browning of age and a few thin spots where mice from years ago nibbled on the card paper. What a gift from my mother to me! She had no idea that a few old "cards" from her childhood could make me so very happy! These cards and my Dad's worn New Testament which he carried with him during his tour in the South Pacific in WWII are among my greatest treasures. How blessed I am to have them. Knowing they belonged to my parents and how much they meant to them, make them even more special and precious to me, their daughter.

Shalom to each of you on this beautiful Mother's Day 2012!

A Spectacular Week
May 6, 2012

A good Sunday morning to you and yours! How I love the first day of the week! There is no better way to begin the day than by stepping outside, and breathing in a breath of fragrant mountain air. There is something blooming now which is literally permeating the air with the sweetest of all smells. As I had my devotion time this morning, and was thanking God for all his blessings, I again thanked him for this beautiful place where I live.

I have had a simply spectacular week; filled with so many diverse happenings and I have seen God's hand in every one. How blessed I was to have had a part in our **National Day of Prayer** here in Sevier County. Our hearts swelled with pride as the many prayers were lifted for our nation, our leaders, and our people. **Ken Jenkins** delivered a masterpiece of a speech as our keynote speaker. We all came together with pride and patriotism for our "One Nation Under God." The **Garlands of Grace** ladies and **Dot Egli** did a splendid job in coordinating this beautiful service.

Yesterday morning . . . well, I have to tell you . . . was a very special occasion and one I look forward to every year on the first Saturday of May. I attended the **Pittman Center Class of '49's** brunch. They made me an honorary member of their class a few years ago. What a time we had! Nothing could top the tales I listened to with rapt attention. These folks are as delightful as any group I have ever been part of. They really enjoy themselves and the only thing wrong was I didn't get to hear all the stories as everyone was talking at once. I would love to have been able to record the conversations and just listen to them over and over. **Mayor Glenn Cardwell** led the group in singing their school song and passed out a list of names of the graduates, those present as well as those deceased. He also listed the teachers' names and the years they taught at Pittman. It was sheer delight as I listened to the folks remember their antics, their teachers, and their years at Pittman High.

Saturday evening was the Open House for the **Pittman Center Heritage Museum** located in our new Elementary School. A guide was stationed at each exhibit to answer questions and explain its history. My station was at the **Dr. Robert F. Thomas** exhibit. What an honor to have his son **Vern,** his wife, and their daughters stop by and introduce themselves. Dr. Thomas was such a learned man who provided so many services to these mountain folks. He served not only as a physician, but a minister; he was truly a servant of the people. **Wilford Morris** boasted he was the first baby Dr. Thomas delivered after coming here. Of course, you know Dr. Thomas also delivered **Dolly Parton**. He served the churches here in Pittman which I now call "my churches" for many years. You can see why I love this place. God is good! All the time!

Daddy's WWII New Testament
May 29. 2011

Many American soldiers who fought in India and Burma during the Second World War are buried in an allied cemetery in North Assam, a separate state in extreme northeast India, separated from the rest of the country by Bangladesh. The writing over the entrance to the cemetery reads: "Tell Them That We Gave Our Todays for Their Tomorrows." Every soldier who has given their life, or offered their life, in the defense of our great country is to be remembered with honor and praise; not only on Memorial Day, but every day of the week, for all the years of our life.

A soldier who dies through the hazards of war and in the defense of our freedom has died for a great and worthy cause. Dying for justice and freedom, a soldier is forever joined with the purposes of God. So when the picnics are in full swing and the joy of the day is at its height, stop, and remember that freedom is not free and give thanks for all the men and women who have fought and died so that we might enjoy this blessed thing called freedom. Wave your flags, wear red, white, and blue, and savor the moments that have been given to you at great cost to others.

My dad was a Navy veteran of **World War II** who served aboard ship in the South Pacific and in the islands. There is a little black book lying on the table beside my bed; one of the few things I have left that belonged to my father. Every night, as I hold this New Testament and read from its yellowed crackly pages, my mind wanders back to the young soldier who held this same book in his hands for comfort in the midst of war; so many years ago and so far from home. How sad he must have been during those years apart from his wife and children back home in Cleveland, TN. How blessed we were to have dad come home safe and sound in 1945. I was five years old.

In the back of this little Testament, there are pages containing the words to hymns and patriotic songs as well as prayers for the soldiers' comfort during their time in service to their country. I am copying one of the prayers:

"A PRAYER ON GOING INTO BATTLE—Almighty God, our Heavenly Father, grant unto us this day such strength and courage in thy service on land, on sea, and in the air, that we may faithfully defend and

preserve the liberties and the lives of all thy dear children who are now suffering from unprovoked aggression and from unjust attack. May thy Fatherly hand ever be over us! May thy Holy Spirit ever be with us, so that we may quickly scatter those who delight in war; and may build an enduring peace founded upon thy holy laws and upon that unselfish good will to all those who love justice and peace, which Thou hast given unto us through Jesus Christ, thine only Son, our Lord! Amen"

Thanks be to God for our soldiers. God bless them, every one.

Shalom.

Zach's Graduation
May 22. 2011

Many of you have attended graduations this year, just as I did. Friday night, I sat in a jam-packed crowd as the Class of 2011 from Grainger County High School walked across the platform to receive their diplomas. Why was I there? My grandson, **Zach Newman**, the son of daughter Mia and her husband Curt, was graduating. When his name was called, my heart filled with pride. The hour of waiting in line to be seated, the loud boisterous yelling and the jostling crowd dissolved into the background. I felt in my own heart what I know Zach's mother would have felt could she have been there. Many of Zach's family and friends were there to support him and honor him.

Looking back to 1958 and Bradley Central High School in Cleveland, TN, memories of my own high school graduation flooded in and I knew just how those graduates felt. On top of the world! On fire! Ready and anxious to meet life head on! Some going to college, some getting married, some joining the military, and some . . . still wondering. A new beginning is underway, a gift to be unwrapped a bit at a time. What new adventures lie ahead? At this moment in time with your diploma in hand, the world is your footstool and you are ready to soar. Limited only by your own strength and desire, nothing is impossible if the will is strong enough to survive. Yet, the immediate thought is . . . no school tomorrow, no alarm clocks, sleeping 'til noon; the future will come as it will.

If I were to give my best advice to the graduates of 2011, I would say to each one that the most important thing in life is to make sure your salvation is intact. Where is Christ in your life? In your list of priorities, what position does He hold? God is a selfish God and He demands first place. *"Thou shall have no other gods before me!"* If you have Him in second or third place, or if there is no place for Him in your life, you are not ready to move forward. There will be many obstacles along with all the accomplishments and you must know how to face them, stare them down, and move on. I assure you, if God is first, everything else will just fall into its own place!

From time to time friends and family may turn against you but Jesus will always be there; to love you, guide you, and see you through. Pray;

then be open to His will. His ways will not always be your ways so how will you know if the path you choose is God's way? It will feel right and there will be no doubt. The greatest ideas formed in a human mind compliant with God's will, live on and bear much fruit.

"Truly my soul waiteth upon God: from him cometh my salvation. He only is my rock and my salvation; he is my defence; I shall not be greatly moved." Psalm 62:1-2 (KJV)

This Is My Father's World
May 15, 2011

Driving home in the cool of the evening with a soft breeze wafting through the open window of my car, I can't think of a thing that would have been more pleasant at that moment in time. The sound of the cicadas reminded me of a mighty army preparing for battle with loud and boisterous song. Maybe Joshua was the name of their leader as they prepared to "fit the battle of Jericho". Even the sound of **Clyde's** CD was drowned out as they sang their mighty song. Listening carefully, I tried to hear the usual sounds of the late evening along the creek bank as the water gurgled along the side of the roadway. There was nothing, only cicadas.

As I passed each field, the green and gold of the landscape was breathtaking. Add to that the black dots of Angus cattle as they fed on the green grass and round bales of hay, and you had a pastoral scene that artists dream of. In this area of East Tennessee, it seems there is always something growing and blooming, something eye catching, in unexpected places. Fields of purple clover and waves of grain touch my soul as nothing else can. How lovely to the eye is all of God's natural creation.

Even the old barns, some almost falling to the ground and others repaired and repainted, bring a wave of nostalgia. I envision the old ladder in the hallway of the barn leading up to the loft where I used to delight in finding a hen's nest full of eggs we hadn't known was there. I smell the fragrant honeysuckles growing along the fence rows; knowing in the center of each delicate flower is a drop of nectar, oh, so sweet.

Just around a curve in the road, an old wooden church comes into view. This small one room building was formerly called a chapel and visions of an old time "preacher man" extolling the Gospel and wiping sweat from his brow with the handkerchief he waves in his hand, comes into my mind. I can almost hear the cracked bass voices of the older men as they join with the sweet sopranos of the young women singing out the old hymns of the church. How they echoed over the hillsides and I can still hear "Amazing Grace" and "When the Roll is Called Up Yonder" as clear as way back then.

Lost in my reverie, I marvel as I look up to the sky and mouth a silent "thank you" to God for allowing me to see, hear, touch, taste, and smell.

With the moon in the sky behind me and the setting sun in front of me, I find amazing beauty in the most unlikely places. Driving along a country road is just another little bit of heaven on earth.

"This is my Father's world, and to my listening ears . . . all nature sings, and round me rings the music of the spheres. This is my Father's world: I rest me in the thought of rocks and trees, of skies and seas; his hand the wonders wrought."

Celebrate

May 8, 2011

Happy Mother's Day! What a wonderful day this is going to be; a day to celebrate mothers and a day to rejoice in our children. I have three wonderful sons and a great son-in-law who stands in for my only daughter who is spending her second Mother's Day in heaven. My own mother is just the absolute best. She is not only a godly mother whom I love with all my heart, but my best friend as well. She will soon be 93 and has returned to our family home in Cleveland after spending the month of April with me here in the mountains.

Yesterday was filled with surprises. I enjoyed brunch with the Pittman High School Alumni Class of '49 down at City Hall. They adopted me about 10 years ago and I attend every year. The food was oh so delicious and the company, well, what can I say . . . I enjoyed every minute. I hung on every word as they were telling their stories of days gone by. I wish I had taken a tape recorder. Everyone was so excited they were talking over the top of each other. I would get the beginning of one delightful story and hear the end of another.

One thing I know for sure, **Ms Pearsal's** ears were burning in heaven as she was revered as a favorite teacher. Someone was asked if **Mr. Quigley** ever hit them with his cane and was answered "no, but I know many who were!" **Ruby** said "Remember when **Blanche** took her algebra book down to the creek bank and set it on fire?" Then she reminisced that if it had not been for the **Booger Town Bus** coming by her house, she would never have been able to attend high school. Of course, **Mayor Glenn Cardwell** was the life of the party as he passed around pictures taken "way back when." **Pauline** delighted in showing me the pictures made on the day they graduated and pointed to a lovely young lady as she said, "that's me." Then she went on to name all the others who graduated that year. The young women were so dressed up; hats, suits, high heels, etc; so very different from today.

So much of our past is still with us in our hearts and minds. What a wonderful gift, the gift of remembrance, especially when it brings with it so much joy and laughter.

When I returned home from the brunch, I found a lovely bouquet of cut flowers waiting for me. There was no name so I don't know who to thank but they sure lifted my spirits. Just as I sat down for a lonely afternoon, a dear friend came bringing a big dish of homemade lasagna! Was it ever good, a new recipe made with Italian sausage. I won't have to cook for the next several days! I am one blessed woman.

So my dear friends, live well, love always, laugh often, and think kind thoughts. Remember to put God first in your life and everything else will fall into place.

A Trek to the Creek

May 15, 2010

Walking down the road in front of the parsonage on a sunny spring afternoon, I'm headed toward my favorite place, a bench just across from the old Pittman Center Elementary School. I love these treks down to the creek and I can feel my heart beginning to beat just a little faster as I near my destination. Taking a deep breath of the clear mountain air and letting it out with a sigh, I take a seat beside the crystal clear waters. It is here, I find my peace.

The sound of the rippling water is soothing as it flows ever so gently over rocks worn smooth from the water's caress. The small stones and pebbles have increased in number from last year and taken on a new design higher on the bank, fashioned by nature and the rains of the past year. Four lazy turtles have crawled out of the water and upon a log jutting up in mid-stream. They are basking in the sun's warmth. It is here, I am reminded of the tranquil moments of my life.

Walking back home, I pass the dark murky pools of water hiding huge boulders, tangled roots, and slithering black snakes swimming gracefully along. The fish gather in these deeper pools and it is here we must step closer to really see what is lying underneath. I see more clearly now, the intertwined roots of the willow tree growing half in and half out of the water. They appear as long skeletal feet with even longer toes dipping in and testing the temperature of the water. Some going deeper than others seeking to find whatever may be found. It is here, I am reminded of the dark, seeking, trying times of indecision and turmoil in my life.

Further upstream and almost home, I pass the bridge and stop to gaze below. I see clear waters once again, rushing over the rocks, dipping down and spewing back up in frothy white bubbles, leaving giant gurgles, giggles, and the harmonious laughter of nature in their wake. Sights and sounds: exciting, exhilarating, clear, dancing, melodious, vibrant and strong, magnificently displayed for all who have ears to hear and eyes to see. It is here, I am reminded of my youth, of love and laughter, energy, merriment; of LIFE fulfilled, and God's great goodness displayed in a single stream of many moods in the mountains.

And as I walked up the drive leading to the parsonage and my home, I saw a tiny weed growing victoriously in a crack of the well-worn pavement!

No Greater Joy
May 9, 2010

A plaque hangs on the wall of my study which reads *"I have no greater joy than to hear that my children walk in truth." 3 John: 4 (NKJV)* That's the first thing that caught my sleepy eyes as I came into my study this morning, barely awake, but rarin' to go. It's Sunday!!! Hallelujah! and, Amen! It's good to be alive!

On this Mother's Day, my prayer is that my children do walk in truth; to know they have a strong relationship with our Heavenly Father; and allow Him to be their guide. Each one has endured "speed bumps" as they have sped along life's highway but God has been by their side; and I'm so thankful. I have tried to teach them that wealth is never measured by the amount of money you have in your pocket, or in your bank account, but by the joy and peace that God puts in your heart!

My own mother taught me what it means to be a "real mother" she was a sweet, unselfish woman who prayed for her children and introduced them to God. Her family always came first as her own wants and needs oftentimes went unnoticed. Her guidance in our home was her ministry, and I truly believe she fulfilled God's intention for her life. Some may have called it dull domestic housework but not my Mom . . . she was always there for me and my brother and she still is at 91!! We didn't have to say "do you love me?" She showed it in everything thing she did and every word she spoke. In my little girl eyes, and still today, I see her as a saint. Hers was a holy calling. She taught us about God and what it means to always "do right." The paths we trod were sometimes filled with doubt and fear, and sometimes pain and sorrow; but we were taught to hold fast to God's hand and we would never go wrong.

My greatest delight in this life is my own children. Each one . . . unique and special, differing from each other in so many ways but held together by a common bond called FAMILY. I am thankful for the good times we have shared, the laughter as well as the tears, and the joy as well as the heartaches. My only daughter, Mia, is spending her first Mother's Day in heaven and I miss her every day of my life. Today will not be an easy one for her husband and two sons. I continue to praise God for her life and for my three sons, son-in-law, and two daughters-in-law who continue to fill my life with joy and gladness and not a small amount of pride.

I have no wealth to leave them, at least nothing material. But one thing I am sure of, they know they are loved and that I thank God for each one of them.

I have learned a lot from my children as well . . . patience most of all. One of the things I remember most was their forgiveness and the laughter in their eyes when I had to say "I'm sorry, you were right and I was wrong!"

"Honor your father and your mother, that your days may be long upon the land which the Lord your God is giving you." Exodus 20:12 ((NKJV)

Always Beautiful
May 2, 2010

Good morning! What a beautiful Lord's Day . . . they are all beautiful to me! I can think of nothing better than getting up every morning in beautiful Pittman Center, Tennessee. I've told you before I am so blessed that God, the Bishop, and the District Superintendent appointed me to this charge almost ten years ago. I have loved every minute of it!

Let me tell you about yesterday morning! Once again my mother and I were invited guests at the Pittman Center Class of 1949's Annual Breakfast hosted by Blanch Moyers. We had the best time! Eating good food and listening to funny stories is about as good as it gets. I just sat back and listened . . .

"Remember when I finally got out of that algebra class? I went down by the creek and I burned that book! I hated algebra!"

"Oh, and do you remember Ms.—? She was a nervous sort wasn't she?

Remember every time we would act up, she would say "Now children, straighten up or we will have to pray.""

"Do you know our class is the only one that still has an annual meeting? There were twenty of us in the graduating class and seven of us are here this morning!" (Whereupon, **Mayor Glenn Cardwell**, a member of the class, read the roll of the deceased members and each one who was absent was recognized and remembered.)

Mom and I sat next to **Ruby** who had us in stitches when she told about the boy who sat behind her who undid the sash to her dress and tied her to the back of the chair during class. When class was over, she couldn't get up . . . I laughed so hard as I mentally pictured this scene.

"Remember our principal, **Dr. Quigley**? Lord, have mercy! I was scared to death of that man!" and on and on . . . wish I had more time to tell you more stories this morning but I better get crackin'. It is time to get ready for church!

Before we left, I was duly sworn in by Mayor Glenn as an honorary member of the "Class of 49" and officially became a "Forty-Niner." What a delightful morning and one I shall long remember.

Memories, passed along to each generation by the elders, keep our history alive. The land and its people will live on in the hearts and minds of those who care to listen, remember, and pass them on to the next generation.

What may seem mundane and insignificant now, will someday be recalled as a 'remember when' becoming the source of many conversations and thoughts as we grow older . . . sitting on the front porch in an old swing or rocking chair; talking and laughing, as we, too, recall days gone by.

There is another time when it is important to listen, listen very closely, and learn . . . to that still small voice of God. In order to hear him we must be quiet. *"Be still, and know that I am God." Psalm 46:10a (NIV)* Do you ever feel guilty when you hear that verse? There are times when guilt almost overwhelms me. *James 1:19* speaks also of hearing, *"My dear brothers, take note of this: Everyone should be quick to isten, slow to speak and slow to become angry," (NIV)* Listen! Can you hear Him?

The Wind's Warm Embrace
May 31, 2009

It's Pentecost!!! Today we celebrate the birthday of the church. The day when the Holy Spirit of God came down from heaven like the sound of a rushing mighty wind and tongues of fire which filled the hearts and lives of the disciples who would now become His apostles. Pentecost brought the Holy Spirit, the third person of the Trinity, which united them, enabled them, and filled them with power and praise.

One afternoon this past week I was sitting in our front yard enjoying the sunshine, the spring blossoms, birds singing, and the sound of squirrels as they chattered away. All of a sudden a strong gust of wind came through seemingly out of nowhere and enveloped me in its embrace. As I shivered, I thought of God's strong arms holding me and I felt so very close to Him. As I savored the moment of that oneness with God I began to ponder on how He speaks to us in so many different ways. God speaks to me through nature; the gurgling of the creek, the sweet fragrance of flowers, the sturdy old trees on this lovely mountainside, little river rocks that move endlessly on their journey, and most of all . . . the wind.

We wonder, "Where did it come from, and where is it going?" *John 3:8* tells us *"The wind blows wherever it pleases. You hear its sound, but you cannot tell where it comes from or where it is going. So it is with everyone born of the Spirit." (NIV)* We can't see it but we know it's there because we feel it, we hear it and we can see the results of where it has been in changed lives and miracles wrought. No one questions the wind's existence even though we can't hold it in our hands or put it in a jar. The wind is as the Holy Spirit of God, the third person of the Trinity, the very hand of God touching and caressing everything that He has created. It's like a mother's goodnight kiss, or a father's big bear hug. It empowers us and comforts us; the hand that assures us He is always there, leading and guiding, providing strength for each new day and joy as we embark on each new journey.

All of this pondering has brought to mind a nursery rhyme my mother used to read to me long, long ago. It was entitled *"The Wind"* and just in case you've never heard it, it goes something like this . . . *"Who has seen the wind? Neither I nor you. But when the wind comes passing through, It says to whitt, to whoooo."* Have an empowering Pentecost my friends!!!

A Sweet Fragrance
May 24, 2009

As I stepped outside into the pleasant coolness of today's early dawn, I was greeted with the sweetest fragrance of honeysuckle permeating the air, bringing back memories of another time and another place. I have always loved the smell of honeysuckles which takes me back to my childhood and to the farm where they grew in wild, abandoned beauty. The graceful tendrils of white and yellow blossoms hanging over the roof on the porch of the old farmhouse where we lived, over the smokehouse, and draping the fence rows, lending an air of indescribable fragrance and beauty to those days of old. Even today as I breathe in deeply, it seems as if God is again bathing this new day in that same fragrant promise of His own sweet love. And I pondered how blessed I am.

We have had lots of rain this spring and though we need the rain, I love days filled with sunshine!! They are so uplifting, spirit filled, joyous, energetic, and they make me happy. I remember a time about four years ago when we returned home from a completely sunless vacation to the beach. We could have stayed home and gone to the movies or read a good book which was about all we could do in the rain! Upon arriving back in Pittman Center, I wanted to physically hug these mountains and blow kisses to the sky! I do need to be honest though and tell you we actually had a very peaceful and relaxing time. I loved the wee hours of the early mornings best of all. I found great joy quietly sitting under a big cabana on the beach, watching and meditating as the darkness turned to dawn and I marveled at the new day being born. Listening to the cacophony of beach sounds, watching the waves rise up to clap their hands in a great crescendo before kissing the shore and leaving behind its treasure of shells and mysterious fragments from the sea, with the winds becoming so boisterous you could hear God speaking *"I AM, that I AM!" Ref. Exodus 3:14 (KJV)*

One morning in particular, was very special. As I was having my prayer time, eyes tightly closed, talking to God like he was right there beside me, I did venture to ask quite meekly, that *if it was His will*, I sure would like a little sunshine that day to dispel the rain and gloom . . . and almost immediately a golden light filled my eyes as if the sun had popped through the clouds and I could see it even though my eyes were still closed. *"Oh! Thank you God!!! That was the quickest any of my prayers have ever been answered!!"* When I opened my eyes, the cloudy, overcast day was still there and even as a frown was beginning to form, I became aware that God had sent me that golden image to remind me of the SONshine of His love which he had already given to the world. Now, may your day be filled with SONshine and the joy in knowing the great *"I AM!"!!*

An Exciting Week
May 3, 2009

Some weeks are just more exciting than others!!! This past week has been full of excitement. First, there was the fire on the mountain at Cobbly Nob and great concern for all the folks who live up there. There was much less damage than we had thought and we gave God thanks. Then on Wednesday night our churches gathered to study the second chapter of John Schnase's book "Five Practices of Fruitful Congregations" and we learned how to have more passionate worship.

And last but not at all least, yesterday morning, my mom and I were guests at the Reunion Brunch for the Pittman Center Class of 1949! Here's where the excitement hit its peak for the week! Very seldom do I get to just sit back, relax, and enjoy what everyone else has to say. I had more fun than if I had been to the church where the squirrel got loose. Pittman Center's **Mayor Glenn Cardwell**, a member of the Class of '49, was our Master of Ceremonies. He brought along an album chock full of pictures and mementos from their high school years. **Blanche Moyers** has been in charge of this brunch bunch for many years now and they all agree she is the glue that holds them together. We feasted on delicious food but that didn't stop the endless stories being told.

"Remember the time **Mrs. Wakeman** *had the cookout for us and forgot the wieners!!!" "And do you remember the Boogertown bus? I tell you if it hadn't been for that bus, we wouldn't have had any way to school." "Remember* **Mr. Squiggly** *and his walking stick? You know he was blind but he knew the page numbers and the book by heart. He sure was a good teacher." "Oh, and I'll never forget our graduation party at the island in* **Greenbrier***! We all packed our lunches and walked over there. It really wasn't much more than a cow pasture, but we sure did have fun. Stayed there all day long!"* And **Anna Pearsall** was remembered by everyone as a great teacher as well as principal of the school. There were so many stories about **Ms. Pearsall**, I couldn't remember them if I tried. **Blanche** remembered that math was her hardest subject and when she finally passed the test, she set fire to her math book!

Cora Huskey was the only former teacher in attendance. Cora is now 95 years old and remembers the years she taught Home Economics at Pittman following her graduation from Maryville College in 1937. Many kind remarks were shared concerning their bus driver, **Willard Parton.** They reminisced about **Glenn Roberson** who taught them the *Virginia Reel* and invoked the ire of a county official running for office who said if he was elected "the first thing he would do would be to get rid of that Roberson man who is teaching our children how to dance!!" I thought that old politician must be rolling over in his grave if he could see what is happening in our schools today! Anyway, **Mr. Roberson** went on to become a college professor so all ended well for him even if he did get criticized for teaching the children to dance.

The morning ended with a trio (who used to be a quartet) singing "A Beautiful Life." The trio was made up of **Glenn Cardwell** singing bass, his brother **Lon Cardwell** singing tenor, and **Carl Shults** singing lead. My, my, what a wonderful morning!

Every day, my love of the mountains and Pittman Center, my parish, is reinforced and becomes more precious to me. I feel the blessings of Almighty God falling mightily upon me every time I wake up and see the beauty of my surroundings. Yesterday afternoon, we were high up on the mountain at a place called the "Pinnacle." It was cool with a slight breeze and a drizzle of rain. The clouds seemed to just sit down on top of the mountains like soft white pillows. There is no day in the mountains which is not beautiful, no matter what the weather.

"You will go out in joy and be led forth in peace: the mountains and hills will burst into song before you, and all the trees of the field will clap their hands." Isaiah 55:12 (NIV). God is on His throne and we are blessed.

My Mother's Face
May 11, 2008

I have always loved my mother's face and the feelings she inspires in me. My mother's face mirrors the *love* she has for me, no matter how unlovable I might be. I have always seen *my own possibility* in my mother's face. I know that she *believes* in me and in what I can achieve and become. I know that any *criticism* from my mother comes from a loving heart and a desire to help me along life's way. In her face, I see not only *wisdom*, but sweet, wonderful, *forgiveness*! *Goodness* shines in my mother's face. Every spanking and every correction Mother ever gave me was always well deserved!!! It was only after becoming a mother myself I came to know just what she meant when she said *"this hurts me more than it hurts you."* I echoed this sentiment to my own children many times through the years of raising them.

In my mother's face I see the *epitome of love*. I know that if the world should turn against me, I will always have my mother's love. My mother always has a welcome answer to a troubling question. She is, and always has been, my *solace* in sorrow, my *quiet* in a storm, my *shelter* when the winds of life are raging and my *light* in darkness. I have always loved *my mother's face* and will continue to do so until the end of time. She is among everything else, my *best friend*!

Today, Mother's Day shares the spotlight with *Pentecost*, the day lightning struck the disciples in the Upper Room. Lightning in the form of enlightenment, like tongues of fire, filled them with the Holy Spirit of God. Jesus said in *John 8:12* *". . . I am the light of the world. Whoever follows me will never walk in darkness, but will have the light of life." (NIV)* Have you ever considered how closely related a mother's love is to the love of Christ? How pure and unconditional. On each of my children's birthdays, I celebrate my own special Mother's Day. They know they are loved beyond measure, just as my own mother loves me. *"I have no greater joy than to hear that my children are walking in the truth." 3 John: 4 (NIV)*

Remember the verses from *Proverbs 6:20-23*. *"My son, keep your father's commands and do not forsake your mother's teaching. Bind them upon your heart forever; and fasten them around your neck." (NIV)*

Cora Deats Huskey

May 4, 2008

What a time I had yesterday morning, along with a lot of other fine folks! I had the pleasure of escorting **Ms. Cora Huskey** to the Kick-Off Breakfast, hosted by **Blanche Moyers**, for the Annual Reunion of the Pittman Center Class of 1949. Oh my, what a lively bunch!!! I just sat there and listened in rapt attention as they told tale after tale that always began with *"Remember when . . . ?* followed by the names of teachers from their high school years and I quickly surmised that a **Mr. Quigley** was a favorite subject. Seems he used to bang (not *rap*) his walking stick on the desk to get the attention of the students. If I heard right, they said he was in his eighties and still teaching! Have mercy!

Our own **Ms. Cora** is now 94 years of age. She was the Home Economics teacher for many years at Pittman. She loves to tell the story of the student who poured actual cream in the butter when she told her to "cream the butter" for the cake she was making. Then there was the young girl who sewed the sleeves in her dress backward. Cora pointed to her head of gray hair and rapping the group to attention she would say *"this is what you all did to me! See this gray hair!"*

A long-time member of **Burnett Memorial UMC** here in Pittman Center; she played the organ in the church until last year when she had a fall in her home and has since had a bit of trouble getting around. Cora was married to **Conley Huskey, the Mayor of Pittman Center**. They had one son, **Larry**, who was a Tennessee State Senator. Both Conley and Larry have passed away and Ms. Cora is alone except for a grandson, **Tyler**, and his lovely wife, **Rachel,** and sons, **Jack**, **Will**, and **Craig**. Her enthusiasm for life is still evident and were it not for some difficulty hearing, she would be the belle of the ball.

We all love to reminisce, to remember good times, and even sad ones, too. And as we think of years that have past, we may begin to feel a bit *old*. However, the Lord has us alive today for a reason and a purpose. Our best days are not behind us but may be just ahead of us! The Scriptures tell us that we are more than conquerors through Christ and no weapon formed against us will prosper. We can still enjoy life by helping others, and creating even more beautiful memories. We can choose to move ahead and live as God intended by renewing our mind, and energizing our spirit that we might enjoy each new day and the surprises it holds. The Lord is always in need of new vessels to be filled and poured out. Be available! Live, love, and laugh!!

My Graduation Week
May 18, 2007

Waking up early as usual, I put on my robe and slippers and headed down the hallway toward the showers. The morning air was quite chilly coming through the open windows but I could already feel the excitement of the day invading my being and permeating my soul. It is another day at the Appalachian Local Pastors School on the campus of Union College in Barbourville, KY. Today, I will complete the 19th of the 20 required courses of study in the United Methodist Church. Next week will be my last class. How blessed I have been to study under so many outstanding professors, including **Dr. Paul Blankenship** (who will be retiring this year) and **Dr. Ken Ramsey**. Many others, I have told you about in the past.

Opening the door and stepping out into the coolness of the early dawn, I am greeted by the sound of birds chirping at the top of their little lungs. One plump robin, the matriarch of her family, has her beak filled to overflowing with fat juicy worms for her little ones; and, oh, the crisp clean smell of fresh mown grass as the morning mist shrouds these stately old buildings. Red begonias and broad leafed hastas adorn the grounds and dappled shade comes from giant old elms. Melodious chords of the carillon chime out the hour and half hour and the hymns of the church waft across the lawn. Friends, words can't do justice, the peace and serenity surrounding me. You might just pretend this is a vacation post card that says "Having a wonderful time, wish you were here."

I will miss my mountain parish this Sunday but will return next week for Pentecost. I can't wait! I have complete faith and trust in the Lay Leaders in each of my three churches and know that I have left everything in very capable hands. I would urge you all to continue to be God-filled, with abundant love and care for each other and for your neighbors. Not one word of dissension do I hear in my churches, because God is present, accepted, and claimed as our own!!! Am I blessed??? You bet I am!!! Over, and over, and over again. God is so good!

And now, my friends, 'til we meet again—May the Lord bless you and keep you. May the Lord make his face to shine upon you and be gracious to you. May the Lord lift up his countenance upon you and give you peace. Amen

Appalachian Local Pastor's School (ALPS)

May 28, 2006

As St. Paul would say, "Grace and peace to you!" One of these days you may get very tired of my expounding on all my blessings; but, with the hope that you have one last indulgence left, I must do it again. And I do it sincerely.

I have just returned from one fantastic week at **Appalachian Local Pastors School (ALPS)** in Barbourville, KY, the oldest city in Kentucky which boasts a small but fine old school, Union College, where ALPS is held in May of every year. The school is sponsored by Red Bird Missionary Conference and the General Board of Higher Education and Ministry of the UMC as an extension of the Course of Study School, Candler School of Theology, Emory University, Atlanta, GA.

What a blessing to study *"Biblical Preaching"* under **Rev. Dr. J. Ellsworth Kalas.** God's leading in my life was affirmed once again when I learned that this year was **Dr. Kalas'** last class . . . and I was in it!!! He retires this year after 14 years of faithful service to ALPS. He is Professor of Preaching at **Asbury Theological Seminary** and served 38 years as parish pastor. He has written several wonderful books including: *"Parables from the Back Side," "The Thirteen Apostles,"* and a major doctrinal study, *"Christian Believer."* Wow! What a preacher! What a gentleman! No wonder he has been sought after and has preached all over the world.

Another blessing was my second class, *"New Testament II"* under **Arthur Wainwright, PH.D.** This true English gentleman and his sweet wife who moved to the US in 1965 were absolutely delightful. **Dr. Wainwright** is so intelligent it blows my mind! He is Professor Emeritus of New Testament at Candler School of Theology, Emory University. An ordained minister of the British Methodist Church, he was educated at Corpus Christi College, Oxford and Wesley House, Cambridge. He is the author of several books on biblical themes, the most recent being *"Mysterious Apocalypse."* A highly respected teacher, he has an impeccable command of the Greek language. The Bible from which he teaches is written entirely in Greek and he translates and interprets *The Word* precisely for his students.

Thanks be to God for having allowed me the privilege of studying under such great and respected men! I will finish my classes the middle of 2007 at almost 67 years of age and I'm just getting started! Retire? Heavens, no! There's a whole lot left for me to say and do before I kick the bucket! 'Lord willing and the Creeks don't rise!'

Andrew's Graduation Day
May 14, 2006

Good morning! What a great day this is going to be! Happy Mother's Day! Yesterday was a very special day as I was with my mother and could give her a hug and tell her I loved her in person rather than a card across the miles.

Yesterday morning also found me sitting in the bleachers of my old alma mater, Bradley Central High School in Cleveland, TN. With the wind blowing through my hair, the warmth of the sun on my back, admiring the brilliant blue sky . . . forty-eight years after my own graduation, I watched my oldest grandson receive his diploma, **Andrew Chase Blair**. Was I a proud grandmother? Oh, yes! Not only proud of this handsome young man . . . but proud he was graduating from a school such as Bradley High. I was amazed and very, very thankful when I heard the beautiful invocation given by Class Representative, **Laura Kinder**. Not only Laura, but the Valedictorian, as well as the Salutatorian, in each of their speeches, thanked God for His leadership and guidance. These were not merely fleeting references spoken softly and quickly, but with loud, shameless pride and feeling. My own faith was restored as I listened to these fine young leaders of tomorrow invoke the name of God with truth and respect!

Today in our Pittman Center churches we will be honoring not only our mothers, but also our graduates. Three bright, lovely, young ladies: **Bekah Tweed, Bethany Kloster, and Cassie Maples** are graduating seniors from Gatlinburg-Pittman High School. May God bless each one as they unfurl their wings to begin that first solo flight as a young adult.

WOW! I'm excited! God is alive and well in our East Tennessee schools! It is now that our young people will find this faith that has been instilled in them put to the test, quite possibly on a daily basis. As we honor our mothers and our graduates, let us lift them up in very special prayers today that God will continue to bless them and to lead, guide, and direct them in all that they do.

The only advice I gave my grandson was to keep God first and everything else would fall into place. Though you may have heard it a hundred times before, that truth remains and it ever shall be. *"Train up a child in the way he should go, and when he is old, he will not depart from it."* (From Memory)

Class of 1949—Reunion 2006

May 7, 2006

Yesterday morning, bright and early, found me driving up the shaded lane to Cora Huskey's beautiful mountaintop home. This spry 92 year-old came to Pittman Center in 1937 just after her graduation from Maryville College and became the Home Economics teacher at the first school in Pittman. I had been invited to accompany her to the annual breakfast at **Blanche (Emert) Moyer's** home for the Pittman Center Graduating Class of 1949. I've never had so much fun! Sometimes, it's just plain good to listen. You learn a lot that way; especially when you are in the company of such articulate, animated, and happy folks.

"Remember our senior trip?" "Oh yes!" "Now where was it we went?" Why we went to the Island over on Pittman Road." "Now that was a big deal for us back then! There's a campground there now but then it was just a pasture. We had fun running and playing, dodging those cow patties!"

"Remember the time all of us girls spent the night at **Mrs. Pearsall's** house? How in the world did she put up with us?" "Where's **June**?" "Oh, she has a granddaughter graduating from nurse's school today and she couldn't come." "Now tell me about . . ." "Well let me tell you this!" "You know there were just twenty of us in our graduating class. We were the '49ers!" "Did you know . . . died? Oh, that's a shame, no I didn't know that." "Remember our principal, **Dr. Quigley**? Lord, have mercy! I was scared to death of that man!"

Good memories, cherished memories, painful memories, shared by the ones who lived them. And on a day like yesterday, we become fully aware of how important memories are in our lives. How often do we say "remember when?" What may seem mundane and insignificant now, will someday be recalled as a 'remember when' becoming the source of many conversations and thoughts as we grow older . . . sitting on the front porch in an old swing or rocking chair; talking and laughing, as we, too, recall days gone by.

There is another time when it is important to listen, listen very closely, and learn . . . to that still small voice of God. In order to hear him we must be quiet. *"Be still, and know that I am God." Psalm 46:10a (NIV)*

Do you ever feel guilty when you hear that verse? There are times when guilt almost overwhelms me. James 1:19 speaks also of hearing, *"My dear brothers, take note of this: Everyone should be quick to listen, slow to speak and slow to become angry." (NIV)*

Listen! Can you hear Him?

JUNE
PONDERINGS

A Dream Fulfilled
June 24, 2012

What a beautiful Sunday morning! What an amazing day I had yesterday! God blessed these mountains with an abundant amount of sunshine and blue sky. It was truly a day that the Lord had made. Each day here is an absolute joy filled with so many interesting things. I have to pick and choose the stories I share with you as time and space prevent me from writing about it all.

Early yesterday morning, my door bell rang and to my surprise there stood the "treasure" of Pittman Center, our **Mayor Glenn Cardwell**. I knew it was going to be a good day right away. He had in his hand one of the *first* copies of his new book ***A Dream Fulfilled, A Story About Pittman Center.***

I have had a love for books since I was just a mite of a girl when I used to beg my mother to read to me. I didn't care if it was a newspaper, I just wanted to hear her voice make the words come alive. I read very little fiction but give me a true story and I will devour it from cover to cover. I told Glenn if he had come to tell me I had won a thousand dollars it wouldn't mean as much to me as that book. I couldn't wait to begin reading. It is very well-written and the stories are historical, factual and down to earth.

Many who read my *Ponderings* do not live in Pittman Center/Sevier County and can't understand why I am so in love with this place. Since the first day I moved here it was like I had come home to a family I never knew I had. I loved them immediately. I still do . . . as I begin my twelfth year as pastor of this Circuit which includes three small Methodist churches. Quickly, I can tell you that all your questions can be answered in this wonderful book. You will learn so many stories that only Glenn knows and we are so grateful he has put forth the time and effort to write them down for posterity. I'll just step up and say, if you want a copy . . . you can purchase one at the Pittman Center City Hall for $13. All the proceeds stay here in Pittman Center (a gift from Glenn) to pay for our new playground and equipment. Glenn has written another excellent book ***The Greenbrier Cove Story*** which is just as rich in history as his new one. It can also be purchased from the Town of Pittman Center City Hall.

Each time I write, or even think, about this place, I remember the words of David in *Psalm 98:7-9a* *"Let the sea resound, and everything in it, the world, and all who live in it. Let the rivers clap their hands, let the mountains sing together for joy; let them sing before the Lord." (NIV)*

Simply put, the Lord God has made it all. We are his people and the sheep of his pasture. Praise Him!

"The Story" I found at Annual Conference . . .

June, 2012

This year, Conference was focused on 'everyone has a story to tell' and finding the story behind the person or place. This is the story I found at Conference this year.

You are all familiar with the fact that I sit and ponder a lot and I did a lot more of it at Conference this year. There was a man attending Conference as a lay member from his church. He was sitting a few rows in front of me in Stuart Auditorium and I immediately recognized him though I do not know him personally. I certainly knew him from his "crucifixion" in all the newspapers and the TV reporters had a field day with making very public all his faults.

What did I do? I made sure I got close enough to read his name tag so I knew there was no mistaking his identity. He still looked much like the man on TV and in the newspapers but there was also a difference that I noticed right away. The deep wrinkles and deep set eyes were not quite so deep anymore. The big eyes now looked at the world with a bit more understanding, his skin was no longer lackluster, he walked, though stooped, with his head held high and he seemed quite peaceful.

Yes, I watched him every day as we were sitting in close proximity in most every meeting, chapel programs, meals, and just walking around on campus. Though I saw very few folks actually talking with him . . . I wanted to go up to him and shake his hand and tell him I was praying for him. I didn't know how he would have taken this gesture from someone he had never met before in his life. Perhaps he would have been uplifted, perhaps not. I will never know as I did not take the opportunity. Now, I am haunted that I missed an opportunity to be a Christian friend to someone that I am sure has lost many of the friends he once had.

Though many folks go to Conference for various reasons, some not quite so noble, this man came to worship. He attended every meeting as lay members to Annual Conference are *supposed* to do . . . not only that, he attended every chapel program and took Holy Communion every morning at 7:45AM. He wasn't on the pier fishing, nor taking in a round of golf, nor walking around with shorts and t-shirt just having a good old time. He was worshiping! I saw him stand, I saw him clap his hands, I saw him lift his hands in praise at the wonderful singing, I saw him pay close attention to the speakers as well as the preachers and he did not nod off. (Something I did a time or two I have to admit.) He was most always alone.

I guess what I am trying to say is, I have changed my opinion of this man . . . who unwittingly became addicted to a drug that will drive you mad when you can't get it. It makes you do things you would never do if you weren't "hooked." It literally changes you from the good and honorable person you once were to a new person, defiled by things of the world disguised as "pain killers."

Would I have looked at this man with such compassion had I not experienced this type of transformation in another person very dear to me? Probably not . . . but when you have looked into the eyes of Jesus . . . you see Jesus in "distressing disguises" as Mother Theresa once said. We think of the familiar disguises of Jesus as being in the lost, the lonely, the hungry, the sad and brokenhearted, and we fail to see the "addicted" and the "prisoners." We forget the human person *inside* . . . the person they really are when not altered by any type of drug or medication.

I am ashamed I formed an opinion of this man without even knowing anything about him except what I had seen on TV or read in the newspapers. You are wondering how I know he has changed without speaking a word to him. I will tell you, his *countenance has changed*. He was an open book to be read at will, not printed in words, but *in his actions*. Remember Moses, when he came down from the mountain? At first the folks didn't recognize him because his *countenance had changed*!! I'm not calling him Moses but he is a man who has changed and he should be given credit for having the "guts," to get out in public and face the scrutiny. This has to be the first and most important step in healing from something that has had control of your life way too long. This is the beginning of *his* new story returning to the honorable and just man he was years ago. He is now in prison and I continue to pray for him.

He may no longer be *judge*, but he is our *brother in Christ*, Richard Baumgardner. He deserves our prayers and our forgiveness.

A Great Gettin' Up Morning
June 26, 2011

"Well, it's a great gettin' up morning . . . fare thee well, fare thee well." Remember that old song? And that it is, my friends. It's always good to see the dawning of another beautiful day here in the Smoky Mountains and Pittman Center.

Now, I guess I better backtrack a little bit here . . . the last few weeks have led me to believe we might be smack-dab in the middle of the monsoon season. I want to sing as I did when a child, *"Rain, rain, go away, come again another day."* A bit of every day seems to be set aside for stormy weather. Which reminds me, if you have rain on your prayer list *please delete it for the next couple of days or so.* Right now, we are soaked, soggy, and sodden.

Lots of folks don't like storms. Some are frightened by them. Well, that's OK. Storms can be terrifying if for no other reason than the deafening noise of the thunder which seems to shake the whole earth as it rolls across the heavens. The flashing lightning declares there is someone, much bigger than we are, in charge of the universe! And the wind can be ferocious! A storm is humbling . . . a storm is awesome . . . and a storm is the most magnificent display of God's omniscience you will ever encounter. He seems to shout from the heavens "Look and see, listen and hear . . . I am the Lord thy God, and thou shall have no other gods before me!" I am . . . the great I AM!!! (certainly I've paraphrased!)

I love storms. I hear God's voice in a storm. I feel awe and wonder in a storm. It is during a storm that His power and majesty are revealed more than any other time. Man has done a lot of great things in this old world, but he will never claim the power that is God's alone.

Humanity gets a little high and mighty when expounding on how far we have come and all the discoveries we have made in so many diverse areas: science, geology, space, history, religion, language, art, medicine, forensics, and on and on.

Do you think we could have done any of it without God's help? Well, nooooo!! Who created our brains, for goodness sake!!! Who gave us the ability to learn? Certainly, no *mere mortal!!!* We can *enhance* our knowledge with effort and diligent study . . . but it all *began* with God! How we use our knowledge, for good or bad, unfortunately, is still our choice.

Remember, *"In the beginning, God . . ."* *Genesis 1:1 (KJV)* And therein begins the story, the greatest story ever told. From Genesis to Revelation; God is an awesome God.

Henry Trewhitt and the
Ramp Festival
June 19, 2011

Good Sunday morning to you! Sounds like thunder out there and it's oh so dark; a perfect morning to get ready and come to church. No, no, don't go back to bed. As I begin my ponderings this early morn, I am reminded that some of the responses which I get from folks who read my ponderings are great stories in themselves. There is one I want to share with you today which is really a great history lesson as well. It is from **Bill McClure**, a classmate from Bradley High School in Cleveland, TN.

*"You mentioned that one of your churches is in Cosby, Tn. I must tell you a story. Between 50 and 60 years ago, my uncle, **Henry Trewhitt**, was a reporter at the **Chattanooga Times** and went to Cosby to cover the ramp festival because **President Harry Truman** was going to be there. While he was there, he was walking across a small wooden bridge that was about ten feet over a small but rocky creek. There was a highway patrol car sitting on the bridge, and as he walked by, the patrolman opened the car door and knocked Henry off the bridge and into the rocks below. It broke his back in three places and his neck in two places, and they weren't sure for a few days if Henry was going to make it or not. He lived, and had to wear a body cast from his waist, up under his chin and included one arm stuck out at an odd angle. He eventually got well, but had to work with weights the rest of his life to keep his back strong.*

*Henry went on to a great career, and was chief diplomatic correspondent for the **Baltimore Sun** and then **Newsweek Magazine**. When he retired he was the deputy managing editor of **US News and World Report** and was a panelist on three of the presidential Great Debates. He asked **Ronald Reagan** the question, "Do you think age will be a major factor in the election". Reagan's reply was, "I don't intend to let the youth and inexperience be a factor in this election." Mondale later said that at that moment he knew that he was going to lose the election. Henry also wrote a book about Robert McNamara called, "**McNamara, His Ordeal in the White House.**"*

Henry died about 5 years ago, but told me one time that he had visited 57 countries in his travels. Interesting for a country boy from Cleveland, isn't it?"
See if any of your older church members might remember this." Bill

There are many of you in this area that will remember this event or be familiar with Henry Trewhitt. I love passing along stories that happened right here in East Tennessee. The Bible says wisdom is good and that we should forever seek understanding. For many of us, this is a learning lesson, something we did not know before. *"Happy is the man that findeth wisdom, and the man that getteth understanding." Prov.3:13-14 (KJV)*

Flip Flops and Combat Boots
June 27, 2010

This past week has been filled with so much "God-Stuff" here in Pittman Center. How blessed is my life in these beautiful, ever-changing, majestic, glorious Smoky Mountains! There is always something new and exciting and each morning as I awake, I can't wait to see what the new day will bring.

One of the highlights of this past week was a wedding at **Webb's Creek United Methodist Church**. They were such a lovely couple; he, standing tall and proud in the dress blues of the US Army and his bride walking barefoot down the aisle dressed in soft white gathers reminding me of a beautiful peasant girl. This was their day! Even the decorations on the table that held the guest book were something I had never seen before . . . combat boots and flipflops! So appropriate! What a blessing I received officiating at their wedding; a soldier returning from a tour of duty in Iraq and the girl who was waiting for him.

These lazy, hazy, crazy days of summer are the best! Each morning when I wake up, sometimes before dawn, I hurry through the house opening all the doors and windows so the cool crisp morning air and the clean smell of the mountains can permeate the house. I love the pungent smell of damp earth after a cooling shower. One minute it will be pouring buckets and the next minute, the sun will be shining and the dark clouds swept away leaving nothing but beautiful blue sky.

Change is coming in this beautiful place called Pittman Center but it moves ahead slowly guided by the goal of always preserving our mountain heritage.

There is a bit of sadness in my heart as the elementary school across the road from the parsonage is now silent. I miss the noise and laughter of children at play and being a neighbor to such a fine school! However, our beautiful new school is now open, just up the road off Highway #321. I would challenge you to find a more beautiful, or well-equipped school anywhere; a very functional, unique structure which includes a museum and is dedicated to excellence in education!

As I begin my tenth year in ministry in this beautiful and extraordinary place, I wonder what the future holds for us. What will happen to the old school building? Are we about to see our first Pittman City Park? Have you noticed all the beautification going on around here? Did you know that all of the land in Pittman Center once belonged to the United Methodist Church?

The settlement that spawned the Town of Pittman Center in the early 1900s has seen many changes through the years. Change is as much a part of life as breathing. I wonder how the changes that are sure to come will affect the lives of the folks remaining and the new ones moving in. I wonder what is in store for all of us. Yes, I wonder . . .

And yet I *know*, that *we too* shall, one day, be changed according to *I Corinthians, 15: 51-52: "Listen, I tell you a mystery: We will not all sleep, but we will all be changed—in a flash, in the twinkling of an eye, at the last trumpet." (NIV)*

This . . . I do *not* wonder about. I simply believe.

Old-Time Baptist Preachers
June 13, 2010

Have you ever met someone you liked instantly, with whom you felt a rapport, that you just knew in your heart was going to be a good friend? God's love is like an aura all around them and you feel good being in their presence.

One of the greatest accomplishments known to man is being able to find joy in living! The way to be strong is to rejoice! And, the most important factor in finding joy is to know you are living a life that is pleasing before God. When you are past feeling the need to prove yourself, when you don't have to put on airs, when you no longer feel the need to build yourself up by putting others down; then, you can find real peace and abundant joy.

Two of the sweetest old-time Baptist preachers are here in Sevier County and to me they embody all of the attributes of living joyously. The first time I met each of them (don't forget I'm a *woman* preacher) they showed no surprise, animosity, or even questioning. I met **Rev. Andy Ball** many years ago at the funeral of an older member of my Shults Grove UMC, **Paul McAlister**. When I was introduced to Brother Andy at the funeral home, he took me aside and asked me to be part of the funeral service. He declared it was only right that I sit with him and take part, and I gladly read the obituary and gave the opening prayer for the funeral service. It takes a *real man* to do that, especially if your faith doesn't believe in women preachers! I had been in Pittman Center less than a year and was still 'wet behind the ears.' Rev. Andy Ball's gesture of friendship and acceptance was a precious gift I shall never forget.

Another dear preacher that I took a liking to the first time we met is **Rev. Melvin Carr**; such a gentle man in every sense of the word; soft-spoken, kind and always smiling. He accepts me as he would any other preacher who loves the Lord and His people. Many are the times Brother Melvin has come knocking on my door with gifts from his garden or delicious apples from his orchard. He always called to check on **Clyde** when he was sick and they enjoyed long talks together. Just last week my phone rang and it was Melvin all excited about a theology book he was reading. He said just as soon as he finished it, he was going to bring it to me to read as well. Now that's a wonderful friend as well as colleague. Both Preacher Andy and Preacher Melvin have the gift of joy in their lives because they know God's grace is extended to all, even women. **Zenith Whaley** (now deceased) was another old-time Baptist preacher-man I called friend and our mayor and his wife, **Glenn and Faye Cardwell**, are devout Baptists and dear friends I cherish daily. Knowing God intimately allows them to see God's grace in others. HE is the Father of us all. Denomination and gender are not relevant, being a Christian is! I am blessed.

"Yet I will rejoice in the Lord, I will be joyful in God my savior." Habakkuk 3:18 (NIV)

Barefoot Days of Summer

June 7, 2009

My goodness, what a beautiful day this is going to be! I couldn't wait to get up. The weather lady said it will be 80 degrees! Now, this is my kind of weather. Nothing like the barefoot days of summer; uh oh, I guess it is still spring! Yesterday the creek was calling me and I went down to my favorite bench and sat there watching the tumbling water, meditating and contemplating on things not so important; just flickers here and there of my wandering mind. I love to go wading but I am going to wait until the murky waters from all the rains clear up a bit. I want to make sure that the snake I found in the basement of the church and dropped into the creek has moved on downstream. I must be more careful of the slippery rock in the river bed. They are so deceptive . . . I remember what happened last year . . . I slipped on one of them and landed with an enormous splash, kerplunk! I must have been a funny sight hurrying down the road, back to the house, dripping wet from head to toe.

Every time I think about this beautiful place, I marvel at how good God has been to me! Me, just a little old gray-haired preacher lady whom God called as his servant in 1981, and *after 19 years,* finally said "Here I am Lord, send me!" I'm so thankful He didn't give up on me . . . and did he ever send me . . . to the most beautiful place on earth and the very best folks you could ever find to be my parish.

Now I've been pondering on this particular time of the year and it was just about now, so many years ago, when Jesus first appeared to Peter and John and some of the other disciples just days after His resurrection.

It was early morning and they had been out fishing all night and as they neared land, John looked toward shore and was the first to recognize Jesus, silhouetted there beside a small fire. Out of his still grieving heart, I can just hear him burst out "It is the Lord!" No wonder he recognized Christ, he was *looking* for Him.

And then there's Peter who recognizes Jesus as well and knows he must now face Him, the One whom he had denied, not once, but three times. Peter, the disciple to whom we can all relate; Peter, the one with the temper; Peter, the one who spoke without thinking; Peter, the one who had deserted Jesus in the time of His greatest need.

Though John recognized Jesus first, Peter was the first to act. Putting on his outer garment, he plunges into the sea, not even waiting for the boat to come ashore. Three times the Lord asked Peter if he loved Him. Three times Peter assured Him of his love. With Peter's final response, "You know that I love you," Christ had drawn a commitment from Peter and assured the other disciples of the bond between Himself and Peter. In this way, He demonstrated His complete forgiveness of Peter. With this exchange, the Lord restored Peter to his position of leadership in the ongoing ministry of the gospel.

And Jesus is just as ready to forgive you and me as he was to forgive Peter. We don't have to quit because we make a mistake. God *really* loves us. To each one, there will come a time when we will hear God speaking directly to us saying "Do you *really* love me?"

Kids Say Profound Things
June 22, 2008

One of the things I enjoy most in my ministry is my time with the children on Sunday mornings. A pastor who doesn't interact with the children of the congregation on a regular basis misses so many blessings. One of my blessings came this past Friday morning at 6:55AM when I received a call from **Catherine**, a precious little Indian girl who was in Cherokee NC. She asked me to pray with her before she went into surgery to have her tonsils removed. We prayed and when I hung up the phone, I sat up in bed and said "Wow!" I was on cloud nine all day long as I pondered the faith of this sweet child.

Everyone seems to love the children's sermon and hearing the sweet, innocent, though sometimes totally unexpected, things they have to say. There are always big smiles throughout the congregation as we listen with rapt attention to these little ones. It can be, however, a trying time for some parents as they wonder what their child might say. Having raised four of my own, I was always one of those apprehensive parents.

I actually asked our pastor at Pleasant Hill UMC Maryville (where I was a member for 26 years) to please not ask my youngest son, Vic, any questions for I never knew what he might say! This is the child that used to chase me around the house with a live frog in his hand when he was only three. I have always been scared to death of frogs, though I dearly love to eat their little legs, all fried up golden brown and crisp.

One Sunday morning when we were having Holy Communion the pastor began by asking questions to see just how much these little ones understood this sacrament. The first question was *"Can anyone tell me what is under the cloth on the table?"* Immediately, and without hesitation, my son raised his hand and yelled *"I know, I know!!! Bread and kool-aid!!"*

Rev. Ray Robinson, a long time friend and pastor from years ago, told me about a time when he was on the radio in Athens, TN. He asked the kids if there was anything they would like to say to the shut-ins who were homebound and had to spend most of their time in bed. He held the mike up to the boy with his hand up. He yelled: "GET OUT OF THAT BED!"

Is it OK to laugh a little in church? Of course!!! Being a Christian doesn't mean we need a long face and sad expression. Christians should be the happiest people in the world. Jesus loved the little children, he gathered them up in his arms, and I know there were many times when he smiled and even laughed out loud at some of the things they said and did.

"He called a little child and had him stand among them. And he said: "I tell you the truth, unless you change and become like little children, you will never enter the kingdom of heaven. Therefore, whoever humbles himself like this child is the greatest in the kingdom of heaven. And whoever welcomes a little child like this in my name welcomes me." Matthew 18:3-5 (NIV)

Daddy
June 15, 2008

Today is Father's Day! My mind races back to the days of my youth when my dad returned home from his tour of duty in the South Pacific during World War II. I was five years old and he brought me a little pair of black boots. I wore those boots until both of them had 'holey soles.' Sunday afternoons were family time and often we made a trip to the farmers market in Chattanooga for fresh vegetables. Daddy would get a big purple eggplant and I could never understand why something so beautiful could taste so awful. My treat was a cluster of grapes knowing they would keep me quiet until I had eaten every one. Oh, and the breakfasts my dad prepared! An excellent cook, he would get up very early while the rest of us were still asleep and have everything ready and on the table by the time we got up. He made the best biscuits I have ever eaten! He called them 'cat heads' and there was always sausage or country ham, gravy, scrambled eggs, and sliced tomatoes out of our garden.

Being born in the early 40s, I was raised in the fifties; the last years of real innocence. Back when we obeyed our parents, didn't talk back, and learned from them the value of education and working hard for what we wanted. We didn't rely on our parents to keep us up well into our adult years as young folks do today. More than anything, Daddy instilled in me the necessity of telling the truth, being industrious, conscientious, and always finishing whatever I started.

My father worked for **Chase Pontiac Company** for many years and I still remember the "Pontiac Chieftain" emblem in neon on the plate glass window. Some Sunday afternoons when the dealership was closed, Daddy would let me go in with him and put a nickel in the big red chest type cooler. There was nothing better to cool you off on a hot summer afternoon than a bottle of Coca-Cola and, of course, a pack of Lance Peanuts from the big clear jar with red letters beside the cooler. The show room was always pristine and shiny. The elevator, open on all four sides, was really more like a lift but it got you to the top floor. My most vivid memory is the unique smell of the garage area. I never quite identified that smell until I was much older and realized it must have been from the lacquer thinner in the big black drum with the wooden lid across it. Walking into an auto body shop today and being met with that same smell, always reminds me of my dad. Well, look at the time!!! Oh my goodness! I better get ready for church! How time flies when I'm pondering!!!

Let's turn our thoughts now to our Heavenly Father and remember his great love for us. *"Because you are sons (and daughters), God sent the Spirit of his Son into our hearts, the Spirit who cries out, "Abba," Father." Galatians 4:6 (NIV)*

Old Concrete Steps
June 1, 2008

Several years ago when I first came here and just after the clearing out of the overgrowth of trees around the parsonage, a set of old concrete steps was uncovered down near the end of our driveway. As I have made my way around the community, talking with anyone who cares to talk, I have learned a lot about the Pittman Center of long years ago. I love history and I love listening to the old folk's tales. I am told this set of steps is all that remains of a very long path that used to lead up the side of this mountain to the office of **Dr. Robert F. Thomas**. I look at this remaining remnant of history and ponder the tales that would be told if only they could talk.

I imagine little barefoot children and grown-ups alike, with emotionless faces, trudging up the hill to the infirmary which was then located right here where the parsonage now stands. All of them, coming to see old Doc Thomas, who could fix most anything that ailed you. *"Why I remember well the times I trudged up that hill to get my tonsils painted with that purple stuff."* When the visits to Doc's office seemed to slow a mite, folks said you could see 'ole Doc' riding his horse all over these hills and valleys; helping with birthing the babies (human and otherwise), pulling teeth, and calming the fever. *"Twarn't nothin' fer him to even doctor yore old horse, or yore cow, if'n it was ailin.'"* Lo, the many years he served here as doctor, dentist, veterinarian, preacher, and friend. *"Why, he even delivered Dolly herself, and likely some of her other eleven brothers and sisters! And did you know she was paid fer with either a sack of flour or cornmeal, one or t' other, can't recollect right now which it was!"*

Pittman Center was established by the New York District of the Methodist Church through the efforts of **Eli Pittman** and **John Burnett**. It was a highly populated and bustling mission town in the early 1900s. Jobs were created, skills were taught and learned, and every Sunday, the Glory of the Lord came down like fire on its people with old-time preachin', prayin', and singin.' And, when you got to marrying age . . . well, church was the best courtin' place you could find anywhere. Sitting on the back pew holding hands, gazing into each other's eyes, or on the long walk home in the dark of the evening you might even 'steal a little sugar' from your sweetie.

If those old steps could talk . . . they would tell of the strong faith, yet meager existence of these mountain folks who worked hard to provide for their families and to care for each other. The first school in Pittman Center was a most welcome sight! Children of all ages and sizes were brought in by horseback and wagon, to partake in the opportunity of an education.

I imagine how it might have been, late on a summer's day . . . way back then. Men coming in from the fields, dirty from plowing and grubbing all day and making a beeline down to the creek to wash up before suppertime. Their women, wearing aprons, are scurrying around the old wood stove, preparing the evening meal of cornmeal mush, fried taters and big slices of red ripe tomatoes right out of the garden. Of course, there is always fresh milk from their old cow grazing peacefully down by the barn. Just as it is getting 'dusky dark' the clap of thunder can be heard in the distance and soon you can hear the steady drops of rain as they begin their feisty dance on the tin roof of the old farm house. Folks sit back in their rocking chairs on the front porch, feeling mighty good that God is blessing and refreshing the earth with rain that will nourish gardens and crops and provide food for their family as well as their cattle during the summer and well on into the bleak winter months. They savor the clean smell of rain now moving on over the mountain and listen to the song of the evening peepers, frogs, and toads singing down by the creek. The straps on their overalls are already loosened as they get up and make their way into the house and a night of peaceful slumber on the old featherbed.

Oh, what tales they would tell . . . if those old steps could talk! *". . . Our fathers have told us what work thou didst in their days, in the times of old." Psalm 44:1(KJV)*

Rozetta Mowery

June 24, 2007

Celebrating the longest day of the year on June 21 is always bittersweet for me. I love the long days of summer sunshine and daylight! Now every day will become shorter and shorter until December 21 when we have the shortest day. Sometimes, I don't like having to go to bed because there is so much left to do, so much to accomplish. I don't like missing one single second of living and loving!! Life is exciting and every day brings new ways to serve God, new things to learn, new folks to meet, new roads to travel, and new books to read. One of my favorite pastimes is reading . . . which reminds me . . .

This year at Annual Conference there was a beautiful Christian lady by the name of **Rozetta Mowery**, who has written a book entitled *"Tragedy in Tin Can Holler."* She was the featured speaker during our Holston Home for Children reporting session. The book is an accounting of her almost unbelievable life which began in Meigs County, TN and moved on to McMinn County, to a place called *Tin Can Holler*. It tells of her courageous struggle as a seven year old girl who survived the murder of her mother at the hands of her own father, a lifetime of poverty, shuttled from one home to another, and the accounting of her stay at the Holston Home for Children in Greeneville, TN. She said her mother's spirit led her to return to the place of her birth and to Tin Can Holler where it all began in 1959, to seek the truth which brought about the writing of this factual accounting.

Folks if you have ever lived in McMinn County, Meigs County, Polk County, or anywhere else, you will not want to miss this book. It is a must-read and I think you will find it fascinating. Having lived in McMinn County from 1964 until 1976 I found many of the names and places familiar. I must tell you . . . it is not for the faint hearted. It is bold, shocking, outrageous, and as I said before, an almost unbelievable accounting of murder, incest, and family secrets. If you like true stories and you have a strong gut, this book will not disappoint you. You can purchase it from Cokesbury (ISBN 978-0-9779680-6-0). It is unforgettable.

"You turned my wailing into dancing; you removed my sackcloth and clothed me with joy, that my heart may sing to you and not be silent. O Lord, my God, I will give you thanks forever." Psalm 30:11-12 (NIV)

Isaac's Salvation

June 17, 2007

The sound of the phone ringing caused me to jump, startling me out of my evening reverie. Answering the phone, I heard the sound of my youngest son's voice telling me that my little grandson, Isaac, had something he wanted to tell me.

Now, most of you will remember Isaac as he visited Webb's Creek a couple of weeks ago and came down for the children's sermon. He is only six years old but he stood and repeated the books of the Bible from memory! I can't even do that!

Listening closely, his sweet voice came on the line and he said "Guess what, Mamaw Alta! I got saved tonight!" Such excitement in a little boy's voice I have never heard as he continued, "I accepted Jesus as my Savior!"

As Preacher Mull used to say, "if that won't light your fire, your wood's wet." There are some things that will make an old grandmother's heart beat with joy and this was one of them. This salvation story took place at Grandview Baptist Church in Maryville where Isaac and his little brother, Ivan, were attending Vacation Bible School. I extol the virtues of VBS! Not only my life, but many others have been changed during this time; not just children, but parents as well. This innocent child found his Heavenly Father that night and he couldn't wait to tell everyone he knew!

The preacher said that night as he was giving an invitation at the close of the service, the minute his last words were spoken, little Isaac jumped up from his seat and made a bee-line down to the altar. No one coaxed him, no one encouraged him, the decision he made was his own as Jesus spoke to his heart. Oh, that we could all possess the boldness and determination of children. The eleventh chapter of Isaiah describes the Messianic Kingdom to come as he says "a little child shall lead them." Perhaps we could all use some guidance.

Today is Father's Day and children everywhere will be celebrating the day with their Dads. I know Isaac has already given his Dad the very best gift he could possibly receive! May every father receive a gift just as rewarding!

"Yet I will rejoice in the Lord, I will joy in the God of my salvation." (Habakkuk 3:18)

Annual Conference—2006

June 18, 2006

Good Sunday morning! Grace and peace to you! This is going to be another beautiful day! I can feel it in my bones.

The cool weather at **Annual Conference** this past week was a real blessing. The only one I saw wiping 'sweat' was Bishop Swanson as he was preaching! Lord have mercy! If I could just preach like that, I would be one blessed woman. Let me tell you, he knows how it's done! And there's not a doubt about it . . . he feels it, he believes it, and he sure *ain't* ashamed to preach it!!! He was shouting glory all over the place!!! I could listen to him all day long and never get tired.

In addition to his fantastic preaching, **Bishop Swanson** handled a myriad of business matters with such diplomacy and tact, I was truly impressed. This is not to say that I *agreed* with all the decisions that were made concerning the ten resolutions that were voted on; but, watching our Bishop handle the business meetings in such a stellar manner was amazing.

I am most thankful to God, the Bishop and **DS Ron Matthews** for sending me back to my little bit of heaven on earth . . . **Pittman Center** . . . for year number six! There is no place on earth I would rather be than right here, serving my Lord. My parish is one of my greatest blessings!!! And, our new Maryville District Superintendent, **Carol Wilson,** was my own pastor several years ago and is so very capable. She will do an excellent job in both leadership and organization!

Oh, I almost forgot . . . Happy Father's Day!!! This day always reminds me of an old hymn: *"Rise up, O men of God! Have done with lesser things. Give heart and mind and soul and strength to serve the King of kings."* Oh that all our fathers could have been, or are now, 'men of God.' What a profound influence for good they would have on our life.

My Dad believed the Bible; especially *Proverbs 29:15a "The rod and reproof give wisdom;" (KJV)* I must have been a holy terror as I seem to remember receiving quite a bit of reproof . . . however, just look how smart I am today! (Oh Lord, forgive me for that wisecrack, I truly pray!) *"Our fathers disciplined us for a little while as they thought best; but God disciplines us for our good, that we may share in his holiness." Hebrews 12:10 (NIV)*

What a wonderful world and what a wonderful life! Live it!!!

A Blind Lady and Her Pony
June 11, 2006

Good morning and how do you do this fine day? Hope you had a restful night's sleep and are rarin' to go (to church that is!). Today is Trinity Sunday, the Sunday after Pentecost wherein we celebrate the Trinity: one God in three persons. No one has ever seen God; but if we love one another, God lives in us, and his love is perfected in us. "Let your light so shine before men . . ."

We are called to believe in things we cannot see . . . and sometimes, we cannot believe some of the things we do see. Let me share with you an email I received last week . . . *"Hi y'all,—we thought we had seen most everything. While at Wally's* (a favorite eating place on #321) *a blind lady came in with a PONY (a miniature). It had a harness handle like a dog. It was well behaved and just stood by the table while everyone ate. It looked like it had a blanket over its back—kind'a thought it might be a diaper. It was a first for us and many more in the restaurant by the looks on their faces."* I have never heard of a seeing-eye "pony" but I am truly thankful to God for the many important uses for all His creatures.

As a pastor, I do a lot of listening and I ponder on what I hear . . . I marvel at how some folks have such a warped sense of what is important in life. Just yesterday I heard someone say *"Did you know she's dating again? I hear he's rich! Her family is delighted!"* Do they ever wonder about his integrity? Is he a good man, an honorable man, and one who knows the Lord? Will he be a good father for her children? There is certainly nothing wrong with being wealthy, but it should never be used to measure a person's worth. Sometimes, it is good to lift up the carpet and peer under the edges.

I am reminded of a verse from *Proverbs: 22:1 "A good name is more desirable than great riches; to be esteemed is better than silver or gold. Rich and poor have this in common: The Lord is the Maker of them all." (NIV)*

A last random thought as my mind is prone to wander this morning (as you can tell). Another comment I heard this past week was concerning an elderly lady in our community who is in the nursing home: *"I don't think she has ever known contentment."* Isn't that incredibly sad?

Oh, that the Holy Spirit might invade all our lives, show us His glory, and present us with the peace that passes all understanding. Perhaps the answer is again to be found in *Proverbs: "He who pursues righteousness and love finds life, prosperity and honor." 21:21 (NIV)*

Lost Sight
June 4, 2006

Good Sunday morning! As I look out the window of my study this morning, I am amazed at how much earlier daylight is coming. There's a little rabbit in the front yard having breakfast on the tiny clumps of clover. That pesky bird who outdid me and built her nest right above our front door is flying out to find her first big juicy worm. A little brown squirrel is sitting on the stump near the drive. The school across the road is silent now but will come alive in the morning with the children's last hurrah as they leave for the summer. I was privileged to speak at their eighth grade graduation this past Thursday! What a delight and honor to be part of this wonderful place called Pittman Center.

As I ponder this morning . . . my mind settles in on the miraculous gift of sight. Of all our senses, sight has to be the most important. At least, it is to me.

A couple of weeks ago while away at school, I awoke early one morning with the darkness still about me and wondered what time it was. I reached for my glasses on the table beside the bed and opened my cell phone to check the time. It was more difficult than usual to read the numbers but I finally made them out after several twists and turns trying to make them more visible. It was only 4:10AM, so I snuggled back down in the bed and slept until the alarm went off at 5:30.

Jumping up, I took a quick shower and again . . . put my glasses on. (I can't see a thing without them!) As I was attempting to apply my powder and paint, I realized I couldn't see! For the life of me I couldn't figure out why everything looked so distorted. I got scared!! What if I were losing my eyesight? Something must have happened during the night!! Oh dear, oh dear! Whatever will I do?

My next rational thought was that my glasses just needed cleaning. So, I reached for the softest towel I could find, and proceeded to clean the first lens and then as I moved to the second lens . . . I found that my fingers and thumb were rubbing together in the space where that lens should have been. Whew!!! Plop, plop, fizz, fizz, what a relief!!! I wasn't going blind after all!!! I finally found the missing lens on the floor beside my bed and went in search of a friend to put the tiny screw back in place which held the lens in the frames. Thanks be to God for that dear friend, as well as the miraculous restoration of my sight!!

"The eye is the lamp of the body. If your eyes are good, your whole body will be full of light." Matthew 6:22 (NIV)

Taking Up Serpents
June 25, 2006

I have told all these folk up here that I am a strong Methodist in the oldest tradition. Wesleyan, you might say. I don't take up serpents! In fact, I prefer putting them down. No religious thoughts in mind . . . more like annihilation!!! Before I came here, I thought snakes were only good for killing. That's the way I was brought up in the country. We didn't want those creepy crawling creatures eating our hen eggs; even worse, our baby chicks! Oh sure, they ate a few mice, too; but, those were for 'Old Tom.' Why, there's no telling how many meals they stole from him. And another thing, those old screen doors on our farm house didn't fit very tight and they could slither in, hide in a cool corner, and then scare the living water out of someone . . . like me!!! Or my grandmother!!! Or my mother!!! No, we didn't like snakes!

I quickly learned that here in the mountains serpents are almost revered!!!! The Great Smoky Mountains National Park Rangers frown something awful if you kill one of these silent stalkers, especially if it is black. My Lay Leader, **George Minnigh**, who is also a park ranger, told me that black snakes are harmless and please don't kill them; just call him and he will take it away.

Well, last Monday night, I looked out the window beside the front door and couldn't believe my eyes!!! The long *white* belly of a snake was climbing (yes climbing!! I didn't even know they could climb!) up the several window panes toward the nest of baby birds over our doorway. It didn't look black so, to me, it was fair game! Out the back door I went and grabbed the snow shovel; I couldn't find a hatchet to hack its little bird-thieving head off. When I got up real close, I discovered my visitor was about four-five feet long with several coils filling a greater part of the window ledge. It was mighty fat, too; probably full of baby mice, I'd say. And . . . on its top side . . . it was black!! Oh no!!

There I stood with the shovel poised to do as much damage as I could when my conscience said, "the 'park ranger angel' will come and get you in the middle of the night if you hurt this harmless creature!!!" So I just sat the shovel on top of it so it couldn't move until morning! (Sounds like something a woman would do, doesn't it?) Surprise, surprise . . . it was gone by the time I got back in the house! It does seem to me, however, that I should have killed that snake . . . if I take a verse from Scripture, out of context, to make my point, (some folks do that about *women preachers* you know) *"Cursed are you above all the livestock and all the wild animals! You will crawl on your belly and you will eat dust all the days of your life. And I will put enmity between you and the woman, and between your offspring and hers; he will crush your head, and you will strike his heel." Gen. 3:14b-16 (NIV)*

And if a visit to the parsonage from a serpent isn't bad enough . . . I learned earlier in the week that a big black bear was taking a bath in the creek in front of our house just after dawn. Guess that puts an end to my future strolls along *that* road in the cool of early morn!

Where am I going with all this??? I don't know. These Sunday morning epistles are just a *preacher's printed ponderings* whom the Lord has blessed by planting her in the mountains she has learned to love with all her heart. *". . . the mountains and hills will burst into song before you!" Isaiah 55:12b (NIV)*

Listen . . . I think I hear them now!!!

A Traipse in the Woods
June 13, 2004

The other day I was walking along the creek bank when I decided to traipse back into the woods above the parsonage for a closer look at nature's bountiful display of plant life peeking from the dark, moist earth. There used to be an old lean-to barn up there when we first moved here but it has long since fallen down. As I kicked around in the debris of what is left of that old barn, my mind wandered back to the time when **Rev. Ralph Cline** was the pastor here. Thought I didn't know him I feel like I did from all the tales that are told about this beloved man. He served this parish for twenty-nine years before he passed away at the age of eighty-one. I'm told he had every sort of fowl you can think of here on the side of this mountain from peacocks to guinea hens and goats were among the farm animals he cared for in that ramshackle old barn. He is remembered quite fondly here in Pittman. You may remember being introduced to him on the Heartland Series on WBIR, some twenty years ago as the "Circuit Riding Preacher." You can still see it in a rerun every now and then.

So many amazing creatures inhabit this beautiful place in the mountains. From the black snake that occasionally slithers across the road to the two little rabbits who love the clover in my front yard and visit frequently in the cool of the evening to nibble and play. Their big brown eyes belie their intelligence as they are ever alert to any movement and quickly hop away to safety under the low branches of the old cedar tree. I found a tiny turtle (or was it a terrapin) not much bigger than a half-dollar nestled in the grass making its way, slowly and steadily, down to the trickling stream at the bottom of the hill.

There is so much 'God stuff' here!!! I marvel everyday at His handiwork! No wonder so many folks make annual treks to the mountains. There are never enough hours in the day to enjoy it all. Living here is so different than anything I have known before. The pace is so relaxed and the folks are truly genuine and friendly. A far cry from the business world I was used to for so many years. I was always in a hurry, always worrying about 'business' decisions; and time and money were such big priorities, *back then*. Business attire was all I had in my closet . . . high heels (ouch), tailored suits, and everything else that goes along with the trappings of being a career-woman on the move. That's

OK for some folks, and I was really quite successful, but real peace alluded me! Thank goodness, God saw fit to change all that when I said yes to Him and the ministry I love. He has given me peace I never dreamed possible.

Folks here never seem to be too hurried to stop for a 'hello and how-are-you' before going on their way. There's still lots of little society things to do if you like; parties, teas, etc. and it's fun to 'dress up' . . . every once in a while. But, the focus is not on what you have, or what you wear, but on living LIFE and enjoying it. God is so good in Pittman Center!

Our church doors are always open, always welcoming, not only to our own but to the many vacationers who visit often and soon become a part of our church family. There is joy in knowing that I am living out my calling as one of God's faithful servants. You might even say I'm still in the insurance business . . . *fire and **life*** that is. But, I don't have to sell it anymore, I give it away. Oh, yes! Did I mention my BOSS? He's the greatest! *"Know ye that the Lord he is God. It is He that has made us and not we ourselves. We are his people and the sheep of his pasture. Praise ye the Lord!"*

JULY
PONDERINGS

"The Joy of Growing Old with God"
July 29, 2012

As I sit in my study this morning, it is barely past dawn and already the little hummingbirds are gathering around the feeder just outside my window. I love to sit and watch these graceful little creatures. When they all gather round they appear as tiny ballerinas pirouetting and flitting about on an invisible dance floor. During these hot days, they surely do like to drink that sweet nectar and the end of each day finds the bottle ready to be filled again. This morning most of the hummers are female but there is one male showing off his bright red throat and getting more than his share of the feast.

There has been so much going on this week. I have been kept busy as there are so many things to do to honor God, and He just continues to pour out his blessings in these beautiful mountains I call home. One event of this past week was my seventy-second birthday! I don't feel older; however, I do see another wrinkle or two. Shucks, these aren't wrinkles; they are just character lines! Yes, that's what they are!

A wonderful book which I have been part of, *"The Joy of Growing Old with God"* arrived from the publisher this past week and we rejoiced at our Author's Reception at the **Anna Porter Public Library**. This book was the brainchild of **Teri Pizza** at the direction of God's distinct instructions. Fourteen authors shared their thoughts in story and poem about the joy of growing old with God. I was blessed to be included as one of the authors. This is a book you can read in one or two sittings and it will leave you with feelings of joy and peace. Local artist **Vern Hippensteal's** beautiful painting of a lovely rainbow, "After the Rain," graces the cover.

Yesterday was our Pastors' Summer Picnic at **Middlesettlements UMC's** "Field of Dreams" in Maryville. We welcomed the new pastors to the Maryville District, ate delicious barbeque and fried chicken and enjoyed our **District Superintendent Charles Maynard's** great stories. A master storyteller, he never fails to leave us laughing.

Driving home in the afternoon my mind was wandering and thinking about many things, both past and present. I welcomed the opportunity to sit with **Bob and Phyllis Bostick** at the picnic. Bob, my first DS, is the one I have to thank for my first appointment to Pittman Center way back in 2001. I told him then and I affirmed it again, he made me the happiest woman in the world when I came to these mountains. It will soon be time for me to take the designation of "retired" and I'm not looking forward to it. My deepest regret is that I waited nineteen years to accept God's call on my life which came first in 1981. When folks ask me what I am going to do next, I honestly say, I'm not sure, but God knows, and I can't wait to find out.

Lazy, Hazy, Crazy Days of Summer
July 1, 2012

Good morning to you! Today is the first day of July and we are smack-dab in the middle of those lazy, hazy, crazy, and very hot, days of summer. Hope you are able to stay cool and please don't forget to check on your neighbors, especially the elderly. We are Jesus' hands and feet doing his work here on earth. You will have blessings like you've never known before as you move outside your comfort zone to help others.

I was blessed to have my granddaughter, **Elle Kate**, who is thirteen, spend a few days with me last week. I found out something I have known for quite some time now . . . I am getting older. In fact after we got home from **Dollywood**, I was one exhausted old woman. The first ride she chose was the Geyser Gulch where I just happened to be sitting on the outside seat and Elle was on the inside seat. I didn't know any better! I was soaked from head to foot and walked around the rest of the day in wet pants, shoes and socks. I didn't feel too bad though, there were many others who looked the same way. After the scrambler, bumper cars, motion theatre, and everything else that moved, plus walking up and down hills for a gazillion miles, we came home with Elle laughing and me dragging.

Another day was just perfect for wading in the creek and Elle loved catching salamanders, crawdads and all sorts of God's creepy little creek creatures. It had been a while since I had playtime in the creek with my grandchildren. I could definitely tell it took a tad more effort to stay on my feet in the water as the rocks were quite slippery. I was very tired after the first thirty minutes but Elle still hadn't caught the exact size of salamander she wanted so I decided to sit on a stool in the yard and watch her as she played in the creek another couple of hours. The hill back up to the parsonage is definitely steeper than last year. I can't figure out how that happened. Where, oh where, do young folks get all that energy?

My sweet mother (*she will be 94 in September*) is spending the month of July with me and we are enjoying each other's company while keeping cool inside. Gives us time to talk and reminisce. The time we spend together is a cherished treasure.

Spending quality with family is so important. Teaching children proper manners and morals should be a priority with all parents and grandparents. And most of all, children should be taught respect. *"Even a child is known by his actions, by whether his conduct is pure and right."* *Proverbs 20:11 (NIV)*

When you have an extra hour, why don't you read again the book of Proverbs? Written so long ago, it is still relevant today. Here you will find some mighty good advice on living. May God richly bless you and yours this day with love and a joy that is everlasting!

Shalom my friends.

Whispering Hope
July 10, 2011

One of my favorite hymns of the church has always been *"Whispering Hope."* Sadly, it is not in our newer Methodist Hymnals as many of the older songs have given way to those deemed by the church hierarchy to be better suited for the church today. Personally, you can definitely say it is because of my age, I prefer the older songs. I know the history of many of them and realize the circumstances in which they were conceived in the mind of the writer. "Whispering Hope" leaves more questions in my mind as to the writer's purpose or reason than I can find answers to the "why" . . . but we certainly know the finished work is a masterpiece of depth of soul and longing.

"Whispering Hope" has its surprises, the first being that it was written by a man, Septimus Winner, yet published under the name of "Alice Hawthorne." The second surprise is that Winner also wrote "Oh Where, Oh Where, Has My Little Dog Gone" and "Listen to the Mockingbird." I guess you might say he was better known for his folk music than his hymns. Third, he was once charged with treason against the government of the United States of America. I wonder what event in his life was the catalyst that caused him to pen the beautiful and soulful words: *"Soft as the voice of an angel, Breathing a lesson unheard, Hope with a gentle persuasion, Whispers her comforting word. Wait till the darkness is over, Wait till life's tempest is done, Hope for the sunshine tomorrow, After the shower is gone. Whispering hope, O how welcome thy voice, Making my heart in its sorrow rejoice."* Published in 1868 this was the last successful song before his death and was based on *Hebrews 6:19 "This hope we have as an anchor of the soul, both sure and steadfast, and which enters the Presence behind the veil." (NKJV)*

Many have been the mornings I have awakened with this melancholy song on my mind and find myself humming it throughout the day. Hope means we look forward to the future with great expectation of our wishes being fulfilled. Hope gives us courage to look for the possibilities of each new day. With hope alive in our hearts we have the assurance that God is with us, come what may. With His help, we can rise to new heights, dream the impossible dream, soar like an eagle, and be at peace with ourselves.

Hope is the quiet solace of our very existence as we pass the days of our life here on earth. And when we pass into that heavenly realm . . . well . . . we see hope realized and truth revealed. What a glad day that will be!

Shalom to you my friends and many thanks to Webb's Creek's organist, **Jane Dean**, who plays "Whispering Hope" many Sunday mornings in our worship service. It never fails to lift me up and I am blessed by her thoughtfulness.

A Meandering Stream
July 17, 2010

Have you ever walked along a meandering stream and thought about where it came from and where it is going? Have you lain in your bed at night listening to its soothing sounds outside your bedroom window? Have you contemplated the wonder of that same stream flowing into a river bringing life and sustenance to all the fish, frogs, turtles, snakes, and flora finding their abode therein? Do you ever just sit and ponder the awesome beauty of its exciting journey; the ebb and flow that provides tranquility, serenity, peace and solace to each who draws near? The mountains and streams outside my front door are two of God's greatest gifts and they bring me joy and make me happy.

A stream of clear flowing water fascinates me! It intrigues me! I want to scoop it up and pour it out and play in it. I want to wade in it, sit in it, watch its endless journey and enjoy its coolness on a hot summer's eve. I like to listen to its sounds like a soft gentle purring, or a mighty rushing roar. I want to sleep with my windows wide open to hear the lilt of its timeless melody. And I am reminded of my **Granddad Musgrove,** many years ago.

In my mind's eye, I see a tired old man coming in from a hard day's work in the fields, slightly stooped and quite dirty from grubbing and plowing. Dust settled into every line of his wrinkled face and onto his neck from the open collar of his faded old work shirt. Beads of sweat form little rivulets down his face as he hunkers down to take a seat on the smooth rock beside the small stream. Bending over, he pulls off his boots, sets them aside, and dips his tired aching feet into the cool water. Sitting there with eyes closed, resting . . . a sigh escapes his lips, a prayer of thanksgiving to God for another good day. Slowly he lowers the galluses of his overalls, slips into the coolness of the stream and begins washing the grime from his body. Rising up, cleansed and at peace, he makes his way along the moonlit path toward the back door of the old farm house, thinking only of the comfort of the feather bed just beyond the squeak of the old screen door . . .

And I know *"The Lord is my shepherd; I shall not want. He maketh me to lie down in green pastures: he leadeth me beside the still waters. He restoreth my soul: he leadeth me in the paths of righteousness for his name's sake. Yea though I walk through the valley of the shadow of death, I will fear no evil; for thou art with me; thy rod and thy staff they comfort me. Thou preparest a table before me in the presence of mine enemies: thou anointest my head with oil; my cup runneth over. Surely goodness and mercy shall follow me all the days of my life: and I will dwell in the house of the Lord for ever." Psalm 23 (KJV)*

Excuses, Excuses

July 26, 2009

The Kingsmen Quartet recorded a song many years ago entitled "Excuses, Excuses." It tells about how folks can always find some excuse for not going to church: Some of it goes like this: *"Well, the sermons they're too long. And, maybe they're too short. He ought to preach the word with dignity instead of "stomp and snort." Well, that preacher we've got must be "the world's most stuck up man." Well, one of the lady's told me the other day, "Well, he didn't even shake my hand." Excuses, excuses, you'll hear them every day. And the Devil he'll supply them if the church you stay away. When people come to know the Lord, the Devil always loses. So to keep them folks away from church, he offers them excuses."*

I think it is true of most everyone that we can find the time to do those things we really want to do but if it's something we're not so interested in we will find some sort of excuse not to do it. A couple of weeks ago my favorite doctor said I needed to walk at least thirty minutes each day. It would improve whatever was ailing me. So every day I kept putting off my walk until the next day with the excuse I was just too busy. Now I have a much better excuse . . . I saw a bear (a big black smoky bear) in the woods behind the church across the road. Why, that bear could sneak up behind me while I was walking and make mincemeat out of me before I knew what was happening . . . See what I mean? Excuses, excuses!

What if God made excuses every time we needed Him? *"Sorry, there's too many others in line. You'll have to wait your turn." "Can you hold on a minute, I have someone else kneeling in?" "Oh no, not you again." "Pray back in a couple of hours I'm busy right now." "Sorry I'm on my way to see those folks down at the beach. I'll be back to the mountains in a couple of weeks. You just take care of things the best way you can until I get back."* Yes, what if God made excuses?

We need to be reminded that our Lord never changes and is in the same place during the good times as well as the bad. He is the Rock that never moves and He is always there to comfort and listen to our needs. He is the Rock we lean on and the strength we cling to. *"For who is God save the Lord? or who is a rock save our God?. It is God that girdeth me with strength, and maketh my way perfect." Psalm 18:31-32 (KJV)*

Jesus Laughing
July 19, 2009

There is a painting on my mantle called **"Joy to the World"** by **Stephen Sawyer** and it is a picture of Jesus laughing; a hearty laugh of pure pleasure! It makes me happy to know I have a Savior who laughs, probably at me as He sees me stumbling along life's pathway. I'm glad He loves me even though He knows me and shares my joy in laughter as well as the pain of my sorrow.

Have you heard the song by Mark Lowery, *Jesus Laughing*? What a fantastic song and one that echoes the way I feel about Jesus! I've preached many times on how Jesus wants us to be happy! Jesus was just as physically human as you or I. He experienced the same feelings we do; he loved, he hurt, he felt pain, he cried, and he also laughed.

Some folks have a problem with thinking of Jesus laughing; they seem to think it might just be just a tad sacrilegious. My goodness!! Don't you think Jesus laughed as he walked along the seashore with his disciples whiling away the hours; or when they were in the boat fishing, or breaking bread together? I cannot even imagine Jesus not laughing and smiling as he held the little children close to him. When I enter that Heavenly City, don't even try to tell me Jesus won't greet me with a smile or even laughter as He bids me "Come on in child, you finally made it!"

I heard a statement sometime ago which I think is absolutely profound. I've been pondering it the whole week. "Just because someone is a Christian, doesn't mean they have to stop dancing. They just need to change partners." Wow, as pastors say . . . "that'll preach!" Have you ever thought about that? Change partners and keep on dancing! This partner will be with you forever; He'll never let you down.

Have you noticed that we all seem to read our Bible a lot more as we get older. It finally makes sense now that I'm 'older' . . . we are cramming for our finals! Don't we all hope God grades on the curve? It's OK to laugh . . . go ahead. Laughter is good medicine and we can all use a big dose every now and then. A lot of us need a facelift if it weren't so expensive. Well, I know how you can get one . . . free. Put on a smile and look ten years younger, instantly!!! Oil of Olay can't come close to competing with a smile!

Live close to the Lord, keep on dancing and don't stop laughing. *"A merry heart doeth good like a medicine: but a broken spirit drieth the bones."* *Proverbs 17:22 (KJV)* And we don't want any dry bones now do we?

Keep smiling!

So Sure of Life

July 5, 2009

One of the first books I read upon arriving in Pittman Center almost nine years ago, was **"So Sure of Life"** written in 1950 by **Violet Wood**. This fascinating account of **Dr. Robert F. Thomas** and the years he spent in Pittman Center intrigued me back then and still does today. As I began a second read this past week . . . I discovered I enjoyed it more now as my understanding of this mountain community has grown with the years I've spent here. All of this being fresh on my mind this morning, I decided to rerun a previous 'pondering' about the old steps at the end of my driveway. Please indulge me as my mind wanders back a few years.

Established by the New York District of the Methodist Church through the efforts of **Eli Pittman** and **John Burnett**, this was a highly populated and bustling mission town in the early 1900s. I would think it was much like our present day, **Red Bird Mission** or **Henderson Settlement**. Jobs were created, skills were taught and learned, and every Sunday, the Glory of the Lord came down with old-time preachin', prayin', and singin.' And, when you got to marrying age . . . church was the best courtin' place you could find anywhere. Sitting on the back pew holding hands, or on the long walk home in the dark of the evening when you could 'steal a little sugar' from your sweetheart's cheek.

In clearing out the overgrowth of trees around the parsonage, a set of *old concrete steps* was uncovered down near the end of the driveway. Those old steps have caused me to ponder on the Pittman Center of long ago; little barefoot children and grown-ups alike, with emotionless faces, trudging up the hill to the infirmary which was then located right here where the parsonage now stands. All of them, coming to see Doc Thomas, who could fix most anything that ailed you. When the visits here slowed a mite, you could see 'ole Doc' riding his horse all over these hills and valleys; birthing the babies (human and otherwise), pulling teeth, and calming the fever. "Twarn't nothin' fer him to even doctor yore old horse, or yore cow, if'n it was ailin'." Lo, the many years he served here as doctor, dentist, veterinarian, preacher, and friend. Why, he even delivered Dolly Parton herself, and likely some of her eleven brothers and sisters!

If those *old steps* could talk . . . they would tell of the strong faith, yet meager existence of these mountain folks who worked hard to provide for their families and to care for each other. The first school in Pittman Center was a most welcome sight! Children of all ages and sizes were brought in by horseback and wagon, to partake in the opportunity of an education.

In late evening, loud claps of thunder, flashing lightning, and downpours of rain frequented the mountains. I can just see the women now, gathering up the children and hurrying to the middle of the 'feather bed' for safety from the lightning. Mothers in aprons are scurrying around the old wood stove preparing the evening meal of cornmeal mush, fried taters, pinto beans and lots of fresh milk from old Bessie grazing down in the bottoms. And, dads coming in from the fields dirty from the day's work; making a beeline down to the creek to wash up before supper time. Oh, what tales they would tell . . . if those old steps could talk!

"We have heard with our ears, O God, our fathers have told us, what work thou didst in their days, in the times of old." Psalm 44:1(KJV)

Picking Blackberries
July 20, 2008

You want to know what is on my mind this fine morning? Blackberries!!! Last evening around 7:30PM, a sweet lady came to my door bearing a delicious homemade blackberry pie. Her husband had called and said she was on her way and it was my birthday pie!!! My 68th birthday will be this Thursday and I can't think of a better way to celebrate than with warm blackberry pie, topped with vanilla ice cream. Yum! Yes I celebrated early, with many thanks to **Wade and Jane Smith** for being so very thoughtful.

This brings to mind another knocking on my door about a week ago. **Kent Green**, and his sons, **Kasey** and **Kendall**, with the biggest smiles you've ever seen handed me a gift of fresh picked blackberries, washed and ready to eat. My first of the season! Don't know where they found them but there must have been sugar in the soil. Those were the sweetest berries I have ever tasted. There was enough for a cobbler but I thought they were more like Lay's potato chips. I couldn't eat just one!!! I tell you folks I like being your preacher!!! You continually amaze me with your thoughtfulness and generosity of your time.

Let me tell you about the last time I went blackberry picking! **Clyde** and I lived in Louisville, TN and there was a small grove of trees and bushes way back on the land behind our house where lots of blackberries grew. Grabbing a bucket, off we went. Right in the middle of picking berries, I was taking in our surroundings for snakes and other varmints when I spied something eerily familiar.

Don't forget I worked in the court system for many years—and I know a few things you wouldn't think a little old gray haired preacher lady would know. I reached for Clyde's hand and whispered for him to look at this gigantic plant and some smaller ones around it. When he did, I whispered again . . . *I hate to tell you . . . but . . . this is somebody's marijuana patch and we better get out of here before we get shot!* We hightailed it back to the house and that was the last of my berry picking days. We did tell the authorities after thinking about it a couple of days, but when they went to investigate . . . the plants had been plucked!!! Someone was watching that crop, and us, just as I suspected!

But this pondering isn't really about blackberries at all. It is more about the random acts of kindness of my parish and the love and care that is being shown every day: not only to me but to each other! *Jesus said "Love the Lord your God with all your heart and with all your soul and with all your mind,' this is the first and greatest commandment. And the second is like it: 'Love your neighbor as yourself.' Matt. 22:37-39 (NIV)*

A Great-Grandmother
July 29, 2007

Good morning! It's time to wake up!! Here it is Sunday morning and time to put on your Sunday-go-to—meeting clothes! What a great week we have had. First of all, God just poured out his blessings all over these mountains with much needed rain. At last the rivers and streams are flowing *over* the rocks instead of *around* them. Fishermen and rafters are once again enjoying the recreation they provide.

Let's begin with last Monday. I had another birthday! I may be sixty-seven but I still feel like a teenager! I know; I know . . . my face and body say otherwise!!! You didn't have to bring that up. And . . . I got lots of sweet stuff for my birthday: pound cake, red velvet cake, almond joy pie, donuts from the Donut Friar . . . Have mercy!! When I *waddle* up to the pulpit one Sunday morning, you will all know where it went! Thank goodness, that big bouquet of beautiful flowers was not edible!!

Thursday, I became a *great* grandmother for the first time. I can't wait to see and hold this sweet little baby boy in my arms. He is **Jayden Chase Blair, son to Andrew and Courtney**. I just love little babies . . . and old people, too . . . and little creatures!

Which reminds me . . . Have I told you about **Roscoe**? Well, when my youngest son was ten years old, he came home from a visit with his dad dragging along . . . a cage, a box of food, and a GERBIL! I never did like rats . . . too much. But, I am tenderhearted and I can't let *anything* go hungry or dirty so he was named Roscoe and I cared for that little feller for five years! When I came in from work he would jump all over his cage and turn flips in his wheel. He loved me *and* he loved salted peanuts! So every evening, I fed Roscoe salted peanuts. One day he just fell over . . . and died! I cried and cried as Clyde put him in a little shoebox, dug a hole, and buried him in our back yard. As I lay in bed that night, thinking . . . slowly, I realized what I had done . . . *I had killed Roscoe; he had died from high blood pressure caused by all that salt.* And then . . . I cried some more.

When I sit down here at my computer at 4:30AM every Sunday morning, I never know where my ponderings will go. You don't either. Sometimes, we are both surprised. Like today! So y'all just love each other . . . as Christ loves you! See you in church!

"Bless the Lord, O my soul: and all 5that is within me, bless his holy name. Bless the Lord O my soul, and forget not all his benefits: Who forgiveth all thine iniquities: who healeth all thy diseases; Who redeemeth thy life from destruction; who crowneth thee with lovingkindness and tender mercies; Who satisfieth thy mouth with good things; so that thy youth is renewed like the eagle's." Psalm 103: 1-5 (KJV)

Dare We Be Honest?

July 15, 2007

Honesty is the best policy; at least that is what I have always been told. I've also heard that little white lies are just as bad as big black ones. I don't think I can honestly agree with that statement. Sometimes I wonder how to be really honest without hurting someone's feelings. Is there such a thing as ever being able to be totally and completely honest at all times, in every circumstance? Just suppose my friend asks me, "How do you like my new hairdo?" What if it looks awful and makes her look ten years older than she really is? What am I supposed to say? "Well, to be honest, it looks awful!" Splat . . . I just picked myself up off the floor! Now be honest, don't we all usually say what we know the other person wants to hear? "Honey, it looks lovely and makes you look so young!" *Liar, liar pants on fire!!*

Perhaps we should take our cue from a little boy who was the ring bearer in a wedding. He was about eight years old and looked very spiffy in his little tux and shiny patent leather shoes. I said to him, "My goodness you look handsome today. Your shoes are so shiny. Are they comfortable?" His reply? "The socks are!" My first instinct was to laugh but thinking more deeply, I realized his was a profound answer! This young lad came up with the most positive response possible. What an excellent way of being honest without saying anything negative!

Reminds me of the Sunday morning **Miss Vida** Reagan (pronounced Videe), a lovely, intelligent sage who has attained the age of 92 years, told me quite honestly something I needed to hear. "Miss Alta, you need to wear more color. You look pale today. Put more blush on your cheeks, and with your gray hair, you shouldn't wear anything grey, or brown, or tan, or even beige. As we get older, we should all wear more color!" What did I do then? I went home and pushed all of those nondescript, colorless clothes to the back of my closet so I wouldn't be putting them on again the next Sunday! I got out a brighter shade of blush for my cheeks and a deeper pink for my lips. Recognizing wisdom and truth, I respect what Miss Vida has to say. She was giving me honest constructive criticism in the kindest most straightforward way! There's no beating around the bush with Miss Vida!! When she speaks, I listen. Honest!

"Apply thine heart unto instruction, and thine ears to the words of knowledge. Yea, my reins shall rejoice, when thy lips speak right things. Buy the truth, and sell it not: also wisdom, and instruction, and understanding." Proverbs 23: 12, 16, 23 (KJV)

An Extraordinary Place
July 1, 2007

These lazy, hazy, crazy days of summer are just what the doctor ordered! Every morning when I wake up, I scurry through the house to open up all the doors and windows so the cool crisp morning air and the clean smell of the mountains, will permeate the whole house. I love the pungent smell of damp earth after the rain and we've been getting a shower almost every afternoon this past week. One minute it will be pouring buckets and the next, the sun will be shining and the dark clouds swept away leaving nothing but beautiful blue sky.

There is a bit of sadness in my heart as I realize the elementary school just across the road from the parsonage will be silent next year. The long-awaited new school just up the road off Highway #321 will open in the fall. We will miss the noise and laughter of children at play and being a neighbor to such a fine school! **Pittman Center Elementary School** is one of the best! God's name is still spoken with reverence and without fear, prayers are lifted without shame, and pledging allegiance to our country's flag holds patriotic fervor. Many of our National Merit Scholarship winners got their start here. Parents are good, salt-of-the-earth folks who support their children *and their children's teachers* as well. They attend school activities and encourage their children to be the best they can be. The principal, Susan Carr, is to be commended for her dedication and commitment to excellence in education.

As I begin my seventh year in ministry in this beautiful and extraordinary place, I wonder what the future holds for us. What will happen to the old school building? No one seems to know. All of the land here in Pittman Center once belonged to the United Methodist Church. The settlement that spawned the Town of Pittman Center in the early 1900s has seen many changes through the years. Change is as much a part of life as breathing. I wonder how the changes that are sure to come will affect the lives of the folks remaining and the new ones moving in. I wonder what is in store for all of us. Yes, I wonder . . .

And yet I *know*, that *we too* shall, one day, be changed according to *I Corinthians, 15: 51-52: "Behold, I shew you a mystery; we shall not all sleep, but we shall all be changed. In a moment in the twinkling of an eye, at the last trump; for the trumpet shall sound, and the dead shall be raised incorruptible, and we shall be changed."* This . . . I do *not* wonder about.

    I simply believe.

The Storehouse of God
July 30, 2006

Prayers have been answered this past week here in the mountains and I suspect in your part of the country as well. We have really had much needed "showers of blessings." Thank you Jesus!

I have probably told this story in my ponderings before but I'm going to tell it again, even if I have. I think of it every time I think of rain! It happened back in the early 70's and our family was living in Athens. We were members of Trinity UMC and **Ray Robinson** was our pastor. We had a long dry spell and everyone was praying for rain. Finally . . . it began to rain, and it rained, and it rained, and it rained, and it got to be *Day 40 of the Deluge*. (I'm not kidding! It rained a portion of every day for at least 40 days!) Having to pass the church on my way home from work, I just happened to notice the sign in front of our church . . . "If you have been praying for rain . . . Stop!!!" How indicative of Ray who always had something to say or do that reached out, grabbed your attention, and caused you to think. When you realized what he was saying . . . it was profound . . . and sometimes incredibly funny. But . . . he always got his point across in a way that was not easily forgotten. (I have always wished I had that ability!)

One of the most important emphases in our lives as Christians is that of prayer, both for our own guidance in our spiritual journey and for the under girding power of the Holy Spirit in our churches! Prayer is the practice of the presence of God in our daily activities; praying that God will bless our efforts in His behalf; that we will be Christ-minded and not self-minded. There is power in prayer for our weakened will and the world's woes.

We need to practice God's presence even as we are distracted by the things of the world; the sorrow and heartache all around us; amid the strife of our country's battles, and in the hustle and bustle of all our days. We need that constant abiding in us and the assurance that we have this great shield always available to us. Someone once said that "No one is poor who can by prayer open the storehouse of God." And what a storehouse of blessings He has!!! Blessings unending! For us! You and Me! God is so good!

"Praying always with all prayer and supplication in the Spirit, and watching thereunto with all perseverance and supplication for all saints;" Ephesians 6:18 (KJV)

Mary Kay
July 23, 2006

Oh, this is going to be a good day! A great day! A wonderful day! On this day sixty-six years ago, my mother was oh so glad to give birth to me. I know she was glad, because I have given birth to four children and every time, I said "whew, I sure am glad that is over!"

I'm pondering today on 'Mary Kay' who seems to become dearer to me every day. Her 'powder and paint' sure helps out by concealing a number of new flaws I seem to discover each morning when I look into the mirror. There is one thing I don't agree with her on, however. She said "a woman who would tell her age would tell anything . . ." My goodness, I'm so glad to be here! It is certainly better than not being here!! God created me, I am here by his grace . . . I believe in rejoicing!!! Every (birth) day is another sweet gift from God that I truly cherish.

There are too many times in our lives when we waste precious time thinking about our yesterdays. Wishing we could go back and relive them or do things differently. It is so important that we understand yesterday is gone and nothing we can do or say will bring it back or fix its mistakes.

As God's children we must focus on the bright future we have ahead of us and not fall for the Evil One's lies as he tries constantly to make us believe that our best days are behind us. My desire is to encourage you that there are wonderful days ahead of you, tomorrows that are even more wonderful that you can imagine.

"For I know the thoughts that I think toward you, saith the Lord, thoughts of peace, and not of evil, to give you an expected end." Jeremiah 29:11-13 (KJV)

"For the grace of God that bringeth salvation hath appeared to all men, Teaching us that, denying ungodliness and worldly lusts, we should live soberly, righteously, and godly. In this present world;" Looking for that blessed hope, and the glorious appearance of the great God and our Savior Jesus Christ;" Titus 2:11-13 (KJV)

"Now unto him that is able to do exceeding abundantly aove all that we ask or think, according to the power that worketh in us," Ephesians 3:20 (KJV)

Moments of Pure Grace
July 16, 2006

We all have our moments of pure grace, moments of sweet delight, special moments when we feel God with us, *oh, so intimately*. In times like these, I get chills as I literally feel Him wrapping invisible arms around me, encircling me with unconditional love. And He invites me to accept His presence. My heart seems to settle somewhere in my throat and I am amazed at the awesomeness of Almighty God; the Creator of all that is and ever shall be.

There are so many ways I experience true communion with God. Like the week we were in Myrtle Beach; I saw a rainbow and thought it had to be the most beautiful I had ever seen. When I looked again, there was a second rainbow right beside the first! And I thought of God reassuring me, twice over, of his great love and mercy. Never before have I seen two rainbows, side by side with colors so vibrant! Each one clearly defined; violet, aqua, pink, and yellow; so magnificent that praises deep within me bubbled up and escaped my lips! *"And the bow shall be in the cloud; and I will look upon it, that I may remember the everlasting covenant between God and every living creature of all flesh that is upon the earth."* *Genesis 9:16 (KJV)*

God's presence is so real in the gurgling of a clear mountain stream; in a cool gentle breeze on a hot summer day; in a bird's warble or the chatter of squirrels high in the old oak tree in our front yard. God speaks to me when I find a shiny new penny in an unusual place . . . and I am reminded "in God we trust." When I see our American flag fully unfurled in the wind, I think of freedom and my heart is glad! I am grateful to those who fought and died on foreign soil so that we might live here in peace. I think of those blessed to return home from war to loved ones who can never comprehend the magnitude of all these soldiers have seen and done. And I think of my earthly father and the goodness of God in keeping him safe during WWII and the time he endured in the belly of a great ship in the Pacific Ocean. *"But thanks be to God, which giveth us the victory through our Lord Jesus Christ."* *I Corinthians 15:57 (KJV)*

God speaks to me in the soothing refrain of a great old hymn of the church and I'm reminded of Charles Wesley as I try to imagine the passion he must have felt as he penned such beautiful words of praise and honor. *"O Sing unto the Lord a new song; sing unto the Lord, all the earth."* Psalm *96:1 (KJV)*

I see God's eyes in the eyes of a caring friend and I feel His touch in their embrace. He joins me in laughter; and in my tears, He feels my pain. I know that everything is in order as He tells me, there is *"A time to weep, and a time to laugh; a time to mourn, and a time to dance; A time to cast stones and a time to gather stones together; a time to embrace, and a time to refrain from embracing;" Ecclesiastes 3:4-5 (KJV)* And I feel His presence. And I know I am loved for God so loved the world that he gave his only Son that the world through Him might be saved. God has made known to me the path of life; and he fills me with joy in His presence.

Be assured that we, His children, shall be kept as the apple of His eye; and hidden in the shadow of His wings from the wicked who assail us. May God bless you today and everyday with the little things of life that bring you fully into His Holy Presence.

Euphoric with Joy
July 2, 2006

We arrived home yesterday afternoon after a week at the beach. I discovered that going to the beach these days is a lot different than it used to be. I used to come back all tanned and beautiful (?) from long walks on the beach and bathing in the sun. Now, the sun causes skin cancer and I better stay out of it. The bacon which tasted so good with my pancakes is now dangerous, fattening and loaded with cholesterol. Anything that is fried, sweet, or buttered isn't good for me, either! If it tastes good, I better spit it out!!! If it feels good, I better not do it! Have mercy!! I thought when I got old I could do what I wanted. Humph!!! Now there are more things I *can't* do than those I *can*. I couldn't even have popcorn with extra butter while enjoying the movie that caused my heart to race. (Was that bad for me, too?)

Well, I do think I may have sinned just a little while I was on vacation. There is nothing that sates my craving for 'something sweet' like a fresh, hot donut. And, I'm supposed to be on a diet! I will tell you a secret if you promise you won't tell. One afternoon while Clyde was napping, I slipped away, crossed the street and hurried up a couple of blocks to the *Krispy Kreme Donut Shoppe*. I entered that sweet smelling haven of mouth-watering confections savoring each moment and left with four donuts! Within less than five minutes, every one of them had just melted in my mouth! Almost euphoric in my joy, I pondered . . . how could anything so good, be so bad? But I didn't ponder too long . . .

Let me get real serious for a minute. This past week was a refreshing and renewing time for me; a real sabbatical! When I am close to the ocean, I feel God's presence so powerfully! It is incredible! Every morning, long before the sun painted the eastern sky with red and gold, I was sitting on the beach drinking in the awesome beauty of sand, sea, and sky. What a magnificent revelation of God's power and might! I watched as the endless white capped waves came rolling in, caressing the shore. And I marveled at the awesomeness of it all, and the order of it all . . . and I communed with God.

Now, I am home, blowing kisses to the mountains I love and more than ready to get back to the Lord's work. May your day and the coming week be blessed by God's own hand.

Shalom!

AUGUST
PONDERINGS

A Sweet Aroma
August 19, 2012

It is a quiet, still morning here in the mountains just before dawn. As I hastened out of bed, I grabbed my robe and ventured outside for my first breath of the cool crisp air. There is a slight tinge of fall in the air even as the summer is still marching along. This is the time of day I love best; the first light creeping over the mountain and the awakening of a new day. It always brings with it the wonder of what the day will hold. How many hearts will open for God's touch through the words he has given me to deliver to His people? I pray for guidance each day but especially on Sunday morning. An awesome task lies before me as I serve the Master of all that is or ever shall be. Lord, strengthen me and prepare me for the day that stretches before me and guide me as I impart your Word today.

Driving up Highway #321 early yesterday morning, I think every homeowner and road crew were out mowing the lush green grass that has sprung up, seemingly overnight, from the abundant rains we have had. Rolling down my window to enjoy the cool breeze, the sweet aroma of fresh mown grass permeated the air. That smell, so crisp and clean is almost heavenly; it defies description. It reminded me of years gone by when I loved to mow our lawn when I got home from work in the evening. It wasn't a chore and was something I found relaxing and calming after a hectic day at the office. Most of all, I enjoyed not having to answer the phone and listen to folks complain because their insurance rates had gone up or explain why their claim wasn't covered by their policy. This was of course, in the years before I became a pastor. I was working in the insurance field. I could write a book about that . . . like the time a girl in a lime green bikini came into my office, mad as an wet hornet, calling me every name she could think of . . . well that is another story better left untold. You can see why mowing the lawn was somewhat soothing after a day like that.

Our sense of smell is one of the easiest ways we connect to our past. A smell can transport us back to grandma's kitchen, to a loved one when we smell the scent of their perfume, and oh, the smell of cedar reminds us of Christmas past and Christmas to come. The sweet fragrance of flowers in spring is like a heady balm to our senses.

We as Christians should always have the sweet smell of Christ all around us. How do we do that? We put away all bitterness, hatred, and malice and replace it with kindness, compassion, love and forgiveness. Listen to Paul's instructions in *Ephesians 5:1(NIV) "Be imitators of God, therefore as dearly loved children and live a life of love, just as Christ loved us and gave himself up for us as a fragrant offering and sacrifice to God."* May we, today, join in that sweet smelling aroma of Christ's Church.

Shalom my friends.

The Cat and the Lizard
August 12, 2012

I have a cat. She is appropriately named **Miss Kitty**. There is nothing she likes better than for me to open the front door and let her sit in front of the storm door for hours on end. Now this storm door doesn't fit so well and a sliver of light can always be seen underneath it. I know that little skinny creatures can slither in so I shouldn't be surprised. Kitty loves it when they do and she pounces on them like a tiger on a junebug.

Last Wednesday, I was deeply involved in studying for my sermon for today and my mind was in Ephesus as I listened to St. Paul expound on unity and anger in the church there. When I heard a great thump! I was so startled I almost fell into the bars of Paul's jail cell and knocked his pen from his hand. It was Kitty! She was playing with the bright blue tail of a lizard that had just lost it. It immediately came to my mind . . . where is the torso of this creature now hiding. I have been looking in every dark crevice trying to find it before it hatches a new tail in the darkness of a baseboard and ends up in my chair, under my bare foot, or heaven forbid . . . in my bed! I shiver to even think of it!

Miss Kitty, lying flat on her belly, took up residence in front of the piano . . . I think I know where the lizard is hiding. I can't lift the piano; I can't even move it just an inch. What am I to do? I think this story is continued until the maimed lizard comes from its hiding place, and slithers to center stage once again. I sure hope Kitty sees it first!

Going back to my being with Paul as he writes to the Ephesians telling them to control their anger and always seek unity within the church. I began to think how anger and temper tantrums make us a lot like the cat and the lizard. Sometimes we are like the cat, ready to pounce on anything that moves and we cause folks to become displeased with us or 'disjointed' in some way. Sometimes we are like the lizard, hiding out and lying low until the storm passes and we are forgiven.

Anger causes us to do some pretty silly things, like yelling at drivers in other cars or screaming at the television set when we don't like what the coach is doing. Anger destroys the unity in our churches and the church, as the body of Christ, is crippled and maimed and unable to function while trying to do its work in the world.

Listen to what St. Paul has to say in *Ephesians 4:23-27(NLT)*: *"Instead, let the Spirit renew your thoughts and attitudes. Put on your new nature, created to be like God—truly righteous and holy. So stop telling lies. Let us tell our neighbors the truth, for we are all parts of the same body. And "don't sin by letting anger control you Don't let the sun go down while you are still angry, for anger gives a foothold to the devil."*

A Day to Call My Own
August 5, 2012

Yesterday, I enjoyed a rare treasure . . . a day I could actually call my own. It is seldom I have a day not planned even before I awaken. In fact, I have become so accustomed to living by a schedule, when a day comes and the calendar is blank, I find myself wondering what I have forgotten. Time is such a precious gift. I did just what I wanted to do and even though it was not an ordered day, it was a good day.

I awoke early, around 4AM, and decided to get some studying in while the house was dark and quiet. I enjoy silence and feast on the hours just before dawn. Looking out my study window, I watched as the day awakened and came to life and knew I was seeing a performance that outshined any performed on any stage, at any time, or in any place. As the actors took their various places in the natural scenery of the mountain, it was almost breathtaking. They needed no training . . . these woodland creatures, born with the gift of knowing their lines as well as their places.

Driving leisurely down Rocky Flats Road in mid-afternoon to deliver the church bulletins to **Shults Grove**, I let my eyes drink in the magnificence of the scenery all around me. As I drove in and out of patches of sunlight, I marveled at the sun-dappled roadway, how the trees seemed to close in all around me and wrap me in a blanket woven by God's own hand. There were places along the way where the density of the foliage permitted only a small opening to view the smoky blue of the summer sky above. Vibrant green leaves on slender branches and majestic firs seemed to dance to music all their own. A gentle swaying to and fro, a dip and a bow, a caress and a touch . . . reminding me of the days of my youth when dancing brought me more joy than almost anything. I let my mind run free . . . remembering . . . as I listened to a CD of love songs from the 50's by *The Platters*, my favorite group from days gone by.

When I reached my destination and climbed the long wooden steps that wind upward from the roadway to the church itself . . . I opened the door slowly and quietly, then reverently walked inside. Immediately I could smell that wondrous 'old' smell that always greets me upon entering this tiny sanctuary. I walked down the aisle between the two rows of pews and came to the altar where I knelt there on the floor of that precious old church and thanked God for bringing me to the peace and joy of this awesome place. How amazing to live where other folks must drive hundreds of miles just to spend a few days in this little bit of heaven on earth. And to think, it is my home! I shall not let a day pass that I don't marvel in its wonder and drop to my knees in thankful gratitude to Almighty God for His blessings on me!!

Surely, goodness and mercy shall follow me all the days of my life and I shall dwell in the house of the Lord forever!

Amen and Amen!

Power Nap
August 21, 2011

Several years ago, it became necessary for me to seek a doctor's advice because of some problems I was having. Oh don't worry, I'm in good shape now but one bit of advice this doctor gave me was to take a power nap each day for at least ten or twenty minutes; mainly because I was working constantly, raising children, and taking no time for myself. I was to use this time to recoup, and refresh. It worked, and to this day, I still try to take a short power nap each day.

So . . . I was lying on the couch taking my power nap and had fallen into a deep sleep. My only companion for the past couple of years has been **Miss Kitty** who is like all cats; she has an attitude. She loves to scratch the furniture and I have to scold her constantly. I was half awakened by her having jumped up onto the couch at my feet and she was pouncing up and down and scratching furiously. I opened one eye and told her to stop and then tried to drift back to sleep. Did she stop? No, I told you she has an attitude. After my scolding another couple of times, I jumped up and was ready to give her a swift swat for not minding.

It was then that I saw she had brought me a "toy" and laid it at my feet. She does this often when she wants me to play with her. When I looked again, my eyes grew big and my mouth dropped open. There where my feet had been was a snake!!! Okay, it was only a baby but it was still about sixteen inches long and about as big around as a pencil. I'm sure it came in under the storm door. If it even showed an inch of itself, I know Miss Kitty grabbed it and pulled it the rest of the way into the house.

As I looked at the poor thing with all the claw marks on its little body, I knew it had to be dead, it wasn't moving. I reached down and gently picked it up and headed for the back door to toss it out. I couldn't bring myself to toss it, somehow it just didn't seem fitting, so I "laid it out" on the rock wall near my carport. Poor snake. As I stood there watching and feeling a bit sorry for it, it lifted its head, and slithered away!!!

I hesitated to tell this story in that some of you may think I have gone to "taking up serpents." God hasn't told me to do this and until then, I'm not, I don't, and I won't!

Get your Bible and turn to *Mark 16:18* which deals with snake handling. A footnote in my Bible reads: *"Serious doubt exists as to whether verses 9-20 belong to the Gospel of Mark. They are absent from important early manuscripts and display certain peculiarities of vocabulary, style and theological content that are unlike the rest of Mark. His Gospel probably ended at 16:8 or its original ending has been lost."* (NIV)

I like to give you something to think about. Perhaps you will want to study more on this.

Summer's Last Hurrah
August 22, 2010

Can you believe it is almost September? My goodness, how quickly the days are flying by! Summer is shouting out its last hurrah and hanging on for all it's worth. Late yesterday afternoon, as I drove back home to these beautiful mountains, I savored the magnificent display of wild flowers in the fields and fence rows along the way. Beautiful purple and gold splashes against a background of green and brown, intermingled with the creamy delicate beauty of Queen Ann's lace, and a garden of tall golden sunflowers, all reaching toward heaven. God's world is so magnificent . . . it takes my breath away.

We too, are created by God, and listen to what he said!!! *"And God said, Let us make man in our image, after our likeness: and let them have dominion over the fish of the sea, and over the fowl of the air, and over the cattle, and over all the earth, and over every creeping thing that creepeth upon the earth. So God created man in his own image, in the image of God created he him, male and female created he them." Genesis 1:26-27 (KJV)* Wow! We are an image (or a reflection) of God himself!!!! What an awesome responsibility that places on us. The very idea that God created **us** to mirror Him . . . it takes my breath away.

Do we truly feel that our life is a portrait of *God's* love, mercy, and grace? Do we stand straight and tall reaching toward heaven? Do we love Him with all our heart and soul, and our neighbors as ourselves? Does our life bring Him honor and glory (remember, we are created *in HIS image*), or do we bring shame on his precious and holy name?

Just as I viewed the creation of God in those wildflowers and saw unspeakable beauty . . . I ponder on the image we are portraying and wonder if it is something beautiful and worthwhile? Is God pleased with who we are? Oh, my friends, I see room for so much improvement!!! I pray that God will grant me abundant grace to become more and more like Him.

"He hath made everything beautiful in his time," Ecclesiastes 3:11 (KJV) and . . . He takes my breath away!!!

"Joy to the World"
August 15, 2010

There is a painting on my mantle entitled "Joy to the World" by **Steven Sawyer**, painted in the year 2000. It is a picture of Jesus laughing; a hearty laugh of pure pleasure! This painting was a gift to me from the members of Shults Grove UMC shortly after my coming to Pittman Center in 2001. It makes me happy to know I have a Savior who laughs, probably at me, many times, as He sees me stumbling and tripping along life's way. I'm glad He loves me even though He knows me, oh so well, and He shares my laughter as well as my sorrow.

Have you heard the song by Mark Lowery, *"Jesus Laughing?"* What a fantastic song and one that echoes the way I feel about Jesus! I've preached many sermons on how Jesus wants us to be happy! And that we as Christians have more to be happy about than anyone. Jesus was just as physically human as you or I. He experienced the same feelings we do; He knew pain and suffering, He felt joy and gladness, He experienced love in its purest form, He knew disappointment, He cried, He was happy, and He laughed!

Some folks may have a problem thinking of Jesus laughing, even laughing out loud. They tend to feel it might just be a tad sacrilegious. My goodness!! Don't you think Jesus laughed as he walked along the seashore with his disciples, whiling away the hours; or when they were in the boat fishing; or as they shared a meal? I find it impossible to imagine Jesus not laughing and smiling as he held the little children close to him. When I enter that Heavenly City, don't even try to tell me Jesus is not going to greet me with a smile or even a great big laugh as He bids me "Come on in child, you finally made it!"

One Sunday about four years ago, **Ray Morris** was our interim pianist at **Webb's Creek**, and he said something I have never forgotten. We had just sung that wonderful song "Lord of the Dance" in our worship service that morning. The words to this song were penned in 1963 by Sydney Carter and it has become a favorite in all of our churches. Ray said, *"Just because someone is a Christian, doesn't mean they have to stop dancing. They just need to change partners."* Now isn't that the absolute truth? Think about it. It is profound.

I've been thinking too, about how we older folks seem to read the Bible a whole lot more now than when we were young. It finally occurred to me . . . we are cramming for our finals! And I wonder if God grades on the curve?

Live close to the Lord, keep on dancing, and please don't stop laughing. "A cheerful heart is good medicine, but a broken spirit saps a person's strength." *Proverbs 17:22 (NLT)*

Prayer-Filled Thoughts

August 8, 2010

Good morning! Another hot summer day is ahead of us and I can't wait for it to begin!! What a blessing to be able to be up and about! Do I get excited on the Lord's Day? I sure do! I get excited about bringing The Word to my people! I love my parish and pray daily for God to work through me to do the things He would do if He were here. I want to speak His words, comforting and reassuring; to do His work as if my feet and hands were His, to care for my Christian brothers and sisters and those who have not yet found our Savior. Yes Lord, help me fulfill the mission of making disciples of Jesus Christ for the transformation of the world.

All creation proclaims the glory of God and we should, too! Go get that cup of coffee or pop open a Diet Dr. Pepper. It's time to get your Sunday-go-to-meeting clothes on. Won't be long before the church bells will be ringing, beckoning you to come, enter the doors of God's house and be greeted by His presence. Sit down, let Him put His arms around you and just be blessed as you forget, for the next hour or so, all the worries and cares of this old world.

As I look out my study window this morning, I see my hummingbird feeder is empty once again. Those tiny little creatures sure can eat. Excuse me for a minute while I go fill it up . . . There, that is done, and they can once again come and feast. I see three birds out there now and instead of eating, they are busy trying to keep each other away. What selfish little creatures who can't realize they could each have a sip at the same time if they weren't so afraid of sharing. There is a side to hummingbirds that I didn't know existed until a few months ago when I got my feeder. They are territorial, they are loud, they like to fight, and they want it all. Seems I've heard of some humans who are the same way. It is sad to think my little hummingbirds are not exhibiting very Christian-like behavior. Guess all I can do is pray for them. Seriously, God is in control and these beautiful little birds are just doing what comes naturally.

I'm pondering this morning on prayer and how so much of my life is filled with prayer-filled thoughts even when I'm not on my knees. It's so easy to commune with God . . . He is our Father, our best friend, and we can tell Him everything that is on our heart. Prayers for guidance fill my days. He doesn't want or ask for long flowery sentences, proper breathing, good diction, or a pious stance. He just wants to hear from us and we will never find a better listener. God hears and perceives, words spoken, and unspoken. He knows our thoughts and feelings better than we do. So, don't *think* about praying—just *"do it!"*

Now you know I can't ponder without injecting some story of my own from my vast repertoire of yore. My Godly Mother instilled in me very early in life, the power and necessity of prayer. She taught me to pray about anything and everything and I did. When I was about seven years old, I got into a little tiff with one of my playmates, **Athana Brown**, and some pretty mean words came out of the mouth of a little girl who definitely knew better! Stomping my way home, I opened the door and found my very unhappy mother who had been on the phone with my friend's mother. Did I ever get a 'good talking to!' Not only that . . . Mom said I had to call Athana and apologize! By now, I was fuming because my friend had told on me. The last thing I wanted to do was apologize!

What I really wanted to do was go back up to her house and pull out some of her pretty little red curls. Trying hard not to show my anger, I picked up the phone to call my friend's number. All the while I was earnestly, silently praying to God that she wouldn't answer. "God, don't let her answer, please." When the operator said "number please" (remember this was about 63 years ago and yes, operators did talk with you back then) I responded, "amen." I still wonder who was more stunned, me, my Mom, or the operator! I think God was just shaking his head all the while, trying not to laugh as he waited for whatever might happen next.

This reminds me of a song my Clyde used to sing so beautifully, "Prayer is the key to heaven but faith unlocks the door."

Sunday Happenings
August 9, 2009

Good morning to you!!! Today is another beautiful Lord's Day and I am up and rarin' to go! I have always loved Sundays! Even when I was a child I knew Sundays were special and they were treated differently than all the other days in the week. There were certain things you did on Sunday, like going to church and reading your Bible and eating fried chicken; and there were certain things you didn't do on Sunday, which was anything that had to do with work. That meant you didn't even sew a button on if it was Sunday, you did most of the preparation for Sunday's dinner on Saturday, and you most certainly did not mow the yard on Sunday! It still pains me to see someone mowing their yard on Sunday. It just seems disrespectful somehow yet I know there are many good folks today with very good excuses for working on Sunday. We have become a bit more lenient to say the least.

Today is a really special day as we are celebrating Holy Communion in each of Pittman's three Methodist churches. What a privilege and honor for me as the celebrant; I am deeply humbled each time I break the bread and lift the cup.

Have you ever been guilty of leaving church saying "I didn't get a thing out of the service!" There were times in the past when I have done this very thing and have heard many others make the same declaration. This is nothing new as the people in John Wesley's day were also feeling the same way about the worship services of the Church of England. Many of the sermons were so elegant and so filled with allusions of classical literature they were over the heads of everyday folk. The singing was less than uplifting and worship seemed not to relate to everyday life and the common folk. Today our worship services are well-planned with hymns, prayers, and other parts of the service revolving around the scripture and the sermon flows naturally and is easily understood.

John Wesley, in defending the Church of England, said how we experience worship depends on how we approach worship. We need to be alive to God with upright hearts, coming with expectant faith, and open to the power and presence of God. Worship requires participation, not merely sitting on a bench. We need to come expecting something good to happen, to feel God's presence, and be touched by his grace.

The Lord's Supper, or the Eucharist, is based on Jesus' actions during the Last Supper as told by the New Testament gospel writers, Matthew, Mark and Luke. Jesus takes the bread, blesses it, breaks the bread, and gives it to the disciples. Likewise, he takes the cup, gives thanks, and gives it to the disciples. The promise of this Sacrament is through the power of the Holy Spirit, the risen Jesus is present giving us these gifts of bread and wine (grape juice in our churches). Jesus pours out himself in love as he offers forgiveness for our sins and the promise of new life in Him.

The United Methodist Church observes 'open' Communion which simply means that everyone is welcome at the Lord's Table. Just as Jesus would turn no one away, neither do we. And so as we partake of the Lord's Supper, or Holy Communion, in each of our churches this day; you will hear the familiar words, "Come, the table is ready!"

Sweet Grace

August 31, 2008

I do love these cooler mornings! Ever an optimist, I can't wait to see what is just around the corner. I love every season and look forward to each one with great anticipation. I really don't have a favorite but autumn is such a beautiful time of the year. As soon as school starts back and the mornings become cooler, my thoughts turn to fall.

My study is in the front of the parsonage with a window that looks out onto the front lawn covered with stately old trees and the side of the mountain across the road. As I sit at my computer and write, I always have an ever changing panorama of God's great big beautiful world just outside my window. The lush green of the foliage this year as well as the deep green of the grass declares there has been lots more rain this year than last. Last year's drought caused most of the leaves to simply die and fall from the trees before the beautiful fall colors could even begin and the grass was like walking on potato chips!

This past week has been filled with non-stop days! There was no time for a power nap during the day and when I finally got to bed each night, I practically fell asleep before my head hit the pillow. I began to think about the miracle of God's *grace* and how it truly is amazing, just as the song says. God can take our crazy mixed up lives, and if we let Him, He will turn them right side up again, He can lead us from a road full of twists and turns to one that is straight. He can take our tired, exhausted bodies and make them feel as if we have been lifted up on eagle's wings . . . through His *grace*, his mercy, and his love.

Once when I had a real job (you know preachers only work on Sunday don't you?) I actually took a vacation. That was when I was VP of the insurance agency. I told the girls that worked for me I didn't want to come back and see my desk stacked with so many files that I couldn't even say *grace* over them. When I walked into my office the following Monday morning and saw the stacks of files, I wanted to turn around and leave again! But then . . . I saw the sign that had been lovingly printed and stuck on top of the stacks! It read *"GRACE!"* And grace was granted me that day, as we all had a good laugh and I took my seat and got busy!

Speaking of *grace*, as I was working on my sermon a couple of weeks ago after returning home from our District Day of Discipleship in Maryville and a visit to the hospital to check on a dear friend, I received a phone call from a sweet lady whose name is *Grace*, **Grace Williamson**. She said *"I'm coming to your door in about ten minutes, will you be home?"* I said *"Yes, come on over."* She came bringing a delicious cake still warm from the oven! Don't tell me God doesn't give us *grace* . . . abundantly!!!!

I Don't Like Gnats
August 29, 2010

Do you have something in your life that you really detest? I sure do, and they are called GNATS! I've told you this before. I don't like them, never have liked them, and never will like them! They absolutely *bug* me to death. I do believe this is the worst year I have seen for those disgusting little flying monsters. How can something so tiny cause so much misery?

The flower pots filled with beautiful red begonias outside my front windows were in desperate need of some serious attention. Yesterday afternoon, I decided I would tackle the task. After about two minutes the gnats called out to each other, "here she is, let's get her!" And, that is exactly what they did. My nose started itching, then it started running, and when I sniffed, I sniffed one of those creatures right up my nose!!! Glory hallelujah, I headed back inside like a bat out of Hades. There I blew my nose like a foghorn and took a nice, hot, soapy shower followed by a blast of refreshing cool water. I had to get rid of the itching, sniffling and cringing. Ah, how good it was to rid my body of every vestige of those horrid little pests.

As I ponder on yesterday afternoon's experience on this early Sunday morning . . . I truly think that Satan and gnats are a lot alike. Constantly *bugging* us!!! So I have come to some conclusions: First, concerning gnats: I will have to learn to live without hairspray and perfume (is it possible?) since that is one reason why the gnats just adore me. Second, also concerning gnats, we need to promulgate the importation, breeding, and nurturing of those little birds called 'gnatcatchers' a little North American bird with bluish-gray and white plumage, a long tail and small slender bill. That should take care of the gnats!

Now, to keep that red-suited, long-tailed, forked-tongue and horned-demon called Satan from *bugging* us every day of our lives, we need to put on the whole armor of God, leave off the hairspray (the things of the world), and strip him of his guise of making things seem right and good, just because they feel that way! It is only in Jesus Christ that we will ever find the peace that passes all understanding.

"Therefore put on the full armor of God, so that when the day of evil comes, you may be able to stand your ground, Stand firm then, with the belt of truth buckled around your waist, with the breastplate of righteousness in place, and with your feet fitted with the readiness that comes from the gospel of peace."
Ephesians 6:14-15 (NIV)

Black Crow Convention
August 16, 2009

I just have to tell you about something that happened on the mountain behind the parsonage this past week!! A gazillion crows gathered for a Black Crow Convention in five of the tallest trees and it lasted for several days! I have never seen so many crows in one place in all my life. They were fellowshipping all over the mountain; one must have been the preacher and the rest the congregation. They were definitely in the spirit, let me tell you!! I think they must have had a rattlesnake passing it from one to the other and cawing their heads off. They were so loud, I thought about calling the Pittman Center Police Department to stop watching for speeders (ahem) and come arrest these annoying creatures for disturbing my peace. I wondered who called that great crow congregation together and what was their main topic of 'caw-versation.' These crows were magnificent creatures, big, shiny, and black. They reminded me of the poem by Edgar Allen Poe, "The Raven" which has been a favorite of mine since my high school days. I guess a raven and a crow are probably cousins, don't you? I ponder on such things . . .

Being serious now, this has really been a great week and yesterday was an especially meaningful day. Laity and clergy alike gathered at Fairview United Methodist Church in Maryville for our District Day of Discipleship as well as our District Conference and Pastor's Meeting. We went in anticipation of a day of learning from skilled teachers as well as a day of fellowship. We were not disappointed and came away with our hearts and minds refreshed and renewed, full of creative and dynamic insight into new possibilities within our churches as we seek to take His Word and Work into all the world.

It's good to come together as God's people seeking to serve Him in all that we do. Salvation and service have always been the two major themes for followers of Christ. We come pledging our support to Christ and His church by our witness, our prayers, our presence, our gifts, and our service.

On my way home yesterday afternoon, I stopped for a late lunch and happened to run into an old friend in the restaurant and we ate our meal together. What a delight to be able to wind down the day with good food and good conversation. It was a very good day!

Jesus said *"Where two or three are gathered in my name, there I am also!"* And He was, and He is!!! Have a great Sunday my friends!

The Darkness
August 10, 2008

Those of you who look for my 'ponderings' early and know that I always get up at 4:30AM on Sunday morning and begin writing, will think something is wrong this morning. Well you are right! Something has been wrong!!! We have had no electricity until now and it is 7:57AM. If you have ever relied on a well to furnish your water, you know you are severely limited when the power is off. Sometimes in the mountains, the power is off for a long time and you never know when it will come back on so you begin to get out the candles and start calling on your ingenuity; such as it is . . . early in the morning . . . in total darkness.

Out came all the candles I could find and also the oil lamp. That provided enough light to get around but I still couldn't see anything clearly. I lit the gas logs, not for the heat, but for the meager glow of light they provided. Now that I could see a little, I began to realize that nature was calling . . . uh oh . . . no water to flush! There's no outhouse here so I decided I would just wait as long as possible which was one of the hardest things I have ever had to do!!! Whew thank God for 7:57AM and blessed electricity.

Back to where I was at 4:30AM! I knew I must bathe . . . how was I going to do that? I can at least brush my teeth, right? Nooooo, so the wheels start turning and I get out the Listerine and wet my toothbrush, then dabbed on the toothpaste. Do you need a good awakening in your mouth in the morning? Get out the Listerine and use it for your water! Every little germ that is lurking there will be burned away and may never return!!!

OK, now that my mouth is fresh as a daisy, I've got to shower. How is this going to happen? I got some bottled water from the fridge . . . which was cold as ice . . . found a fresh pack of wet wipes and though I used the whole pack and am now freezing to death, I'm clean as a pin. Thank goodness I shampooed my hair in last night's shower with real running water.

I must go get my makeup on or I will scare everyone away from church this morning. This I did verrrrrry carefully in front of the only window I have that is not shrouded by trees. It may be a little askew, but it's on! At least I can see to fix my hair before I have to take off across the street to my first service at 9:15AM. I now have a much greater respect for the words from Genesis "And God said "Let there be light!" and there was light." Amen!!!

Classmates—Bradley High School Class of '58

Saturday Afternoon, August 18, 2007

Last Thursday began like any other summer day, bright blue sky, the sun a brilliant gold, and the weather hot as Hades! Well, *maybe not quite that hot* . . .

But then everything changed as the Gals (Babes) of '58 began arriving for another mini-reunion at Millie's (**Mildred Miller**) lakehouse for lunch and getting reacquainted. Then it was on to Muggs' (**Marguerite Miles**) lakehouse next door for our dessert. Well, I could stop here . . . as that really sums it up . . . but I don't think you *really want* me to, do you? I didn't think so.

I've got to tell you some of the things that happened and how much fun we had. There were 21 or 22 of us (we were never still or in the same place long enough to be counted) and we laughed, cried, prayed, ate, remembered, gave thanks, told funny stories, talked about everything we could think of; books, ponderings, friendships, husbands, men, etc. and last but not least . . . our own **Bill McClure**. Since Bill is the glue that holds the Class of '58 together, he is, of course, quite special to all of us and we wanted to let him know it. (You'll read more about this later in another paragraph.)

Those who arrived early had a definite advantage over the late comers. As each car drove up, we would stand back in the shadows from the windows and guess who they were before they got to the door. When they came in we all began clapping and calling them by name. Then they had the tough task of figuring out *who we were*. We agreed that **Linda Bell** and **Maureen Olsson** were two that had changed the least. Of course none of us have really changed that much except for some of us having gray hair and a few wrinkles. I can't see why so many of them didn't recognize *me*.

I heard so many stories from our high school years, I laughed until my stomach was actually hurting when I heard this one: *"Do you remember when we were taking Drivers Ed? Oh, what was our teachers name? Mr . . . oh I can't remember his name. But one time when Mary Ellen was driving and we were in the back seat . . . he told her to "turn right here" and she didn't realize he was directing her to turn right at the next street . . . so she made an* immediate turn right ~ into a corn field. There we sat in the middle of that corn field and we were cracking up in the back seat laughing our heads off . . . Boy, did he get mad at us!"

Here's another: *"June, do you remember when you used to have that little Nash that never would run?" "Yes and it was always stopping at the worst places." "But don't you remember those times when we would pretend it wouldn't run just so we could meet boys as they would come over and try to fix it. We sure did meet a lot of guys that way." "Well, yessss . . ." "Wasn't that how you met Larry?" "I sure did, I met him down at the Sugar and Spice."*

And another: *"Betty how did you meet your husband? You are so quiet, I can't believe you married a police officer!" "To tell you the truth, I didn't like him at all the first time I met him and didn't care if I ever saw him again. We actually met because my roommate was dating his roommate and that kind of threw us together. I didn't see him again for a long time after that and the second time, he was all dressed up in his uniform and was he ever handsome! We were sort of accidentally thrown together again but this time, it was different. We began talking, found out we really liked each other, started dating, fell in love and you know the rest."*

Well, that was just three of the stories I overheard but some of them I can't repeat here for fear of retribution. Needless, to say we all caught up on the latest news. Oh my, what a good time we had! There were many that have attended our mini-reunions in the past that could not be with us in body this time but we knew they were with us in spirit: **Marty Fulbright, Lynda Lippard, Martha Jones, Marguerite Ferrell, Julie Kirkpatrick, Patsy Pritchett,** and many others.

Now back to Bill . . . Millie made a phone call to him on speaker phone and we all said "hi" and told him we had a present for him. We tried to get him to come by Millie's house but he was working in the hayfield and literally "trying to make hay while the sun shined." I won't tell you what the present was just in case he hasn't yet received it. I don't want to spoil his fun. Just as soon as he does . . . he better send out an email describing it so you will all know what it is.

Both Millie's and Muggs' lakehouses (homes) were incredibly warm and welcoming with southern hospitality and their great personalities shined through in their individual decors. Millie had just purchased a framed creation of a fish made out of various pieces of cloth pieced together with tiny stitches like a quilt. Such intricate and creative skill! It was quite unique.

Our lunch prepared by **Millie and Gayle Hicks** was a sumptuous chicken salad, garden peas and vegetables in vinaigrette dressing, sliced tomatoes, fresh and hot baked bread and our favorite dish of all was a grape salad. It was absolutely delicious and had all the ingredients that I love; grapes, nuts, cream cheese, sour cream, brown sugar over the top . . . oh my I'm licking my lips now just thinking about it.

Following lunch and another hour of non-stop chatter, we walked next door to Mugg's house and there she had a table laden with two big cakes; one a pound cake with white icing and the other a chocolate cake with chocolate icing. They were so moist and delicious they just melted in your mouth. A big bowl of huge strawberries and icy cold drinks of spring water were set out for all to enjoy. We ate and ate and talked and talked. Finally, the day had to end and we all headed back to our homes; our tummies stuffed and our minds full of 'more tales" to tell and memories to share.

I'm sure we all join in a resounding "thank you" to Millie and Muggs for the delicious food and warm welcome. We all agreed "we must do this again . . . and soon!" Those of you who didn't make it to this mini-reunion, make your plans now to attend the next one . . . we'll let you know when. It was a day of memories made, renewed friendships, warm hugs, good food, great fun, and wonderful fellowship! It just doesn't get much better than that. And yes, we must do it again . . . soon! This day reminded me of two verses of scripture: *"A friend loves at all times"* and, *"A cheerful heart is good medicine." Proverbs 17:17, 22 (NIV)*

We all had a big dose of medicine that day and left feelin' mighty fine.

Rev. Mattye Kirby-Bowman
August 5, 2007

This morning I am remembering the life of the **Rev. Mattye Kirby-Bowman** who at 99 years of age passed away Friday morning at Asbury Acres Health Care Center in Maryville. Many of you will remember her being honored a couple of years ago at Annual Conference when we celebrated Women in Ministry. She was the first woman minister in the United Methodist Holston Conference. Mattye was my friend! What a lovely, charming, articulate, and funny lady! She was always a delight to be around; with a twinkle in her eyes, you couldn't be in her presence without being caught up in the spirit of whatever was on her mind at that moment.

Several years ago, Mattye realized it was time to move from her home to an assisted living facility. Her concern was what to do with her extensive doll collection which, over the years, had taken the place of the children she never had. Mattye lovingly referred to each of them by name. She made the decision to give them away and each doll found a new home. I was the grateful recipient of one of them, much to my surprise. At that time, I was a certified lay speaker and member of Pleasant Hill UMC in Maryville where Mattye preached for a number of years.

One of the things I remember most about Mattye was her humor. She always had a joke or funny story on the tip of her tongue. She loved to laugh and she loved to make you laugh. Many were the times when we would visit in her home for the sheer delight of her company.

About three years ago, Mattye summoned me with a phone call requesting a visit and not to tarry long about it but to come quickly. She wanted to give me all of her old sermons, neatly hand-written and lovingly kept throughout the years. What a treasure!! She knew I would appreciate them and she wanted me, as another woman minister, to have them. They are in a safe place and maybe someday I might *try* to preach one of them. Somehow I have always found it very hard to preach someone else's sermons. Mattye was *one of the best* and you sure didn't go to sleep while she was preaching. You hung on every word and marveled at her deliverance. I'm going to miss her. But . . . I delight in knowing that heaven is in for a real treat as she marches in triumphantly!

"Blessed are the pure in heart, for they will see God." Matthew 5:8 9 (NIV)

Making Bread
August 6, 2006

Good morning everyone! It's still dark outside as I'm writing this morning. The house is quiet and my mind is wandering as usual. Actually I'm fast-forwarding, to the time when school bells will once again be ringing in Pittman Center; one of the sure signs of the coming fall.

I look forward to each new season, bringing its own special flavor and uniqueness. As fall approaches I begin thinking of more hearty fare on our table. Hot soups and warm breads . . . Bread! Let me tell you about a special birthday present this year. A bread maker!!! Yesterday, I decided to make my first loaf of delicious, crusty, fresh baked bread.

After watching the video that came with the bread maker, I read the instruction book and all the recipes. Each one sounded better that the other and I finally decided on a loaf of "nine grain bread." After a trip to Food City to purchase all the ingredients (about $83 worth before I finished having fun in the 'new to me' bread making department), I was ready to begin. Hold on to your seat! I followed the directions to a 't.' The ingredients must go into the loaf pan in just the right order, liquids on the bottom, dry ingredients next, make a little hole in the center of the dry ingredients for the yeast. So good, so far . . . then I made the proper cooking selections and sat down to study a bit while it was baking. Poof . . . in about three hours I went back to retrieve my delicious loaf of bread.

Lifting the lid . . . oh my! Oh my! Such a sorry sight I've never seen! My heart fell to my stomach in disappointment. It seems I didn't get the little kneading paddle on tight enough . . . it came off . . . thus, the bread was not kneaded!!! Go ahead and laugh . . . I've got one better than that. Wait until I tell you about the time I tried to store up some chestnuts for the next year!!! Don't think I'm through with the bread maker. Not by a long shot! I'm glad the directions said I might need to *make a few loaves to get the knack of it*. At least I know I'm not ready to start delivering loaves of bread to all my friends, *yet*! But, I will; just wait and see.

Jesus is the true bread of life; the bread that sustains us; the bread that never fails; the one that is perfectly 'risen!' In Him we find real sustenance.

"For God is the one who provides seed for the farmer and then bread to eat. In the same way, he will provide and increase your resources and then produce a great harvest of generosity in you." 2 Corinthians 9:10 (NLT)

SEPTEMBER PONDERINGS

A Tree Fell

September 9, 2012

After taking a few days off last week to visit my mom in Cleveland, I am now back in my beloved Pittman Center and the mountains I call home. The time I spent with my mom, my brother and sis-in-law is always a time of renewal. We eat together, laugh together, and reminisce about all that has happened in our lives. What a happy and blessed time I had. I returned refreshed and renewed. God is good!

On the way down to my hometown of Cleveland, TN my GPS quit working. All I could get was a blank screen. Panic tried to set in before I thanked God I was near a Wal-Mart and could pop in and buy a new Garmin right away. I have no sense of direction as everyone knows and am completely lost without my GPS for guidance and directions. Knowing I was going on a one day trip to Atlanta while I was away, that GPS was as necessary to me as air to breathe. The new one is great and it got me there and back safely. One new feature tells me both the speed limit on the road I am traveling and the actual speed I am going. My foot was able to lift up a bit now and then and I didn't get stopped for speeding one single time. God is good!

Speaking of God being so good, it was during this time away from home that a huge tree fell on the parsonage. Had I been there I would have been terrified at the noise I am sure it made, if not the damage it did to the carport area and the roof. Especially if it happened in the middle of the night and I'm quite sure it happened on Wednesday night, the first night I was away! I didn't have to worry longer than a few minutes after I was first informed on Friday morning when my housekeeper arrived to clean. I soon received a phone call from **George Minnigh**, my lay leader, who assured me all was well and the damage was being taken care of. He, along with a helper, spent many hours on the roof during one of the hottest days we have had, cutting up the debris of the fallen tree and getting it off the roof so a tarp could be put over the eight holes in the roof. The job was completed before it began raining. Didn't I just say God is good!

During every trial in my life, the calming verse from *Romans 8:28* is always with me. *"And we know that in all things God works for the good of those who love him, who have been called according to his purpose." (NIV)*

I repeat it in my head, over and over, and all is well once again. When you get to be my age, now seventy-two years, your thoughts tend to run amuck at times. To realize there are more years behind you than in front is a sobering thought. To realize that your body simply can't do what it used to do is something else you have to get used to. One thing I know, God is as real to me today as he has ever been. He has seen me this far and He will not desert me now. I have the assurance of His love, His strength, and His grace. What else do I need? Or, what else do you need? He is our ALL, this ever-present loving God.

Shults Grove Homecoming—2011
September 25, 2011

Good Sunday morning once again!!! It's going to be a great Lord's Day I can just feel it in my bones. The morning air smells fresh and clean from the good rain we've had this past week. I love to smell the rain, it reminds me of summer evenings in my childhood when my granddad and I would sit in the swing on the front porch of the old farm house, watch it rain, and talk and talk. As I would hear each new sound coming from the woods I would question him, "what was that?" He would tell me stories about whippoorwills and tree frogs and hoot owls and all sorts of interesting things. I learned to smell the rain even before it got to our house. I liked to think that God was giving the earth a good bath. Living on a dirt road, the rain settled the dust for a little while and the mud puddles were always fun to play in.

Strolling on down memory lane reminds me, last month we celebrated another Homecoming at **Shults Grove UMC** on Rocky Flats Road in Cosby. What a time we had! I just stood back and watched as folks greeted loved ones they hadn't seen in years. The younger ones were being introduced to the older ones and each had a tale to tell on the other. It seems that with each passing year there are more folks missing from the original church family as God calls them home. There is still quite a gathering as the other two churches in my charge, **Burnett Memorial and Webb's Creek**, come to celebrate with those who are left. The long tables were laden with delicious food . . . fried chicken, ham, meatloaf, green beans, corn, fried okra, sliced tomatoes and cakes and pies of every conceivable kind!. Makes my mouth water just thinking about it, even if it is a month later and only five o'clock in the morning!!! Around one o'clock in the afternoon, we all gathered in the sanctuary of the church and enjoyed the great music and singing of the Sutton Family Singers. How they lifted our spirits, and touched our souls.

Traveling down Rocky Flats Road always brings memories of days gone by. Fences built completely of rocks stacked on top of each other, leaf strewn pathways leading back into the woods and to the old cemetery up behind the church. What memories come to mind as folks pass each gravestone, reading the names and dates etched into those granite slabs!

Slabs of stone mark the final resting place of fathers, mothers, husbands, wives, sisters, brothers, sons, and daughters; little babies who died before they even tasted life, their tiny sip carving out a special place in the hearts of parents who learned to accept sorrow early on.

When you climb the long wooden steps built by **Paul McAlister**, an old saint of the church, and enter that precious little one room church you are met first . . . with the smell . . . which I love. Most folks would probably not appreciate the old, musty smell but I do. My mind is suddenly filled with scenes from days gone by . . . how I wish those old walls could talk and tell us the stories of long ago; of the different preachers that have stood behind that sacred old hand-hewn desk; and of all the folks that have found the Lord within those four walls. What a time they must have had; preachin' prayin' singin' shoutin'! If I could hear once again, the mournful sound of the old hymns being sung from the heart of the mountain people: "Where the Roses Never Fade," "What a Day that Will Be," and "Rock of Ages." And, I wish I could hear them lift melodious voices singing "What a Friend We Have in Jesus" "Amazing Grace," "Standing on the Promises," and "Love Lifted Me."

"*. . . Our fathers were under the cloud, and all passed through the sea; And did all drink the same spiritual drink: for they drank of that spiritual Rock that followed them: and that Rock was Christ." I Corinthians 10 1, 4 (KJV)*

Cloudy Skies
September 18, 2011

Walking down my drive toward the City Hall, the early morn was cool and crisp beneath a canopy of cloudy skies. Underlying notes of autumn were in the air as leaves drifted down from their lofty perch to settle in little whirling patterns on the ground or riding on the current of a clear mountain stream. The third Saturday in September was upon us and we would be celebrating another Heritage Day here in Pittman Center; a great tradition now going on for twenty years or more.

What an honor for me to be asked each year, to open up this day with prayer and then our Methodist Singers liven up the group with favorite hymns of the church. **Mayor Glenn Cardwell** shared his thoughts on the rich history and traditions of this almost sacred area. As I wandered the grounds the day came alive with sunshine breaking through the clouds and sounds of laughter filled the air. The dog show was one of our best with one of Burnett Memorial's own, **Rylee Genseal** and her beau, winning first place with their little dog dressed in a tutu. **Vicki Webb** had her dog which is always a favorite "working" dog. The **Flores Family** and the women of Burnett Memorial, were selling homemade hot tamales . . . yummee. Thanks to **Rosa and Maria** who gave us both the recipe and directions for preparation. Tamales are definitely a favorite and I brought several home to go in my freezer for a cold winter night's fare. Hill's Creek Baptist's talented youth both sang and played for us and their booth featured lots of good food, especially fried "taters." Oh my, if I could have eaten all I wanted, I would be fat as a bear.

One of the booths that drew my attention featured watercolor prints of **Lynn Brownell** who used to work for **The Mountain Press.** When I saw her name I knew we knew each other but we had never met in person. What a talented artist she is. Many area craftsmen were present selling their wares. Such a great variety of talent is always present in these mountains!!! I love to read and quickly found my way to **Donnie Lamon's** booth featuring three of his books entitled "Riding to Newport," "Country Voices," and "Christmas in the Holler." I came home the proud owner of all three signed copies and can't wait to begin reading. How I love this area, and I never tire of reading and learning more of its history and tales of yore.

My text for today's sermon is *Exodus 16* and deals with the steady complaining of the Israelites to Moses. Seems they were not satisfied and wished they were back in Egypt. Folks, when you love the Lord and he is the Savior of your life, HE becomes your satisfaction. You stop complaining and start "counting your blessings." Yesterday was a real BLESSING just being a part of a crowd of people who came together in this very special place to enjoy and celebrate our mountain heritage.

May it ever be so.

Kodak Moments
September 12, 2010

Good Sunday morning to you! It is now September and I'm excited! As the weather cools off in the mornings I can almost hear the trees settling down from the glorious days of summer. As they begin to don their beautiful orange and gold attire of autumn and wait for their winter's rest; they know God will watch over their naptime.

While sitting at my desk one morning last week, a flash of brown rushed by my window. Quickly, I got up and hurried down the hallway and into the middle bedroom to get a better glimpse. There stood a handsome young deer, nonchalantly looking around. Then with a lift of his head, he trotted off down the hillside toward the church across the road and was out of sight.

Coming back to my study I continued working having all but forgotten the young deer. Soon there was a movement, quick as lightning, past my window going back in the way it first came. I knew his mother was close. I went quietly out onto the carport for a closer look and there they were . . . posing tall and proud, looking straight at me. A mother and child stood there creating a scene of such magnificent maternal beauty. It was a Kodak moment for sure! I grabbed my camera, focused and clicked! Click! Click! Well, shucks! The batteries were dead! By the time I put in new ones . . . the Kodak moment was gone. How sad! But I have that beautiful memory which can't be taken away.

As a Christian, we all have Kodak moments we wish could last forever. At first we are so excited to be a child of God we can't do enough to please Him. We are excited about going to church, being His hands and feet as we help others, and enjoying the fellowship of other Christians. It is all so right and good! Our Father is so close we can actually *feel* His presence. Life is good.

Then when troubles come our way, and they will, we are so quick to blame Him. And the inevitable question rises to our lips, *"Why me, Lord?"* It is easy to drift away from the church, to drift away from our First Love, to go back to the old way of living and to push God aside. The picture is not so pretty any more. After a few years of worry and confusion, we realize it wasn't God who moved and made the picture fuzzy. We click and find that our own battery has died because *we* drifted away. We remember that first Kodak moment, years ago, as a new child of God, and we want it back. Our battery needs to be recharged. We seek and find . . . God is still there, just waiting to make that connection. And we can smile again . . . hold it . . . Click! Ah, life *is* good! In Christ!

Jail Ministry
September 13, 2009

Good Sunday morning everyone!!! What a beautiful morning, dark and cool, with just the beginning of dawn creeping over the mountains. I only wish my thoughts were as calm and serene as the morning . . . but they aren't.

As many of you know I have a passion for jail ministry. I do not have the time nor the inclination to do this full-time, but I am determined to do my small part. I have befriended a young lady who is an inmate of a County Jail. Her visitation time is Tuesday evenings at 8PM and pastors coming to this facility must now visit at regular visiting hours just like everyone else. This would mean I would be coming home very late at night and now that I am alone, it is something I choose not to do. This is to explain why I have chosen to keep in contact with this young lady by mail with words of encouragement and news from the 'outside.' Her own family wants nothing to do with her so my letters are something she looks forward to.

Yesterday, my last letter was returned marked "unable to deliver." In the same mail I also received a letter from my friend telling me she was told they had returned my letter because it contained 'religious material!' I am ready to bite nails! My letter was marked all over the front to "return to sender.' They had judged the content of my envelope by the return address which indicated I am a "reverend." I never knew a preacher couldn't write to someone incarcerated in that facility.

How are we to minister and encourage as the Scriptures dictate? Let's look at *Hebrews 13:1-3 "Keep on loving each other as brothers and sisters. Continue in brotherly love. Don't forget to show hospitality to strangers, for some who have done this have entertained angels without realizing it! Remember those in prison, as if you were there yourself. Remember also those being mistreated, as if you felt their pain in your own bodies." (NLT)*

Last year, this same jail denied me pastoral visitation privileges because I didn't have anything to PROVE I was a pastor other than my 'church's identification card' and my driver's license. I was told I would have to return home and bring my license back with me. Sure . . . I had already driven over an hour just to get there. I wonder how many pastors carry their preaching license with them? It seems I have a lot to learn!

I am told by a former chaplain of this same facility, they don't really want preachers there. I can understand that some of the radicals may have given others a bad name but I can also name some police officers who have given other police officers a bad name as well. Yet, they have authority over the rest of us and like it or not we must abide by their rules even if it has nothing to do with breaking the law!

Most folks who need our help are not found in our church pews on Sunday mornings! If we are to minister to them, we must go to them! No wonder the rate of recidivism among inmates is so high. All they learn is to become more hardened while they are incarcerated. Without hope and encouragement, how can they feel otherwise? They remain lost! God forbid!

We as Christians and ministers had better start taking notice of the privileges that are being taken away from us. One day soon we will again become the silent majority and I do mean SILENT! And I am sad.

Grandaddy's Swing
September 6, 2009

Good Sunday Morning once again!!! It's going to be a great Lord's Day I can just feel it in my bones. The morning air smells fresh from the good rain we had yesterday afternoon and evening. I love to smell the rain, it reminds me of summer evenings in my childhood when my **Grandad Musgrove** and I would sit in the swing on the front porch of the old farm house, watch it rain, and talk and talk. As I would hear each new noise coming from the woods I would question him, "what was that?" He would tell me stories about whippoorwills and tree frogs and pond frogs and all sorts of interesting things. I learned to smell the rain even before it got to our house. I liked to think that God was giving the earth a good bath. Living on a dirt road, the rain settled the dust for a little while and the mud puddles were always fun to play in.

Strolling on down memory lane reminds me, last week we celebrated Homecoming at Shults Grove UMC on Rocky Flats Road in Cosby, and it was great! What a time we had! I just stood back and watched as folks greeted loved ones they hadn't seen in years. The younger ones were being introduced to the older ones and each had a tale to tell on the other. It seems that with each passing year there are more folks missing from the original church family as God calls them home. There is still quite a gathering as the other two churches in my charge, Burnett Memorial and Webb's Creek, come to celebrate with those who are left. And . . . those long tables laden down with delicious food . . . fried chicken, fish, ham, meatloaf, green beans, corn, fried okra, sliced tomatoes and cakes and pies of every conceivable kind!. Makes my mouth water just thinking about it once again, even if it is a week later and only five o'clock in the morning!!!

Traveling down Rocky Flats Road always brings memories of days gone by. Fences built completely of stones stacked on top of each other, leaf strewn pathways leading back into the woods and to the old cemetery up behind the church. What memories come to mind as folks pass each gravestone, reading the names and dates etched into those granite slabs! Slabs of stone mark the final resting place of fathers, mothers, husbands, wives, sisters, brothers, sons, and daughters; little babies who died before they even tasted life, their tiny sip carving out a special place in the hearts of parents who learned to accept sorrow early on.

When you climb the long wooden steps built by **Paul McAlister**, an old saint of the church, and enter that precious little one room church you are met first . . . with the smell . . . which I love. Most folks would probably not appreciate the old, musty smell but I do. My mind is suddenly filled with scenes from days gone by . . . how I wish those old walls could talk and tell us the stories of long ago; of the different preachers that have stood behind that sacred old hand-hewn desk; and of all the folks that have found the Lord within those four walls. What a time they must have had; preachin' prayin' singin' shoutin'! If I could hear once again, the mournful sound of the old hymns being sung from the heart of the mountain people: "Where the Roses Never Fade," "What a Day that Will Be," and "Rock of Ages." And, I wish I could hear them lift melodious voices singing "What a Friend We Have in Jesus" "Amazing Grace," "Standing on the Promises," and "Love Lifted Me."

Heritage Day—2008

September 21, 2008

Cool, crisp, autumn mornings have arrived in the mountains! It's a great morning and I'm anticipating a great day as well! And guess what happened yesterday!!! It was our Annual Heritage Day here in Pittman Center and what a fun time we had!!! Each year I have the distinct privilege and honor of opening the Day with prayer and the Methodist singers have the first spot on the program. I was glad to see so many show up from Burnett Memorial and Webb's Creek to sing and if I say so myself, they did a good job belting out those beautiful old hymns; thanks to **Jerry Huskey** and **John Eakin's** booming voice, keeping us all in tune.

If you missed the festivities this year, you missed a spectacular fall day, full of fun and good times. The performers, from first to last, were excellent! I especially enjoyed the **Highlanderettes** who took us back to The Fifties with their rendition of *"Sincerely"* and kept everyone's rapt attention with both the singing and choreography of *"Boogie Woogie Bugle Boy of Company B."* Their director, **Ruth Lewis**, does a fantastic job with these very talented girls from Gatlinburg-Pittman High School.

Oh, yes! Have you ever heard 'old harp' singing? This is an old and unique tradition where the notes are sung rather than the words. There were so many fa so las, and do ti dos; I sat there in amazement as I watched and listened to the perfect sound of each note sung. I had heard this kind of singing years ago but had no idea there is still a group that carries on the tradition and travels all over these parts, keeping it alive. If you would like to invite these **Old Harp Singers** for your festivities or church events, you can get in touch with them at 865-428-0874 or go online to www. oldharp.org.

The crafts were spectacular this year from leather works, original acrylic paintings that rival the best I've ever seen, basket weaving, homemade soaps, creams, candles, jewelry, colorful fall flower arrangements, kettle corn, creations of every kind and food galore!!! Folks, you name it, and it was there! What talented folks we have in this almost magical part of East Tennessee. There were even hens and chickens and lots of beautifully groomed dogs who participated in the dog show competition. **Diandra**

Trotter was in her element as she introduced each dog and owner. She is such a dog lover!!! I missed the end, but heard a blood hound was the winner.

Now, I've waited until last to say very much about the food. Why? Because I think I sampled almost everything there and had to waddle back home. No kidding, the bratwurst and grilled onions were excellent, and the funnel cake would melt in your mouth. Of course, I found one vendor that had Diet Dr. Peppers which was just perfect to wash down all the food.

If you think I'm always bragging about this place where I live, I am. If you want to find just a little bit of heaven on earth, come visit Pittman Center. Heritage Day is the third Saturday in September of every year, and every year it just gets better and better. Make plans to come and be part of this great old-time celebration of a land and its heritage. I never fail to thank my God every single day for putting me in this place. I am exactly where I'm supposed to be.

"Lord, you have been our dwelling place through all generations. Before the mountains were born or you brought forth the earth and the world, from everlasting to everlasting you are God." Psalm 90: 1-2 (NIV)

Nicknames

September 14, 2008

Have you ever wondered why parents name their children some of the names they do? And . . . usually, as soon as they are born, they give them a nickname which sticks with them until they start school. Their teacher begins to call them by the name on their birth certificate and they wonder "who's that?"

We have some of the cutest little girls (Cherokee Indian) who attend our church. They are precious! They are known as **"Little Bit" "Becky" and "Scooter."** My own little grandsons have nick names: **"Boogie" and "Spanky", "BJ" and "Zach".** My oldest son **Chase** and my oldest grandsons, **Andrew** and **Ethan**, have never had nicknames. My two younger sons were **"John-John" and "Lil Vic."** My daughter has been **"Mia"** all her life, though her real name is **Maria Luise**. Her teachers always told her she spelled her name wrong; it was supposed to be Louise and she had to explain her mother used the Spanish spelling. My brother **Ralph** was **"Swifty"** in high school. Wait a minute! I never had a nickname! Did I miss something? Guess if I ever had one, they would have called me something silly like "Short Stuff" anyway.

I ponder what's in a name and how it came to be, especially if it is an unusual one. Therein dwells some beautiful stories! Dale Carnegie teaches us to always call people by their name; "to them it is the sweetest sound on earth."

Our Lord himself had many names . . . we know exactly who *Yahweh* is, or *The Great I Am*. What about *Emanuel, Savior, Lord, Redeemer, Prince of Peace, Jesus the Christ, King of Kings, Lord of Lords, the Messiah, the Holy One?*

"Therefore God exalted him to the highest place and gave him the name that is above every name, that at the name of Jesus every knee should bow, in heaven and on earth and under the earth, and every tongue confess that Jesus Christ is Lord, to the glory of God the Father." Philippians 2:9-11(NIV)

"Fear not, for I have redeemed you: I have summoned you by name: you are mine." Isaiah, 43:1b (NIV) HE knows *my name*; HE knows *your name*; we belong to Him!!! Now, that's something to shout about!

Fall, Mom, and Mia

September 23, 2007

Good Sunday Morning! Fall is in the air! Can't you just feel it? Wow, we are having such cool mornings even though the afternoons are still quite warm. It is such an incredibly beautiful time with the red and gold leaves dotting the mountainsides and with every little gust of wind, they fly through the air as if on angel's wings. Every day is special ~ but some days are a little more special than others. Yesterday was one of those extra special days and today is going to be another one.

First, let me tell you about yesterday which was a wonderful family day in Cleveland as we celebrated Mom's 89th birthday! Dad died at 47 years of age and Mom has lived alone the past 44 years. My parents had only two children, me and my brother **Ralph**. With our children, grandchildren, and great-grandchildren, we have increased Mom's family to a total of 32!! Mom has one living sibling, a **brother** who came from his home in Bowling Green KY to be with her on her special day. She received oodles of birthday cards and many of them were from her beloved friends here in Pittman Center and from several classmates of mine who have known her through the years. (She said "Thank you!" to everyone.) Yes, thank you Lord for a very good day!

Now, for today!!! I have more good news! My daughter, **Mia,** will be announcing her calling and decision to enter the ministry this morning during the worship service at **Pleasant Hill UMC** (Blount) where she has been a member since we moved to Maryville in 1976. She has been a Certified Lay Speaker for a number of years and has delivered God's message many times. Most of all she has a compassionate heart and is willing to go and do! She shared with me last week about an encounter she had with God similar to Jacob's when he literally wrestled with God all night long. *(Genesis 32:24)* Mia wrestled with her decision all night last Saturday night as she wanted to know, *beyond a shadow of a doubt*, that God had truly placed his hand on her life. I have been so excited I could hardly contain myself. "I have no greater joy than to hear that my children walk in truth." *3 John: 4 (KJV)*

May the Lord bless you all, each and every one. May He fill you with greater joy than you have ever known and may you know His perfect Shalom!!!

Heritage Day—2007
September 16, 2007

Yesterday we celebrated **Heritage Day** here in Pittman Center. The Methodist singers led by **Jane Dean** opened up the day at 9AM and we did a pretty good job if I do say so myself. **Clyde** was able to be there and he and **Diandra Trotter** sang two duets and he played the piano. What a day it was; cloudy and cool in the early morning with bright sunshine and blue skies into the afternoon. I had the time of my life! Music rang out over these mountains all day long and the dancing and clogging made me wish I were about fifty years younger.

And, oh the delicious food! Of course, I had to sample as much as possible. I tried the funnel cake first with lots of powdered sugar and found it to be yum-yummy. Then on up to the big black drum with the fire under it and the biggest ear of roasted corn you've ever seen, dripping with melted butter. Just a little later came a bowl of 'fried taters' seasoned with onions, hot and tasty right out of a big iron skillet and for dessert, a fried apple pie like my Grandmother used to make, and all of it washed down with several glasses of sweet iced tea. You'll be glad to know I passed up the chicken and dumplings as well as the cotton candy! Now Clyde does not branch out quite as much as I do and he had a cheeseburger from the Volunteer Fire Department's stand which is always one of the most popular.

Oh, and if you won't tell anyone . . . I confess, I brought home a fresh-baked loaf of **Brian Papworth's** beer bread. I'll bet my reputation as a preacher is ruined already! Seriously, if you haven't tried beer bread, please do. It is excellent!!!

These mountain folk can't be beat when it comes to creativity and fine craftsmanship as was shown in the lovely hand-made quilts, jewelry, handbags, leatherworks, paintings, needlework, and homemade soaps and creams. I came home with some of **Alison Houston's** 'Rocky Flats Cucumber Melon Hand, Face and Body Cream' as well as her Kitchen Soap; guaranteed to take the smell of onion and garlic off your hands when cooking.

Before leaving, I just had to have a Pittman Center t-shirt and sweatshirt! **G Webb's** design of the covered bridge at Emert's Cove adorns the shirts and he was personally signing them. There was such a line for his coveted signature that I tucked mine under my arm and will see if I can't corner him after church today. By the way, G's dog didn't win the dog show but I understand G won first place for the best dog *owner*. He sat, stood, and rolled over . . . better than all the rest! The dog show was a delight with so many beautiful and unusual breeds. Our own **Diandra Trotter** served as MC and this pretty lady did an excellent job!

Would it surprise you to know that God wants His people to have fun and be happy? In fact, we have more reason to be joyous than anyone!!! David said it best ~ *"Shout for joy to the Lord, all the earth, burst into jubilant song with music; Let the rivers clap their hands, let the mountains sing together for joy; let them sing before the Lord." Psalm 98: 4, 8 (NIV)*

Streams are Fascinating
September 9, 2007

Have you ever walked along a meandering stream and wondered where it came from and where it is going or if its bare bottom during a drought might become a bit embarrassing? Have you imagined the way it feels to have refreshing crystal clear water flowing over your bed after a season of rain or felt the wonder of knowing that you provide life giving sustenance for so many fish, frogs, turtles, snakes, and flora; can you imagine the excitement of knowing you provide recreation in abundance for mankind and thirst-quenching water to all who care to sip from your cup; or the awesome tranquility, serenity, peace and solace you can give to each one drawn to your tranquil beauty and unique charm? Such is a stream . . .

Water fascinates me! It intrigues me! I want to scoop it up and pour it out and play in it. I want to wade in it, sit in it, watch its endless journey and enjoy its coolness on a hot summer's eve. I like to listen to its sound so awesome, like a soft gentle purring, or a mighty rushing roar. I want to sleep with windows wide open to hear the lilt of its timeless lullaby. And I am reminded of my **Granddad Musgrove . . .**

A tired old man coming in from a hard day's work in the fields, dirty from grubbing and plowing. Dust settled into every line of his wrinkled face and onto his neck from the open collar of his faded old work shirt. Beads of sweat form little rivulets down his face as he hunkers down to take a seat on the smooth rock beside the small stream. Bending over, he pulls off his boots, sets them aside, and dips his tired aching feet into the cool water. Sitting there with eyes closed, resting . . . a sigh escapes his lips, a prayer of thanksgiving to God for another good day. Slowly he lowers the galluses of his overalls, slips into the coolness of the stream and begins washing the grime from his body. Rising up, cleansed and at peace, he makes his way along the moonlit path toward the back door of the old farm house, thinking only of the comfort of the feather bed just beyond the squeak of the old screen door . . .

And I know *"The Lord is my shepherd; I have all that I need. He lets me rest in green meadows; he leads me beside peaceful streams. He renews my strength. He guides me along right paths, bringing honor to his name. Even when I walk through the darkest valley, Or the dark valley of death. I will not be afraid, for you are close beside me. Your rod and your staff protect and comfort me. You prepare a feast for me in the presence of my enemies. You honor me by anointing my head with oil. My cup overflows with blessings. Surely your goodness and unfailing love will pursue me all the days of my life, and I will live in the house of the Lord forever." Psalm 23 (NLT)*

Magical Mornings
September 2, 2007

Did you miss me last week? I missed you! There is nothing like a sick computer to keep a little old gray haired preacher lady quiet. What did we ever do before computers? I guess the answer is 'we got along just fine,' but, we must admit, they sure make life simpler with their ease and spontaneity!

Now I sit here . . . pondering at my desk in the wee hours of a new day and I'm thinking . . . there is something magical about the morning . . . something special; something that says everything is going to be alright. It's like a beautiful present each day, all wrapped up, just waiting to be opened, poured out, and enjoyed. I was standing out on our front stoop moments ago, in the time just before dawn, and it seemed as if the mist hanging over the mountains was like curtains on the stage of life being opened, ever so slowly, to the beat of my heart and the applause of my soul. It's another Sunday morning, another sweet Lord's Day, another day to live, to love, and to serve God.

No matter how dark the night before, no matter what might have befallen you, there is JOY in the morning. There is excitement, vitality, and happiness . . . a new day has come. It comes with a clean slate and what is written thereon is up to you. So if you haven't quite started your day, go look in the mirror and for a full two minutes, at least, think happy thoughts. Exercise your mind in pleasant paths just as you would exercise your muscles on a fragrant hiking trail. Be determined to live, love, and laugh!

Yesterday, I had fun! It was my grandson **Isaac's** seventh birthday and his party was at the Jump Zone in Maryville. Caught up in the pure happiness of the moment, I slipped off my shoes and as soon as the big inflated truck was clear of children and I was out of **Clyde's** sight, my daughter **Mia** and I, climbed the inflated ladder up to the very top where we took a seat and full of laughter, screams and giggles, slid down the steep slide at breakneck speed landing in a pile, on our backs, at the bottom. It was so much fun that we did it again and the second time was more fun than the first one ~ but somehow, though I had the *want to* real bad, I didn't have the energy for a third time. By now, Isaac had found us and he blurted out "Mamaw, did you have fun being a kid again?" Yes I did!!! I love mornings, I love presents, I love birthdays, I love people, and I love life! Speaking of which . . . is exactly what you make it!!!!

"Make a joyful noise unto God, all ye lands: Sing forth the honour of his name: make his praise glorious." Psalm 66:1-2 (KJV)

One of Them Bikers?
September 17, 2006

Is it morning already? It feels like I just went to sleep and it was time to get up again. Well, that is *almost* true as it was very near midnight (a little over five hours on the road) when I got home from my Hebrew Bible Class in Pulaski. I was fortunate to make the trip with a fellow pastor; **Gregg Bostick**, who is also a huge Tennessee Vols fan and quite anxious to get home to see as much of the game as possible. (I've said a prayer for him this morning. That one point loss probably resulted in a huge headache.) I don't think the speedometer on his Mercedes was *under* 80mph from Pulaski to Lenoir City where I said "Thank you Jesus," picked up my own car, and headed home to beautiful Pittman Center. (Just kidding Gregg, you are an excellent driver.)

So here I am on Sunday morning reflecting on my weekend on campus at Martin Methodist College. I woke up early, around 4:30AM yesterday morning, and soon discovered it was only 3:30AM their time! I decided to stay up anyway and after whiling away some time in my room, I went down to the lobby for a newspaper and DDP (Diet Dr. Pepper). The night clerk was behind the front desk and I said "Good morning" in my usual chipper voice. She yawned, "Mornin' . . . you with them bikers?" Taken by surprise I wasn't sure I had heard her correctly. She repeated "You with them bikers?"

Quickly, I responded "Oh, no, I'm with the preachers!" I was beginning to feel a slight prick in my morning bubble. As if that weren't barb enough, she continued . . . "Well, you know they do have them 'over the hill' gangs now. So I didn't know." My morning bubble no longer resembled a bubble at all and completely deflated, I found myself wallowing around in my waning ego.

Seriously, it was a great class! **Brady Whitehead, Sr.**, from Lambuth University; was the professor and he is always excellent!! He is retiring as the Director of the Course of Study at the end of this year and will be greatly missed. Not only is he a good teacher but a real friend to all his students. *"The law of the wise is a fountain of life . . ."* Proverbs13:14a (KJV)

My dear friends, I must take the rest of my few minutes left before time for my first service to take a last look at my sermon.

Peace!

OCTOBER
PONDERINGS

Seeds of Doubt and Pessimism
October 27, 2012

Ray Robinson was my pastor for several years at Trinity UMC when I lived in Athens, TN. Later, he became a dear friend and very important in my ministry journey. He was a profound, yet delightful preacher who could hold your interest like a magnet . . . I learned a lot from him. In one of his emails he said to me, *"When I preached in Korea, we visited in homes. The host greeted us at the door, and then we went into the living room, sat on the floor, and bowed our heads for prayer. I asked the Pastor what the prayer was. He said: "It is our custom, when we enter a home, to pray 'God, bless this home and this conversation.' Just think, Alta, what if we prayed "bless this conversation" every time we communicate—with family, on the phone, at the post office, at church, wherever."*

We get up in the morning and we feel great, like we can conquer the world and then someone or something sneaks up and literally pulls the rug from under our feet and we go sprawling in all directions. Other folks' response to our own life's situations can sometimes make us or break us . . . if we let them. You know what I mean . . . hasn't it happened to you, at least once?

From the time we began this journey of life, we have developed goals of one kind or another. Some were easy to reach and yet as we grew older, many seemed almost unattainable. Don't allow selfish and pessimistic comments keep you from reaching your potential. Stay as far away as possible from pessimists! Avoid being anywhere near them as their attitudes can be quite contagious.

When seeds of doubt and pessimism are sown in our path and we allow them to take root and thrive, we defeat ourselves. If we are alert, we can keep this from happening by taking the stance of the *Little Engine that Could*. We begin by thinking "I think I can, I think I can," and then, "I thought I could, I thought I could," and finally, "I knew I could, I knew I could!!!" With persistence and perseverance, impossibilities can be turned into possibilities, and we can become possibility thinkers. Movers and shakers, ready once again, to conquer the world.

If we can see ourselves the way God sees us, we will know that we can be victorious in every endeavor. By not allowing our minds to even think defeat we become the victor. The Bible asks us in *Amos 3:3 "Can two walk together, except they be agreed?" (KJV)* When we are in agreement with God's Word we believe that he will help us reach our goals. Just as we must avoid every hint of deterrent from our life's goals, we should never be a deterrent in someone else's life.

Let us consider these words from *Ephesians 4: 29-32*: "*Let no corrupt communication proceed out of your mouth, but that which is good to the use of edifying, that it may minister grace unto the hearers. And grieve not the holy Spirit of God, whereby ye are sealed unto the day of redemption. Let all bitterness, and wrath and anger, and clamour, and evil speaking, be put away from you, with all malice: And be ye kind one to another, tenderhearted, forgiving one another, even as God for Christ's sake hath forgiven you. (KJV)*

Autumn Glory
October 21, 2012

Autumn has come to the mountains! The trees are at their peak of color and the mountain roads are alive with folks who have come to take in their beauty. They come year after year to enjoy scenery that we are blessed to have every day, in our own backyard. Feisty October winds have been kicking up their heels this past week and with every gust, leaves are sent flying through the air to soar and twirl before coming to rest in a carpet of color on the still green grass.

Every season of the year comes alive with its own splendor and fall presents its beauty in the changing color of the trees and foliage. Within the past week or so, the bright colors of red, yellow, orange, green and purple have painted the mountainside with great brush strokes of color and it is absolutely breathtaking. Folks from far and wide will be coming to the mountains to enjoy this wondrous scenery. How privileged and blessed we are to live in this little bit of heaven on earth!

I love to walk in fallen leaves; kicking them up in the air and watching them fly around with each step. I love to hear their crunch under my feet, and smell their earthy aroma. Soon there will also be the smell of smoke permeating the air as bonfires are lit and leaves are burned while children dance in delight in the firelight's glow. Autumn's unique smell makes a walk in the woods so enjoyable as you breathe in the scent of *change* in the air. God's world is ever changing and each one fills our senses with pleasure like none other.

The mountain streams are crystal clear and sparkling in the sun's golden rays. They flow so gently during this time of year. **Barry Phillips**, one of our church members, has decorated the front of Burnett Memorial Church with a colorful display of pumpkins, berries, mums, cornstalks and bows of orange and yellow. Tonight we will be having our Harvest Supper when all three churches come together for a great time in the Lord as we share lots of good food, wholesome fun, and fellowship. What a joyous time we will have, eating together, talking, catching up on the latest sports events, and in the middle of it all . . . every heart will be giving thanks to our God for all that He has done for us this past year, for all the provisions He has given us, and for all His blessings. God is good! All the time! God is good.

"Let the heavens rejoice, let the earth be glad; let the sea resound, and all that is in it; let the fields be jubilant, and everything in them. Then all the trees of the forest will sing for joy; they will sing before the Lord, for he comes, he comes to judge the earth. He will judge the world in righteousness and the peoples in his truth." Psalm 96:11-13 (NIV)

All Saints Day
October 30, 2011

Today is the day before that devilish holiday known as Halloween; a day which sees ghosts, ghouls, and goblins knocking on every door shouting, "trick or treat." Yet, I want to focus on the following day, Tuesday, when we raise a joyful salute to Christians who have paved the way to glory.

Tuesday is **All Saints Day,** a day for remembering the Saints with the New Testament meaning of "all Christian people of every time and place." We celebrate the communion of saints as we remember the dead, both of the Church universal and of our local congregations. For this reason, where this day is observed, the names of persons in the congregation who have died during the past year are solemnly read as a Response to the Word of God. In our own churches we remember those who have entered that heavenly realm this past year, **Viola McCarter** and **Erma McAlister,** true saints of this earth now rejoicing with the saints in heaven.

The observance of All Saints Day began in the Church, somewhere around the fourth century, as they honored Christians who had been canonized, designated saints by the Pope, and solemn rites were spoken for all loved ones who had died. Besides looking back, the day calls for Christians to examine whether they are living lives that future Christians will be able to honor. It is a day, especially for young people, to reflect on what they are doing here and where they are going. Many folks believe that our Christian ancestors left a path for believers (us) to follow today, sort of like a roadmap for us to follow in our walk with Christ. They were the pioneers in that they set the pattern and it is left up to us to live lives that are pleasing to God.

The Apostle Paul, in his letter to the Hebrews, reminds the Jewish Christians of a "cloud of witnesses" made up of their own ancestors. Today we remember our loved ones and declare their value to the church. Those who have passed on have left a legacy as strong Christians by serving their Lord faithfully as well as caring for their neighbors and serving their communities. They fulfilled their journey in this life and now they have eternal life and are experiencing joy evermore. Their example when living is motivation for us to lay down the sins that threaten us and anything else that would keep us from being all that we can be here on this earth and following them into life eternal.

Death is sure and certain. Not one of us will escape it. The question is, "Are you ready?" We know not the day or hour that we will meet our Lord in the air and readiness should be the goal of every human today; to live lives pleasing to God and to be "bound for the promised land!"

Muscadines
October 09, 2011

Good morning! It's Sunday again and I'm filled with excitement and anticipation of all the wonderful things God has in store for us today! We don't need a calendar to tell us that autumn is here once again. I always look forward to the beginning of October as I know the muscadines are ripe. I have some friends who live in Maryville, **Dural and Carolyn Howard**, and they have a vineyard with row upon row of these woody vines laden down with large, sweet, juicy, plump, purple muscadines. I made a visit this past week and came home with a bag filled with the most delicious fruit of the vines. I had almost half of the bag eaten by the time I got home and the floorboard around my feet was covered with the dark, empty hulls. What a wonderful fall treat! Yummeee!! I love muscadines!

The coming weeks, filled with warm sunny days, will take on a slower pace and a quieter time. The laughter of children again drifts up the mountainside to fill my ears with joy at the orderliness of the year. Leaves once verdant and vibrant during the summer months are now beginning to change color and let go their grip on branches preparing themselves for a long winter's nap. Slowly pulling free, they drift downward and come to rest on the ground, creating a patchy brown cover on dry, crackly grass. Feisty fall winds will begin picking up speed, their velocity enticing a glorious shower of red, gold and orange as the leaves float down upon the earth like dancers enjoying a beautiful waltz.

How blessed we are to live in a place where we are able to experience each individual season in its own time with its own special beauty and unique offering. Fall is a fantastic time of year; like a great drama with the earth as a stage, it closes the curtain on summer and opens it anew to reveal the preparation for the coming of winter.

For many folks, fall is their favorite season. For others, it is a sad time reminiscent of death and dying. Each of us possesses the ability to create our thoughts and mood for each day. God allows us that freedom and remember, my friends, with Him all things are possible! I prefer to think of fall as a time of rest, a time to slow down, a time to relax and enjoy God's handiwork at its best. Just as an artist takes his palette of color and creates a beautiful scene on canvas, the mighty hand of God brushes over the mountainside and leaves behind an incredible masterpiece of color and design.

The cool mountain streams are now so clear they appear as glass, rippling over smooth stones and mossy logs still and serene, giving no hint of the raging flood waters of the past spring. Falling leaves are again in evidence as they fall from limbs above the waters drifting gently down onto the surface of these crystal streams to be carried away like a child on a carnival ride. The gurgle of the stream and the peaceful hum of nature fill my senses as I sit on my favorite bench beside the waters; pondering, watching, and listening as God speaks to my soul, ever so quietly but oh so firmly.

"Great is the Lord, and most worthy of praise, in the city of our God, his holy mountain. It is beautiful in its loftiness, the joy of the whole earth." Psalm 48: 1-2 (NIV)

The Body and the Blood
October 3, 2010

Today is one of my favorite Sundays; World Communion Sunday. Christians all over the world will be supping at the Lord's Table today. Some folks actually stay home from church when communion is served and I've never understood that. One thing I do know, it's not that way in our Pittman Center parish. Folks here are usually asking "when are we having communion again?" Everyone looks forward to this most meaningful time with our Lord.

As I lift the bread and the cup in remembrance of Him, I am filled with a sense of profound gratitude that I have been found worthy to serve this sacred meal. We remember, it is the Lord's table and not ours . . . therefore as the Lord would turn **no one** away, neither do we!! Everyone is invited to partake of the sacred elements as we confess our sins and seek our Lord's forgiveness. If our prayers are sincere, we arise from His table knowing we are forgiven!!

As you all know, I usually have a story relative to whatever I write about and today is no different. However, this story is so profound, you may have to give it a second, or even a third, thought. I have related this story before but it deserves to be heard again.

Several years ago, I was serving communion to a child who had never taken communion before. I gave him the bread, **"Joey, the body of Christ, broken for you"** . . . and then the cup **"Joey, the blood of Christ shed for you,"** he hesitated only a moment before taking them both and gulping them down. I saw that his angelic face carried small furrows across his forehead as if he were deep in thought.

When the service was over little Joey was seen upchucking on the lawn of the church. As I went over to him, he said "Miss Alta, that didn't *taste* like blood." Do you get it??? With pure innocent faith, that child was willing to drink the 'blood' that was offered to him. Do any of us, as adults, have that kind of faith? We better have!!!

Listen to the words from *Matthew's Gospel, Chapter 18, verses 2-4: He called a little child and had him stand among them. And he said: "I tell you the truth, unless you change and become like little children, you will never enter the kingdom of heaven. Therefore, whoever humbles himself like this child is the greatest in the kingdom of heaven." (NIV)*

Year of the Pear, Walnut and Pinecone

October 26, 2008

The Chinese have a way of naming the years; 2008 is the Year of the Rat, 2007 was the Year of the Pig, and 2006 the Year of the Dog! Well, the Chinese don't have anything on me. I declare the appropriate name for *this* year to be the ***Year of the Pear, Walnut, and Pinecone***!!!

Every bough of every pear tree I've seen this year has been literally loaded down with luscious green and yellow fruit. Walnuts ping on the tin roofs of houses and barns and fall to the ground in heaps. They are huge this year! All along the roads and highways you will see greasy spots that look as if Wesson Oil has been poured everywhere the walnuts have been crunched into pulp by car tires. And the pinecones!!! My goodness, they are in abundance! Especially up the hill from the parsonage. I was out gathering some of the prettiest ones to help with Christmas decorations for the Festival of Trees, and while foraging, I stepped on a walnut hidden under the mounds of fallen leaves. I almost kissed the ground. Down on one knee struggling to regain my balance, I finally had to sit flat down on the ground so I could get up again. Better watch where you step this time of year; you never know what is lurking under all those fallen leaves (maybe even a snake)!

Fall is definitely in full swing here in the Smokies!!! It is a great time for that visit you've been planning. God has been most generous with his paintbrush dipped in the splendid colors of red and gold dotting the hillsides. The trees are aglow with blazing color! Oh yes, have you seen **Jim Gray's** new painting entitled "Autumn Breezes"? It is awesome how he has captured both the beauty and Spirit of the mountains this time of year. Jim is such a talented and creative artist!!!!

As I look around me and drink in the magnificence of this masterpiece of creation, I wonder how anyone can say there is no God. Who could fashion a tree, or make a flower, or even a bee? How could anyone believe our own bodies evolved from apes? Who made the ape, or the fish, or the birds. Who made a lion, a bat, or a gnat? Who made that little red worm hidden under the rock so flat? Who made the earth and the fullness thereof??? Only God and God alone!!

The Bible tells us explicitly *"In the beginning, GOD"*. . . and that says it all. God *was* the Beginning, He *is* the Present, and He *will be* our Future. Praise Him!!

Fiftieth High School Reunion
October 2008

Good Morning!!!! Where do I begin? First of all, let me assure you, all is well. I've had tons of queries about my health and Clyde's health since there were no *ponderings* this past Sunday morning. Well, folks I must tell you I was attending worship service at **West Cleveland Baptist Church** with my sweet little mother on that day. She was ninety years old this past September. This was the church of my youth, though it was then known as **Victory Baptist**. It sure has changed since I left fifty years ago! The church is now a big beautiful brick building and the sanctuary is equipped with the latest in video and audio systems. I remember a rather small wooden building with a wood stove quite primitive according to today's standards. The men always sat on the right side and the women on the left while we sang the old hymns of the church to the accompaniment of a lone piano.

Now for confession time: both Friday and Saturday nights, I was attending my fiftieth high school reunion in Cleveland, TN. We all found it hard to believe that it had been fifty years since we were the graduating class of '58 from Bradley Central. It was the most fun I have had in a long time! If it hadn't been for those name tags with our graduation picture, we wouldn't have had a clue who some of our best friends were. Fifty years has a way of changing us! I didn't always wear glasses, have gray hair and wrinkles!!!!

The change in all of us is definitely for the better. We seem kinder, gentler, more compassionate, more humble, less competitive, and much more appreciative of each other and life itself. Back in the fifties, we couldn't wait to grab life with all the gusto we could muster; to get away from home and be on our own. We now have more years behind us than we have in front of us. We are all aboard the same boat, sailing upstream, enjoying the warmth of the sun and the wind at our back. What beautiful memories we all have and more being made each day.

Clyde didn't go to the reunion with me as he was not feeling up to par. He stayed with my mom and they watched *Cops* and *America's Most Wanted*, Mom's favorite TV shows. They also watched the Tennessee Vols get beat on Saturday afternoon. It was good to be with my family as we don't get to see them very often. Time away is scarce as I am still working full time in the ministry that I love. We spend very little time away from our home in Pittman Center. When you live in the most beautiful place on earth, there is really no reason to go anywhere else.

This entire weekend I've been reminded of my homes . . . the home where I was born, the home where I spent my childhood, the home of my teenage years, and all the other places I have called home throughout the years. Inevitably, we all come to have thoughts of another home, our eternal home. *"Jesus answered and said unto him, "If a man love me, he will keep my words: and my Father will love him, and he will come unto him, and make our abode with him." John 14:23 (KJV)*

Shalom, my friends.

Corridors of Time
October 23, 2007

Greetings in the name of the Lord! Sunday was Laity Sunday in our United Methodist Churches and having excellent lay leaders to fill the pulpit in each of my three churches, we headed down to Cleveland to spend a couple of days with my **Mom,** my brother **Ralph,** and his wife **Willie.**

What a delight to sleep in my old bedroom and enjoy the warmth and love that permeates my childhood home. Mother has always loved company and her home would rival the finest Bed and Breakfast you could find anywhere. Sunday morning found us traveling familiar roads to the church of my childhood, West Cleveland Baptist (formerly Victory Baptist). It was good to join in singing many of the old songs I remembered so well. My brother's wife is part of their Ladies Trio and they sang a beautiful rendition of "What a Beautiful Day." As we were on our way to lunch, we drove by another church where I attended VBS every summer. Back in the 40's and 50's, it was known as **Grace Methodist Church**, now it houses the **Cleveland UMC District office.**

Last night, we were privileged to attend the **Holston Home for Children Dinner. Pat Summit** spoke on being "united" as a *team* working toward making children's lives better that might not otherwise have a chance. A shining example of just what can happen in a child's life through Holston Home, **Rozetta Mowery** shared painful memories of an early childhood where her father murdered her mother by stomping her to death and how she and her siblings were taken to Holston Home and spent the next several years. Now a devout Christian and mother of three children, she has written a book *"Tragedy in Tin Can Holler"* that chronicles her life and the circumstances surrounding the death of her mother.

As we journey down the corridors of time, we must each stop and reflect on the steps we have taken; our hopes and dreams that have come and gone, some fulfilled and some not yet fully known. We ponder our accomplishments as well as our failures, the opportunities we have had, the family that has loved us, the friends we have made along the way, the lives we have been privileged to share, and the spouse that has allowed us to know the meaning of love at its fullest.

We shall ~ in all our ways acknowledge the God of our salvation ~ we shall trust in Him ~ and He shall direct our paths. Be thankful . . . I am!

Snap, Crackle, and Pop

October 7, 2007

Fall has come to the mountains! Leaves are covering the ground and you can hear them snap, crackle and pop with each step. What a beautiful time of year as trees of yellow gold are tucked into the still green of the mountainside! Soft roses that will soon become deep reds are popping up here and there making their own appearance in the colorful palette of autumn.

If you are wondering whether you should make a trip to the mountains this year, may I tell you they are absolutely beautiful even now and in another week or two they will be a splendid sight indeed! I love walking through the leaves, kicking them up, sending them flying in all directions like dancers pirouetting in the air. The air smells so wonderful this time of year and the sound of crickets as they chirp so loudly it seems their lungs must surely burst from the effort; stopping only long enough to catch their breath before continuing their endless song. Only God could create such a masterpiece as the sights and sounds of autumn.

We have such finite human minds it is hard to conceive the love and mercy God has for His creation. His love is from everlasting to everlasting and offered with such clarity and purity of purpose there is nothing necessary to receive this great gift of love. The Bible tells us that we love God because He first loved us. When we think of His goodness and mercy, it is impossible to fathom the depth of His love for us or the love we give in return to our Creator. We should ever be filled with thankfulness for all He has delivered us from and the wonderful future He holds for us in His loving hands.

I pray that you think about all that God has done in your life and see how His grace has covered you every moment; even when sin and bad choices have sent you spiraling into the depths of despair. Always remember that God loves you more than you can possibly imagine and nothing that you have ever done can stop Him from continuing to love you and receiving you unto Himself.

"As a father has compassion on his children, so the Lord has compassion on those who fear him; for he knows how we are formed, he remembers that we are dust. As for man, his days are like grass, he flourishes like a flower of the

field; the wind blows over it and it is gone, and its place remembers it no more. But from everlasting to everlasting the Lord's love is with those who fear him, and his righteousness with their children's children ~ with those who keep his covenant and remember to obey his precepts." Psalm 103:13-18 (NIV)

Stuck in the Elevator
October 29, 2006

As I look out the window of my study this morning, it is still dark . . . and I ponder the darkness. One of the greatest contrasts in our lives is from darkness to light. The Scriptures use this contrast over and over again. Genesis reveals in the beginning, darkness covered all that was and God said "let there be light, and there was light. God saw that the light was good, and he separated the light from the darkness."

Late one Sunday afternoon I got out of my car parked at the end of our drive and quickly made my way across the street to the basement door of the church. **Clyde** would wait for me in the car as it would take only a minute to retrieve the dish of bread pudding left for me that morning in the refrigerator of the church.

Once inside the basement, I opened the elevator door, reached inside and flipped on the light. Stepping inside, I closed the door behind me and pushed the button that would take me up to the next floor. Immediately, the power went off, the light went out, and I found myself standing there engulfed in darkness! It was black as pitch! I tried to open the door; it was locked! I began pushing buttons, slowly at first then randomly jabbing at them trying desperately to find the one I hoped would restore the power, thus the light, and release the lock. It didn't happen.

Standing in the dark, I remembered in my haste I hadn't noticed the floor of the elevator when I got in; what if that big black snake was lying there, all coiled up on the floor behind my feet . . . or, what if there was a spider just waiting to drop into my hair . . . or, a blue-tailed lizard climbing up the wall! After about fifteen minutes I thought of Clyde waiting for me in our car across the street. Surely, he would miss me soon and come to see what was taking me so long. I wondered if he could hear me if I whistled . . . I can whistle real loud, and I did . . . until I was out of breath. He didn't hear me. Maybe I should sit down and wait . . . No!! I couldn't sit down . . . I might sit on that black snake. Forcing myself to calm down, I knew I would have to draw on my great ingenuity if I was to get out of that elevator anytime soon. Clyde must be taking a nap, he wasn't even missing me!!! He was really going to get it . . . if I ever did get out!!!

I said a quick prayer to Jesus to keep me safe from the snake, lizard, and spider just in case they were in there with me and then began gingerly feeling around the top of the door with the tips of my fingers . . . just when I was about to give up, I found a small button at the very top and standing on my tiptoes . . . I pushed it!!! Hallelujah! Thank you Jesus! I heard the lock on the door click and I was a free woman. From darkness I stepped into the light. I saw it . . . and believe me . . . it was good!

Breaking the Bread
October 1, 2006

Today is World Communion Sunday. I have been privileged to invoke our Lord's blessing on the elements and to serve at His Table many times over the past six years in each of my three churches. Yet after all these years, I am still humbled by this awesome privilege. To think that a little girl from Fairway Drive in Cleveland, Tennessee, could have grown into a person counted worthy to serve at the Lord's Table! Wow!! It makes me smile!

Holy Communion is a blessed and sacred time; a time we draw close to our Savior and remember His sacrificial love. What love He deserves from us in return! As we kneel today to receive the bread and the cup, there will be untold numbers of others, all over the world, who will be communing as well. May we, each one, earnestly repent of our sins and give Him thanks for all His blessings.

There are times, when in my position of 'pastor,' I find both embarrassing and funny moments blatantly displayed in the view of my entire congregation. Some have happened in our most sacred and reverent moments. There is no place for me to run and hide so I stand there and stumble through with as much dignity as I can muster. Lord, forgive me for the times I have even wanted to laugh out loud! One of those embarrassing moments came during one of my first communion service.

One of the first things I did as the new pastor of the Pittman Center Charge, was to let the folks who supplied the communion elements know that I preferred to use a single loaf of uncut bread so that it could be broken. No wafers, please! True to my request, at our first communion, a beautiful loaf (or should I say 'round') of bread was on the platen alongside the chalice of grape juice. I picked up the bread to break it at exactly the time I repeated "Jesus took the bread, broke it"—I tried to break the bread . . . I tried, and I tried again. I don't think the crust of that bread could have been broken with a sledge hammer!!! Finally, I was able to tear a very small piece off with much twisting, using both hands, and probably some grimacing!!! The bread that was served had to be dug from the *inside* of that beautiful shiny crust!! Needless to say, I specified the exact type of bread to be used from that day on.

Keep smiling my precious friends! Be filled with the joy of living!

Falling Leaves
October 24, 2004

"The falling leaves pass by my window; autumn leaves of red and gold . . ." What an absolutely beautiful week we have had! The trees in the mountains are really struttin' their stuff. The air is full of the sweet earthy smell of fall and there is a sense of excitement as the earth makes preparation for the frosty days of winter. The days go by, not without a struggle, holding on as long as they can, savoring the warmth of the sun and the coolness of the night until they will soon be past and gone.

Fall is a great time to play in the leaves which is exactly what I did yesterday afternoon. You have to understand that 'play' to a *slightly* older person is not exactly like 'play' when you were a child. God blessed us with the invention of the leaf blower! Whoopee!!! What great fun and there was a ton of leaves on the drive and in our yard. My youngest son Vic is spending a few days with me and he came out and told me it was getting dark and maybe I should come in and watch the TN Vols game! I'm not much of a football fan *except for the final score* so I immediately found work to do in my study; a good excuse to just *listen from 'afar.'*

Folks around here always get excited about football, especially when the Vols are playing. There are many parents of school age children who must attend the various sports events they participate in, be it basketball, football, soccer, tennis, or dance. I remember years ago when I was a 'karate mom' for my 'karate kid.' **Vic** received his black belt in Isshinryu Karate when he was barely eleven years old. Yes, I went to all his tournaments and a few of them were on Sunday. I didn't like it but when I had to choose between his tournament and church, I went with my child. It's human nature to want to support our children. But, we should *never* forget to *support God* as well. It is also His nature to support His children (that's you and me) and He is always on the sidelines cheering us on.

I can't help but wonder . . . what would happen if all of God's people said "enough is enough, my child will not be participating in a game, tournament, etc., on the Lord's Day." I think we simply would not be put in the position of having to choose between a sports event and our commitment to assemble ourselves together as a community of faith in church on Sunday.

"As the Father has loved me, so have I loved you. Now remain in my love. If you obey my commands, you will remain in my love, just as I have obeyed my Father's commands and remain in his love. I have told you this so that my joy may be in you and that your joy may be complete." John 15: 9-11 (NIV)

The Old Pear Tree
October 26, 2003

What a bountiful fall we are having! Gracious, it seems like all the trees are crying out! *"Hey, look at me, I'm beautiful, my boughs are weighted down with the fruits of my very being!"* *"I'm the most striking one on the mountain side!"* *"My leaves are brilliant red and I stand out among all the glories of the gold!"* *"Well, don't forget me, I'm still green and I hold my own all year long. I'm the one you come seeking when you celebrate our Lord's birthday!"* And on and on, I can hear the *silent, crying out,* in declaration of God's wonder!

Driving down Highway #416 I enjoy noticing the subtle changes of the landscape throughout the year. There are two old scraggly pear trees sitting in a field, off to the right of the road. Funny, I never noticed them before . . . and then, one day . . . I glanced over and there were two old pear trees absolutely laden with pears! There were so many of them, their limbs were bent over almost touching the ground with the weight of their abundant, ripe fruit. It was like they were saying, *"Ah ha, you never noticed us before. We were just part of the background; but you didn't know what we had in store. Look at us now! We may be old, but we can still produce fruit with the best of the young ones. Maybe even more! Why, we'll be providing delicious pies, jams, jellies, and preserves for many tables during these fall mornings and even into the cold of winter. We may rest a bit next year; you know, that's kind of the way it goes with us pear trees. Even when our fruit has been picked and we begin to fade into the background once again, don't forget about us!"*

There is a grand old walnut tree beside the driveway of the parsonage which has born an abundance of walnuts. They are falling everywhere and will provide food for many of the small creatures crouched among the fallen leaves and nestled in the hillside. Seems everywhere you go these day, there are oily patches on the pavement where cars have squashed oodles of fallen walnuts. An enormous, *old to the point of being ancient,* pecan tree thrives in my daughter's yard in Maryville. It, too, is chock full of pecans! Of course, her yard is also a haven to a bountiful supply of squirrels and birds, along with all the children of the neighborhood, as each one is grabbing pecans for their own.

Nature's bounty is a declaration from God our Creator telling us that life goes on. Life is good, life with Christ in it, just gets better and better.

293

We don't have to wait for eternity to enjoy God's blessings. Eternity begins the *very moment* we accept Christ into our heart. Our one desire should be to make *our lives* fruitful, producing many souls for the Kingdom.

I lift up mine eyes unto the hills, from whence cometh my help. My help cometh from the Lord, which made heaven and earth." Psalm 121:1-2 (KJV)

NOVEMBER
PONDERINGS

Crown Him King
November 25, 2012

Good frosty morning my friends! It's going to be another beautiful day and I can't wait to get started. Our church year ends this week and next week will be our first Sunday of the Advent Season. On this last Sunday in our church year, we celebrate Christ the King Sunday in all our churches. Just in case you might not remember; this is a special day celebrated since the 1800s when all the world's great empires, American, British, French, German, Spanish, Russian and even the Japanese, were all at war, or thinking about war.

The Pope decided since the world was being torn apart by all the fighting, he would write a letter in which he dedicated the world to Christ the King. It was his intention to remind these warring nations that God is present with all people everywhere and that He alone was King. This celebration at the end of our church year reminds us that Christ will return at the end of time as ruler over all the earth.

As our precious Lord stood face to face with Pilate and was asked if he was a king, he replied: *"You are right in saying I am a king. In fact, for this reason I was born, and for this I came into the world to testify to the truth." John 18:37 (NIV)* This is the only place in the scriptures where Jesus mentions his birth and when he does, it is to emphasize his reign as King over all the earth and to testify to the truth. Even then, Pilate didn't understand . . . as he finally asked Jesus "What is truth?"

Are we any better than Pilate? Do we know truth? When we speak of our Lord, do we *really* know Him? Is He the ruler of our life, or a mere word that we know should be spoken with reverence and awe yet we don't fully understand why or who He really is? Or worse yet, have we reduced our King, our Master, our Savior and Lord to a mere word spoken *in vain*?

How can it be that the greater part of our society today has become so hardened to who Jesus really is that they reduce His precious name to an abhorrent part of speech? When I hear someone use the Lord's name *in vain*, "Oh my God," or when these words become mere initials "OMG;" I cringe as I wonder if these people have even a small clue as to who He really is. My heart breaks every time I hear these words spoken in vain and surely our Lord's heart is ripped to shreds. Is this the way we thank Him for giving His life for, not only us, but for the whole world?

Oh, that we may always speak His name with praise and thanksgiving on our lips; that we can know Him as our King! That we can know He alone is Truth!

Aaron and His French Harp
November 18, 2012

The wooden planks of the old front porch squeaked as the tiny figure walked across the boards, down the rickety steps, and out into the yard. He was just a mite of a lad, no more than four years old. He turned his face toward the eastern sky and shaded his eyes from the sun. Yes, sir, it was a mighty purty day. Looking around the yard for a place to sit down a spell, he saw the old railroad tie down near the mailbox and quickly walking toward it he took a seat. He could hear his chickens cackling over in the chicken yard and knew he needed to go over and play with them for a spell but, first, he had something more important to do.

Reaching down into the deep front pocket of his little overalls, he brought out one of his prized possessions . . . a French Harp. Holding it in his hands he ran his fingers over the grooves and then the holes that produced the notes; getting the feel of the instrument he held in his hands. Putting it to his hips, he took in a mighty gulp of air and began to play, blowing mighty puffs of air into the instrument and leading a bit with his tongue, he produced a mighty tune, getting louder and louder as he played. Surely that would bring him a crowd . . .

Grandma and Grandpa Sutton had been watching the youngster from the window in the kitchen of their farmhouse. They were wondering what he would do next as this was a child who never failed to surprise and amaze them with the things he said and did. A few minutes later, Grandma walked out into the yard, letting the screened door slam noisily behind her. "What are you a' doin,' Aaron?"

"I'm going to collect me some money, Grandma! When folks drive by, they will hear my music and they will stop and put some money in my cap."

Grandma couldn't help smiling and replied, "Well, I wish you luck, but what do you need money for?"

"Don't you see Grandma," he said with a big smile on his little freckled face, "it was just this morning me and Daddy was talking and, I told him I'm gonna need me a truck pretty soon and He said I would have to pay for it myself so I thought I better get started taking up a collection right now." A child's mind is sharp and wise.

The Scriptures say "train up a child in the way he should go and when he is old he will not depart from it." We muse about other things that are small but unusually wise: *"There be four things which are little upon the earth, but they are exceeding wise: The ants are a people not strong, yet they prepare their meat in the summer; The conies are but a feeble folk, yet make they their houses in the rocks; The locusts have no king, yet go they forth all of them by bands; The spider taketh hold with her hands, and is in kings' palaces."* *Proverbs 30 24:28 (KJV)*

And a little child will lead them.

Screams in the Night
November 11, 2012

It was on a clear and cold night in November about twelve years ago that it happened. I was awakened by the shrill screams of a woman in pure agony. They pierced the night like a bolt of lightning. It was without a doubt the most frightening sound I have ever heard and the screams were coming from the mountain directly behind our house. Quickly waking Clyde up, I told him I must do something quickly or this woman was going to die. Her screams suddenly stopped as quickly as they had started. I jumped up and ran to get a pencil and paper and wrote down the exact time (2:08AM) they first began so that I could tell the detectives when they came to investigate her murder. I knew the exact time would be important!

Clyde sat up on the side of the bed and listened intently. He turned to look at me and started smiling. I could not imagine how he could smile while this poor woman who was screaming in the night was not only being beaten, but was also being tortured. She would be dead soon if we didn't get her some help. Nothing in the world could cause those blood curdling screams except someone being killed slowly and painfully. I grabbed the phone book and was looking up the number of the Pittman Center Police and then remembered all I had to do was get the phone and call "911."

By this time, Clyde was up and running around the house after me. When he finally caught me, my heart was racing 90 miles a minute. I was going to get that woman some help, some way, if I had to climb that mountain behind our house. At last, Clyde grabbed me and physically restrained me until I calmed down. Softly and gently, he spoke, *"Honey, don't you know what that is? It's a panther?"* To which I replied, *"Well, no I don't know that it's a panther, I've never heard one before and I hope I never hear one again!"* When it was all over, we both had a good laugh. Funny how sometimes things, and even people, are not what they seem to be.

This reminds me of the Scribes in these words from *Mark 12:38-40* from the *KJV*. *"And he said unto them in his doctrine, Beware of the scribes, which love to go in long clothing, and love salutations in the marketplaces, and the chief seats in the synagogues, and the uppermost rooms at feasts: Which devour widows' houses, and for a pretence make long prayers; these shall receive greater damnation."*

Jesus is teaching that privilege creates responsibility and denounces the scribes for the way they were living which was contradictory to the Scriptures they taught others. Their judgment would be even worse than those who had never heard the scriptures. We need to remember, people can be fooled, but it is impossible to fool God. In fact, it would pay us to consider the Source of all that we have, and all that we are, and all that we shall ever be. Jesus gave His all so that we might find our all in Him.

Gideons' Good Work
November 4, 2012

That extra hour of sleep last night was just what I needed! I woke up this morning renewed, refreshed and ready to greet the world. Hope you remembered to set your clocks back or you are going to be an hour early for church this morning! There's really nothing wrong with that. Perhaps you can use that time to reflect on some of the things that are truly important in our fast paced life; things that really matter. First of all, God is good! He is always ready to listen, he never leaves us alone, and he really cares for us. After all, he is our heavenly Father and we are His children. We know how special a father's love can be.

Today is Gideon Sunday in our churches in the Pittman Center Circuit. **Gideon Art Belt** will be speaking at Burnett Memorial and Webb's Creek and **Mayor Glenn Cardwell** will speak at Shults Grove in our afternoon service. I always look forward to hearing what the Gideons have been doing for the past year and listen to the stories of how their Bibles, found in so many public places, now translated in many languages, have changed the lives of folks who happened to have picked one up, opened its pages, and found there, the answer to their needs and been given hope for the future. What a good work the Gideons are doing!

Last night, I was privileged to be one of the presenting authors at the *Vintage Views of Gatlinburg and the Great Smoky Mountains* celebrating *100 Years of Literacy and the Founding of the Pi Beta Phi Elementary School*. Our book, "The Joy of Growing Old with God" is an inspirational book revealing how each of our fourteen authors found hope and joy through their faith as they grew older. It is filled with letters, poems, testimonials, artwork, and essays that share the spirit and enthusiasm we have for life with God in our later years. It is meant to encourage those younger than ourselves to keep the faith in their coming years. They can become some of the best of all. Profits from the book will be donated to our public libraries for the purchase of children's religious storybooks. Our first check will be presented to the Anna Porter Public Library next week. Local artist, **Vern Hippensteal**, provided the artwork for the book's cover, **Teri Pizza** was coordinator, and I served as editor.

It was my pleasure and such a delight to meet so many other authors who have written books pertaining to this region and chronicling our mountain heritage. One of these was Aileen Fowler with the Smoky Mountain Historical Society; another was **Carroll McMahan** coordinator of The Upland Chronicles, a weekly column of mountain heritage stories in *The Mountain Press*. **Glenn Cardwell** presented his two books on Pittman Center and Greenbrier Cove. **Bill Landry** was there with his book, published in 2011, "Appalachian Tales & Heartland Adventures" on East Tennessee history. And, these are only a few of the great authors who were guests of the evening.

When we consider great books, there is none that can compare with the Word of God contained in the Scriptures of the **Holy Bible**. A complete library is contained within this one book. Beautiful hymns and poetry can be found in the book of Psalms, amazing love stories in the Song of Songs, profound books on the law, on judges, rulers and kings, history, prophecies, and "sayings of the wise" in the book of Proverbs, mostly attributed to Solomon. No matter what genre you are looking for, you can find it in the Bible and in reading, you will be introduced to the Creation, the love of God, the sacrifice of His Son, and the indwelling of the Holy Spirit, the Great Three in One, our Most High Triunal God. Take it in your hands, peruse the pages and be blessed.

The Animals Bowed at Midnight
November 20, 2011

A very good morning to you, one and all! Today is Christ the King Sunday and we officially enter into our holiday season (Holy Season). Holidays comes from the two words 'holy days.' And so they are! Holy, as we anticipate the celebration of the birth of our Savior. The next few weeks will be days of preparation, of awe and wonder, and I am still very much a child at heart when it comes to Christmas. The magic of Christmas still lives in my heart and it has nothing to do with Santa; it's all about a newborn babe!

One special memory (*which I have been asked to repeat every year*) is of my Granddad taking me and my brother by the hand and leading us down to the barn at midnight on Christmas Eve to see the cattle kneeling. I remember bundling up in my heavy coat and my breath making little white puffs as we walked down the moon-lit pathway in the cold night air. Everything was so quiet and still. We had just heard for the umpteenth time the old story about how the cattle would all be kneeling at midnight to honor the birth of Jesus. I remember tugging on Granddad's hand to walk a little faster. I couldn't contain my eagerness to see the cattle kneeling. And as I finally gazed in wide-eyed wonder at the sight before me, I thought those cows and Old Bess, Granddad's old mule, just had to be very close to God; otherwise, how would they know *this* was Christmas Eve?

Walking back up the path to the house, we would turn our eyes skyward looking for the brightest star and when we found it, we just knew it was the very same "Star in the East" which shown the night Jesus was born. I can still feel that sweet innocence of childhood on a cold star-lit winter night.

Oh, and the smell of cedar!!! Nothing brings back Christmas memories so vividly! We always had a live cedar tree in the hallway of our old farmhouse, far away from the fireplace which served as our only source of heat. How the sweet fragrance of cedar permeated that room! There is nothing to compare.

Christmas is another star-lit night; a young girl barely in her teens giving birth for the first time, her worried husband by her side; the sweet sound of a newborn baby's cry mingling with the silent darkness of night.

The lowing of the cattle as they fall to their knees, one star growing brighter than all the rest, the miracle of Jesus, the Christ-child, the King of Kings, the Lord of Lords, the Alpha and Omega, the first and the last.

And now we come to the Last Sunday after Pentecost, the last Sunday of the Christian year, *Christ the King Sunday*, a celebration of the coming reign of Jesus Christ and the completion of creation. May your heart skip a beat!!

All the World is a Stage
November 28, 2010

Good morning and welcome to the First Sunday of Advent, Act I, Scene I, the exciting time of the year when we prepare for the birth of our Lord.

One of my favorite things to do is visiting the Cumberland County Playhouse and seeing a really good play. I haven't been there in quite a while but I have moved it to the top on my "to do soon" list. A sense of excitement invades my very being as I sit there waiting for the play to begin. When the curtains are drawn open, I can't wait to step into that other time and place for the next couple of hours. The last play I saw there was "Cats" and it was absolutely delightful.

I sit here pondering this morning, thinking that all the world *really* is a stage. Each morning God opens the curtain on a new scene and a new set . . . one in which we assume the major role as we interact in the lives of all those around us. We take the stage making our appearance as either, happy with a smile and kind words, or, we portray an old 'Gloomy Gus,' assuming the dark side of our personality. We are in charge! Will we have an SRO hit or will folks be scurrying for the exit, wishing they had neither visited nor been a part of our life?

During my many trips up, down, and around these winding mountain roads, I see the lush green curtain of summer enveloping the roadways, blocking out all view, is now wide-open! Leaves have turned loose their summer's grip on the branches and, falling to the ground, have allowed a much clearer view of the stage. Looking into the panorama of autumn's fields and mountainsides, I see so many things I never realized were there! Beautiful homes, rustic cabins, weathered barns, winding paths, crystal streams, suddenly appear as if overnight. They were there all along just waiting for the curtain to open and their act to begin. Against a constantly changing backdrop, God reveals His handiwork.

If we allow God to take center stage in our lives, He will draw the curtain wide-open and shine the spot-light of his love into our heart that will reveal His glory! In today's first scene, we will light the candle of HOPE in our advent wreath. As we look at the light of this candle, we celebrate the hope we have in Jesus Christ! And from the prophet Isaiah, written some 750 years before Christ's birth, we read these words: *"O house of Jacob, come ye, and let us walk in the light of the LORD." Isaiah 2:5 (KJV)*

Much Quieter Now
November 14, 2010

Most Sunday mornings find me pondering on the past or on the day ahead. Very rarely do I ponder on the future. Not so this morning! I have come to realize that many of the sights and sounds I came to take for granted have now become a part of the past for me as well as for future pastors who will come to call this parsonage 'home.'

Many changes have taken place within the past couple of years here in the hub of Pittman Center. It's much quieter now. The halls of the old **Pittman Center Elementary School** are no longer filled with the melodious voices of many children. The old school building just across the road from the parsonage, sits on land once owned by the United Methodist Church. No longer am I able to watch from my front door the children at play, hear their shouts and happy laughter, or watch soccer practice on the field by the stream. I miss the sound of the school buses as they rumbled along, the early morning clang of trash cans being emptied into the huge trucks long before daylight, the rows of cars filling the parking areas and lining the roadways when there was a ball game, or Fall Festival. I miss watching the children grow from kindergartners into smart and well-mannered preteens. They were taught well and the school produced many National Merit Scholarship winners. Four of them were from just one of my small churches, Burnett Memorial UMC. They learned respect and knew what it was to be loyal to their country and the principles on which it was founded. Their heads were bowed in prayer at every opportunity.

A beautiful new school is now open a couple of miles away on a wooded hillside just off Highway #321. It is a state of the art school that still carries on its great tradition of academic excellence and loyalty to God and country. This is progress, this is change, this is inevitable if we are to grow and prosper. Such is the way things have always been from the beginning of time and such is the way they will continue as time goes on.

This area as it is was once known will undergo many more changes. What will the future hold for this old school building and the land it sits on? I wonder as I ponder on future things. I wonder but I don't worry because I know that for as long as possible this area will be dedicated to preserving our mountain heritage.

There is one thing in our lives that we can always count on . . . the constant never changing love of God. Our Lord does not leave us and never moves away. He rejoices in the good times and is there to see us through the bad ones. *"As for God, his way is perfect; the word of the Lord is flawless. He is a shield for all who take refuge in him. For who is God besides the Lord? And who is the Rock except our God? It is God who arms me with strength and makes my way perfect." Psalm 18:30-32 (NIV)*

"He heals the brokenhearted and binds up their wounds. He determines the number of the stars and calls them each by name. Great is our Lord and mighty in power; his understanding has no limit. The Lord sustains the humble but casts the wicked to the ground. Sing to the Lord with thanksgiving." Psalm 147:3-7 (NIV)

In my broken and untrained voice, I too, sing to the Lord with thanksgiving! Amid all the changes around me, I have confidence in the future and so much for which to be thankful. You do too!

Seasons of our Lives
November 7, 2010

My first glimpse out my window this morning revealed the myriad of trees on the mountainside, some with a few of the last leaves of summer still hanging on and others already stark and bare. The trees are shrouded in fog and dampness waiting for the warmth of the rising sun. And I ponder on these trees. Each one carries a story all its own, a story of constant change, from glorious color to drab bare limbs, from energetic growth to times of peaceful rest and all of it closely parallels our own life's span.

Fall brings rest and a slowing down as the trees prepare for their long winter's nap. The dark green of the dogwood, oak, and maple turns to vibrant red, yellow and gold as they shout their last hurrah. Ready to release their clothing, the gusty winds and pounding rain toss their leaves to the ground, and soon they return to the earth from whence they came. I like trees . . . I think they are fascinating!

In the dead of winter the stark bare trunks and branches of the older trees reveal dark silhouettes of aged, skeleton-like figures with grotesque arms reaching in all directions. Trunks bent and branches gnarled and broken. The younger trees stand tall, boasting straight trunks and graceful limbs, like outstretched arms of the lithesome ballerina full of effortless grace. On the outside, the trees appear dormant, barren and defenseless; but on the inside, there is still the sweet sap of life just waiting for God's call to wake up!

Spring brings the trees out of their deep sleep, clothing them in delicate spring green of new life. Ah, so beautiful! Tiny, coiled leaves emerge from the pregnant branches, as wee buds begin to form and adorn the trees with the first hint of flowering fruition. We wait and watch as they evolve into the magnificent splendor of nature's intent.

Summer finds the trees filled with spontaneity, maturity and provision. Almost overnight, they burst forth, robed in their finest array. Luscious foliage, flowers and fruit clothe them in unimaginable splendor. They preen and boast while providing shade from the heat and rest for the weary who languor beneath their branches. Children climb their sturdy limbs to seek adventure while passing lazy summer days. The fruit trees provide nourishment to be savored and enjoyed and even preserved for the cold winter days ahead.

So are the seasons of our lives. Think on these words from the book of Ecclesiastes revealing the meaning of life, even as it is questioned. *"He has made everything beautiful in its time." Ecclesiastes 3:11a (NIV)* Not just the trees my friend, but you and me!

Magnificent Tapestry of Christmas
November 29, 2009

Today we leap into the dawning of a fresh new day . . . one that heralds an awesome and holy adventure. **Advent** is one of the most beautiful and meaningful seasons of the Christian Church Year. The first Sunday in Advent begins the four weeks of preparation for the coming of our Savior. I love the mood of Christmas with all its anticipation as we cherish each day that brings us closer and closer to the birthday of Jesus.

My mind wanders back to the Christmases of long ago when we lived on a farm in rural Tennessee; the day we went to the woods for our Christmas Tree, and the fragrant smell of cedar as it permeated the hallway where the tree always stood. The few precious ornaments kept packed away in a small trunk so very carefully all year long were brought out only at this holy time of year. Wow! It was so exciting to open up the lid of that old trunk and let our eyes feast on those tiny sparkling ornaments. All of them were glass and quite fragile. I was always praying that I wouldn't drop one as they were hung with great care on the tree. My older brother always got to hang the ones near the top of the tree and I, being the baby of the family, hung the ones near the bottom. There were little red and green ornaments shaped like pine cones, and other pretty round ones in gold, silver, and blue. And of course, the silvery icicles tossed on the lovely green branches.

The days of anticipation before the birth of the Christ Child are always full of special sights, sounds and smells. The pure white of snowflakes as they gently cover the earth; the incredible sound of Christmas bells from each tiny jingle to the final loud clangs; Luke's story of Christmas being read aloud as everyone is gathered around a cozy fire; lovely Christmas Carols being sung everywhere you go; and little country churches alive with children's voices as they present the annual Christmas Play wearing costumes fashioned by a loving mother or grandmother's hands. Churches filled with the fragrant smell of evergreen branches adorning the windows, red holly berries, and candles giving off their warm glow; the smell of cookies baking; the rustling of paper as gifts are wrapped and hidden from prying eyes.

Savor each moment my precious friends, and prepare for the magnificent tapestry of Christmas being woven before our very eyes. Let your imagination run wild and go to that other time and place so long ago, Bethlehem and the manger holding God's Gift to all the Earth.

Shalom!

The Robbing of Matthew Henry
November 22, 2009

Thursday is Thanksgiving and I can't wait!! Now, I firmly believe we should be thankful *every* day of the year; however, it is good to have one special day set aside to gather together with family and friends and be thankful for God's goodness. If a poll were taken of a hundred people, asking them to name one specific thing they are thankful for, there would probably be a hundred different answers. Actually, it would be quite hard to narrow our thankfulness down to just one thing. We are so blessed in this country to have an abundance of everything we could possibly need. There is food on our table, warm clothes on our backs and shoes on our feet; a bed to lie on, a jingle in our pockets and most important of all . . . the blessed gift of freedom to worship God and to live according to our own beliefs and desires with no fear of retribution.

Matthew Henry, the famous scholar and Bible commentator, was attacked by thieves who robbed him of his purse which contained all the money he owned. He wrote these words in his diary: *'Let me be thankful first, because I was never robbed before; second, because, although they took my purse, they did not take my life; third, although they took my all, it was not much; and fourthly, because it was I who was robbed, not I who robbed.'*

This story reminds me of *I Thessalonians 5:16-18. "Be joyful always, pray continually, give thanks in all circumstance, for this is God's will for you in Christ Jesus." (NIV)* How different our lives would be if we could look at life with a positive attitude and seek the good in every situation. Our thankfulness and our joy as Christians does not depend on circumstances. It comes from what Christ has done, and it is everlasting.

I am thankful for answered prayers, for the *divine calling* on my life to serve the Lord with gladness and the blessing of being the Pittman Center Methodist Pastor. I am thankful for the faithful love of a good husband for so many years, for a loving family, for four wonderful children who love and are loved, for grandchildren who make my heart sing and for a precious Godly mother who taught me, early on, about 'leaning on Jesus.' That faith which she instilled in me as a very young child, has been my rock throughout my life. I am so thankful!!

My prayer is that each one of you will have a blessed Thanksgiving Day! Be thankful for all the things money cannot buy, for the priceless blessings that only God can provide.

Torrential Rains
November 15, 2009

This past Tuesday night brought torrential rains to the mountains. Wednesday morning I was up early ready to begin a busy day. When I looked out the window I could see that Webb's Creek had flooded once again and cars were being diverted away from the danger of the deep water over the road. Later in the day when the waters had subsided, I drove up Webb's Creek Road which was strewn with leaves, twigs, and branches left behind by the wind and water. The swollen, muddy streams running beside the roadway, were thundering along carrying their great burden of logs, limbs, and other debris from higher up the mountain. *And, I began to ponder how closely these ever-changing waters parallel our own lives.*

The turbulence of the water, with its swirls and eddies, was so great that you had to look closely to determine which way the water was actually running. There are times when we too, seem not to know if we are coming or going! Our lives are filled with so much *busyness*, we become frustrated with the heavy load we insist on carrying. Our tasks get to be overwhelming and as they pile up, we feel the din and confusion of turbulence as we face our own *inability to restore order.*

As each of the following days of the past week came and went, the troubled waters in the streams changed back, little by little, to the clear tranquil ripple and flow that reveals their peaceful nature. And the sun broke through and warmed the earth like a happy smile.

So are the days of our lives, turbulence comes, but it doesn't stay. This path of life has puddles! If we can't jump them, we need to be ready to pull on our boots, step right in, and walk straight through. God gives us strength for our journey and hope for the future. With Him, we have no fear. We simply take hold of His hand and claim His peace as He calms the waters of our soul and the sunshine of His love flows in.

May each of you find great joy and many blessings today and in the coming week. Be thankful for all that God has wrought in your life . . . the food on your table, the roof over your head, and the clothes on your back; for loving families and special friendships over the years; and for memories of those we have known and loved and are now at home with Jesus. God is so good, my friends!!! His mercy endures to all generations.

"So do not fear, for I am with you; do not be dismayed, for I am your God. I will strengthen you and help you; I will uphold you with my righteous right hand." Isaiah 41:10 (NIV)

First Frost of Winter
November 8, 2009

This past week, as I gazed from my bedroom window into the early dawn, I saw the first frost of winter sparkling icy and cold on the roof of Burnett Memorial Church. Unbidden, a myriad of thoughts began flooding my mind; thoughts of the cold winter days ahead and how they always seem to bring with them a bit of sadness to some folks. Ailments, tolerable and sometimes forgotten in the bright happy days of summer, come creeping back as we awaken to chilly mornings and fewer sunny days. Folks prone to depression seem to become more so and even the holidays bring gloom and sadness.

Many years ago, I worked as a Deputy Probate Clerk in Athens, TN, in McMinn County. The months of November, December, and January had the highest probate activity of the year; for the number of deaths always rose in those three months. I truly believe if we all make a special effort to let the sad, the lonely, the elderly, and the depressed know how much we love and care for them . . . we can make a very real difference in their lives!!!

Many times we forget that we are ALL in Christ's ministry together. Each of us, using our diverse gifts and talents, has something meaningful to offer!!! As we make plans to enjoy the holidays with family and friends this year, why not think of someone special who would otherwise be alone or lonely, and invite them to join you. Pick them up and when you return them home, send a small gift of flowers, a plate for the next day's lunch, or even a book of devotions or positive thoughts, to remind them all week long of your love and care. A phone call or card during the week will let them know you're thinking of them. God will bless and magnify your efforts in His Name.

Straight from the Bible: "Then *shall the King say unto them on his right hand, Come, ye blessed of my Father, inherit the kingdom prepared for you from the foundation of the world: For I was an hungred, and ye gave me meat; I was thirsty, and ye gave me drink: I was a stranger, and ye took me in: Naked, and ye clothed me: I was sick and ye visited me: I was in prison, and ye came unto me. Then shall the righteous answer him, saying, Lord, when saw we thee an hungred, and fed thee? Or thirsty, and gave thee drink? When saw we thee a stranger, and took thee in? or naked, and clothed thee? Or when saw we thee sick, or in prison, and came unto thee? And the King shall answer and say unto them, Verily I say unto you, inasmuch as ye have done it unto one of the least of these my brethren, ye have done it unto me." Matthew 25:34-40 (KJV)*

Magical Snowflakes
November 23, 2008

There is something magical about the first snowflakes of winter. Young and old alike enjoy watching the tiny flakes silently floating past the windows and gently cover everything they touch with a coat of icy white. In Friday's early dawn, I could see the first dusting of snow as it lay cold and sparkling on the rooftop of the church across the road. It wasn't much; just enough to get me excited about the days ahead and start me pondering. We don't have as much snow as we used to, even here in the mountains. Snow has become quite a luxury and our hope for a beautiful blanket of white on Christmas morning is usually dashed with the dawn.

I remember the excitement I felt as a child on those cold crisp days just before Christmas. I began on the day after Thanksgiving, begging Granddaddy to take me into the woods so I could pick out our perfect Christmas tree. When he couldn't stand my pleading any longer, with a gruff sigh that couldn't hide the smile on his face, he would take me by the hand, stop by the woodpile, pick up his ax, and off we would go. I always picked a small fat cedar with lots of branches. Ah, I can still smell the fragrance of that tree as it filled our big old farmhouse. If I could have put that childhood feeling in a bottle . . . what a treasure it would be!! I could open it up any time I wanted and let that wondrous feeling envelope me all over again.

If I could describe what it feels like to know God in a very real and personal way, I would use the analogy of the pure wonder of a child at Christmas. It's like having the feeling of Christmas in your life all year long as God to showers you with gifts of love, joy, peace, and laughter. Laughter is good for you!! Have you ever watched and listened to a child giggling so joyously it causes you to join in? Nothing is more innocent or more beautiful than the pure delight of a child. That's how God wants all His children to feel. Rejoicing always in that which He has given us; not because we deserve it, but because He loves us that much! Our Father's earnest desire is to pour out blessings on us that we could never have imagined, nor even dreamed possible. This Thanksgiving I hope you remember to be thankful for all your blessings: family, friends, food on the table, shelter from the cold, a place to be, something to do, and someone to love. Live life to the fullest, love like it's your first love, and laugh out loud.

How about you today? Do you know the joy of having Christ in your life? If you do, be thankful as I am. If you don't; my friend, I am praying for you with all my heart, that you will seek him and find him. *"I have come that they may have life and have it to the full." John 10:10b (NIV)*

Joy in Giving Thanks
November 18, 2007

And so this morning . . . we find ourselves four days away from Thanksgiving Day! My prayer for each of you is that you will be surrounded by friends and family, that you will join hands in a prayer of thanksgiving for the many blessings you have received, and those yet to come. May you know the joy of shared friendships, the thrill of being able to reach out and touch those you love, may you bask in a feeling of perfect peace and contentment, may you have stomachs sated from an abundance of delicious fare, and hearts filled to overflowing with the pure, sweet love of God.

We all have memories of Thanksgiving Day from the past and I am certainly no different . . . though you might find my memories a little different that yours. I always loved Thanksgiving because my Dad would do the cooking. He was the best! We didn't have turkey very often as we all preferred chicken, fried up golden brown and delicious in a big iron skillet, mashed potatoes and gravy, green beans, cranberry sauce and the inevitable pumpkin pie. Oh, and I almost forgot my Mom's homemade rolls that would melt in your mouth.

Back to the pie, I didn't like pumpkin pie then and I'm not thrilled about it now, though I eat it. I much prefer chocolate, coconut, lemon, pecan . . . yes, pecan, that's the one I like the best . . . yummy! You will never guess what I considered the best part of Thanksgiving Day . . . my afternoon nap! I would rather take a nap than anything else I know . . . I still would. I can remember curling up on the big iron bed and Mom covering me with my own little Dutch Doll quilt that my Grandmother had made. It had girl dolls and lots of pink. The one she made for my brother had boy dolls and was mostly blue. I would sleep soundly without a care in the world. Oh how I remember the peace that pervaded our home as I slept and flames danced in the fireplace making the room all warm and cozy. Life was good . . . on Thanksgiving Day.

We shouldn't save up our 'thanksgiving' for just one day out of the year, we should be thankful *every* day and never fail to let God know it!!! For his love that surrounds us, His peace that fills us, the golden sun in skies of blue, puffy white clouds suspended in space, green grass, dew, spring flowers, dark ominous clouds rolling over each other telling us a storm is brewing, lightning and thunder, rain, a luminous harvest moon lighting up the night sky, autumn leaves, sparkling frost, and the pure delight of waking up to snow covering the ground. These are just *some* of the things for which I am thankful. *"Enter into his gates with thanksgiving, and into his courts with praise: be thankful unto him, and bless his name."* *Psalm 100:4 (KJV)*

Frost Glistens in Moonlight
November 14, 2007

Stepping outside several mornings this past week, I could see frost sparkling like tiny crystals of glass on the roof of the church across the road, glistening in the moon light. The crispness of the early morning air enveloped me like a shroud and I shivered as I drank in the dawn. Breathing in deeply, letting my lungs fill and then slowly breathing out, I could feel myself coming alive. The sleepiness that didn't want to let go is leaving and I feel energy coursing through my body. Before returning to the warmth of my kitchen, I take a last look around, drinking in the dark beauty that surrounds me.

A few colorful leaves, still clinging to branches of the trees, seem reluctant to give up their hold as they appear frozen in the stillness. The school is quiet now but last night it was filled with the noisy laughter of happy people, as they enjoyed their annual Fall Festival. The creek is so low there is barely a sound from the water. The stillness is such that you wish you could bottle it up and keep it for another time and place. The quietness, the serenity, the peacefulness, all join hands in saying "Good Morning" before the hustle and bustle of the day begins.

There are times when we all need to experience *quiet*. It is something I crave like a thirsty soul in the desert. Quiet gives peace, tranquility, and a sense of self which seems to get lost piece by piece as we go through the *days of our lives*. So many times of turmoil, times of giving, sharing, serving, learning, being, chips away at who we are and we must find a place alone to get quiet and recoup. It is in quiet moments we find a blank canvas waiting for our thought pictures to create the masterpiece that is in our minds. When we need to rest, when we need to study, when we just need to 'be' we seek solace away from the crowds.

I am and always have been a workaholic. Seldom will you find me idle. As I get older, I seem to realize more and more that I have fewer days ahead of me than are behind me. There is so much to do, so much to see, so many places to explore, and so many interesting people to sit down with and listen to their tales of *life lived*. Most of all, I want to learn the skill of being quiet more often and to walk even closer to God . . . to seek quiet times to get to know Him better, to feel his arms enfold me and feel the deep abiding peace that passes all understanding. There are times when God seems to get lost in the shuffle of the *business* of life and we need to be obedient as he says *"Be still, and know that I am God."*

May Your Heart Skip a Beat
November 26, 2006

A very good morning to you, one and all! Today is **Christ the King Sunday** and we officially enter into our holiday season (Holy Season). You do know that the word 'holidays' comes from the two words 'holy days' don't you? And so they are! Holy, as we anticipate the celebration of the birth of our Savior. The next several days will be days of preparation, of awe and wonder, and I admit I am still very much a child at heart when it comes to Christmas. The magic of Christmas is still as real as when I was a child. And it has nothing to do with Santa!

One special memory is of my Granddad taking me and my brother by the hand and leading us down to the barn very late on Christmas Eve to see the cattle kneeling at midnight. I remember bundling up in my heavy coat and my breath making little puffs of *smoke* as we walked down the moon-lit pathway in the cold night air. Everything was so quiet and still. We had just heard for the umpteenth time the old story about how the cattle would all be kneeling at midnight to honor the birth of Jesus. I remember tugging on Granddad's hand to walk a little faster. I couldn't contain my eagerness to see the cattle kneeling. And as I finally gazed in wide-eyed wonder at the sight before me, I thought those cows and Bess, Granddad's old mule, just had to be very close to God; otherwise, how would they know *this* was Christmas Eve? Walking back up the path to the house, we would turn our eyes skyward looking for the brightest star and when we found it, we just knew it was the very same "Star in the East" which shown the night Jesus was born. I can still feel that sweet innocence of youth on a cold star-lit winter night.

Oh, and the smell of cedar!!! Nothing brings back Christmas memories of my childhood so vividly! We always had a live cedar tree in the hallway of our old farmhouse, away from the fireplace which served as our only source of heat. How the sweet fragrance of cedar permeated that room! There is nothing to compare.

Last night as I was driving home along Hills Creek Road, I looked to my left and saw an old farmhouse just off the main roadway. Smoke was barreling from the chimney as mightily as from a roaring train passing in the night, only there was no sound. The windows glowed softly with lamplight from within, a huge wreath of greenery hung from the frame of one of the upstairs windows and my heart skipped a beat. Funny how my heart still does that!! And you know what? I'm glad it does because I know I have not been hardened by a world that commercializes Christmas, with folks running over the top of each other snatching up bargains before dawn. Too many folks today forget that Christmas is not about worldly things but all about a tiny babe in a manger who would grow up to be Christ the King.

I know that life is all about choices and I choose to believe in the silence of Christmas; a star-lit night; a young girl barely in her teens giving birth for the first time (she must have been scared), her worried husband by her side; the sweet sound of a newborn baby's cry mingling with the silence and the darkness of night. The lowing of the cattle as they fall to their knees, one star growing brighter than all the rest, the miracle of Jesus, the Christ-child, the King of Kings, the Lord of Lords, the Alpha and Omega, the first and the last.

And now we come to the Last Sunday after Pentecost, the last Sunday of the Christian year, *Christ the King Sunday*, a celebration of the coming reign of Jesus Christ and the completion of creation. May your heart skip a beat!!

The Breaking of Day
November 19, 2007

To me, there is nothing as beautiful as the breaking of day! I love to travel in the early morning hours and watch the sun coming up over the horizon.

Saturday morning found me, once again, driving along Highway 68 toward **Hiwassee College** in Madisonville, TN. It had been dark when I left my room but soon the first glimmer of light began forming in the eastern sky. I watched as the sun slowly made its first appearance and thought how absolutely breathtaking was the scene before me! The sun's beams danced upward into the cloud stratus and each horizontal layer of grey became tinted with soft peach, coral, orange and finally a vibrant, brilliant gold! I was witnessing in this dawning, the painting of a magnificent canvas; a *Master*piece of the Creator's own hand. And I said, yet aloud, "Thank you God for this beautiful world!"

Coming home to the mountains in late afternoon, I marveled at the sight of a sleek white-tailed deer as it came up the steep embankment on my left and darting directly into the path of my car. Thank goodness, I was driving slowly as I had been savoring the beautiful, and ever changing, scenery of the place I now call home. Looking around with startled eyes, the young buck made a quick dash up the embankment to the right. Being much steeper than the frightened deer had anticipated, about half way up his footing was lost on the uneven rock formations and he came scooting back down with a thump on his rump. Quickly he jumped up and again darted down the side of the roadway until he came to the drive of **Laurel Branch Baptist Church**. There he found surer footing and was soon out of sight under cover of a dense growth of trees.

Trees that were sporting branches of beautiful fall colored leaves only days ago are now barren as cool winds have whipped through, stripping them of their coats of many colors. With branches resembling skeletal arms reaching out in all directions, they bear no shame in the revelation of their nakedness. Leaves which once covered them will once again become part of the soil of the earth from whence they came; and nature's cycle will begin again, in the warmth of spring.

God's order in the universe, the earth, the sea, and the sky, is breathtaking! The morning surely declares the glory of God! Live life! Enjoy every day!!!

No Sense of Direction
November 12, 2006

Many of you know that I can't sing very well. I'm just not gifted in that area. Only a few of you know that I have very little *sense of direction*. My Dad used to say he could take me to the courthouse square, turn me around twice, and I couldn't find my way home! Not long ago, someone told me they knew exactly what they were getting me for Christmas this year; a compass, a roadmap, and a thing (can't remember what he called it) to put on my car to tell me which direction I was going. I **do** know the sun comes up in the East and it sets in the West. Woe unto me if it's a cloudy day!!

This past week, I have really felt, quite profoundly, this lack of a sense of direction. I literally felt like a leaf in a whirlwind. Or maybe I felt a little more like Jonah ~ swimming around in the innards of a whale's belly trying to find the button that would pop open its mouth, spew me out, and let me get on my way to Nineveh! The Lord has so much for me to do! Which way do I go today? Well, actually today is not a problem because it is Sunday and my place on Sunday is in the pulpit of each of my three churches. And that is where I will be! Will I see you there?

Did you know **Clyde** and I were on vacation this past week? One of my parishioners said if this was vacation, he would stick to hard labor! Talk about plans made to be broken!!!! Not one of our plans came to fruition. As circumstance would have it, on Friday before our vacation was to begin, I took Clyde to the hospital with pneumonia (he's still there); and on Monday, my eighty-eight year old mother who lives in Cleveland, took a nasty fall and broke a bone in her pelvis. Along with being concerned over my husband's health and my mom's injury, I was also trying to complete Charge Conference reports at home. You do see what I mean, don't you?

Before I go, let me tell you about a wonderful book my dear pastor friend, **Betty Shirley**, sent to me; *"When I Lay My Isaac Down"* by Carol Kent. This is a mother's *true* story of her abiding faith in God during a time of great personal crisis; and for a time, she also felt the sense of loss of direction. The book has spoken to my own heart. Carol tells her story as she weaves the threads of her testimony into every page. It is a book that also speaks of forgiveness. Our Lord's very nature is to love and forgive. He gives us HOPE as we choose to be like Him, follow in his footsteps, and seek his face.

"Trust in the Lord with all your heart, and lean not on your own understanding; in all your ways acknowledge Him, and He shall direct your paths."—Proverbs 3:5-6 (NKJV) •

DECEMBER
PONDERINGS

The Spirit of Christmas
December 23, 2012

Today we rejoice as we light the fourth candle in our Advent Wreaths, the candle of LOVE which joins those of HOPE, PEACE, and JOY. Let me jump ahead a couple of days and wish you a Merry Christmas and Happy Birthday to Jesus!!!

The true meaning of Christmas is found as we share our gifts and graces in a world that has become cold and insensitive, uncaring and materialistic. Look around you and let the Spirit of Christmas invade your life; contrary to that of a politically correct society. Every day and every night should be Christmas as we await the Second Coming of our Savior, the day and hour no one knows. We welcome each new, and perhaps holy, encounter that comes into our life as God presents those *spiritual* gifts that we all desire: His love, mercy, grace and His forgiveness.

Long after the songs of the angels have been sung and the star in the sky has stopped shining, the real work of Christmas begins: we look for the lost, we attempt to heal the broken-hearted, we seek love between brothers and sisters, we feed the hungry, we help hearts heal and feel the music, we spread the Word, and we worship Him. We are happy amid the sadness, we find hope where there was none, we anticipate, we wonder, we wait, smiling, weeping, laughing, mourning, we sing and we pray. It is a most blessed thing to allow the mood of Christmas to enter our lives.

We think, here we are Father, your children, each of us with our own individual wants and needs. The constant reaching out for that special moment of intimacy with you, the light that will overcome the darkness in our lives, the gentle laying on the altar the burdens we are no longer able to bear, the way we say we will give it all to you . . . yet, before we leave, we pick them up and drag them away with us once again. Why Father, can we not trust you more? Why, Father, do we not believe? Why do we continue to disappoint you . . . as well as ourselves?

God of our hearts and lives, hear us as we ask you to accept us, poor and meek as we are, calling on you for help, for encouragement, for enlightenment. Let your Spirit of Christmas permeate our souls today. Let that same Spirit take up permanent residence for all the days to come.

We thirst for your blessings, let them pour down upon us like rain from heaven; soothing, comforting, reassuring, and full of peace.

Father we know and learn from our past, we rejoice in our present, and we anticipate with awe the future you will set before us. Let us be messengers of your peace as we share the tidings of great joy. *"For unto you is born this day in the city of David a Savior, which is Christ the Lord."* Luke 2:11 (KJV)

Joy to the World
December 16, 2012

We continue our countdown to Christmas Day and find ourselves in the Third Sunday of Advent. Today we light the candle of Joy and realize that in Christ we find our real joy. He gave us the greatest gift ever given, the assurance of salvation, and it is in that we can know joy, and hope, and peace. Christmas is all about the Christ Child and His Holy Birth so many years ago in a stable in a manger. Christmas continues each day of the year as we watch and wait for His Second Coming when He will accept each one of us into His Kingdom, the Kingdom of God.

Many of you know that my precious Mother has been very sick and hospitalized a couple of times in the past few weeks. I have been taking my days off each week and even some vacation days to travel to Cleveland and help my brother and sister-in-law provide much needed care for her. She came home from the hospital with hospice care assigned and we were told she would probably not make it the rest of the week, nor certainly no more than two weeks. My little Mom is a strong willed lady and she has proven them wrong as she continues to struggle onward and is into her sixth week of recovery. At ninety-four years of age she continues to amaze and bless our family.

As I help Mom get dressed, I feel the bones in her shoulders revealing the bare eighty pounds of her frail body. I want to hug her and kiss her with love and gratitude for all she has done for me and my brother throughout the years. I wish I could take her in my arms and comfort her as she did me. I wish I could take her pain away. I take her sweet hands in mine and think of all the work they have done. I am so thankful that God has given me this opportunity to care for the one who cared for me. I am blessed beyond measure that she has survived despite the odds against her. It is in my precious Mother that God reveals Himself to me through the unspeakable joy of her never ending love. She is the Christmas gift I cherish above all others. God will call her home in *His own time* and I have the assurance she will live forever with Him.

We should ever be thankful for the wonderful gifts God gives us each day: the gift of life itself, our health, a warm fire, food to eat, clothes to wear, friends who care, and family who love us. The beauty in nature and in all God's creation is ours to share: animals, birds, and pets to delight our hearts, the sun to light up our days and lift up our spirits, the gifts of sight, sound, touch, taste, and speech, the ability to love and be loved, and the pure joy of laughter. God's gifts are free and always there so each of his children can enjoy a blessed and happy Christmas Season. Make it merry, make it holy, and make it bright!

It is Well
December 9, 2012

Today is the Second Sunday of Advent and in our churches we will light both the first Candle of Hope and today's candle, the Candle of Peace. Oh, that there could be peace; peace over all the earth; peace in our hearts, and peace in our homes, peace in our land and peace on foreign soil. I imagine if I could have just one wish granted, it would be for peace.

When I think of peace, I think of the calm assurance that comes from daily walking with our Lord and Savior, Jesus Christ. He who was born on Christmas Day so long ago with one purpose, to give to us the gift of salvation, full and free. How blessed we are when at last we can say, it is well with my soul. I remember the words of that precious old song written by Horation Spafford back in 1873 . . . *"when peace, like a river, attendeth my way, when sorrows like sea billows roll; whatever my lot, thou hast taught me to say, it is well, it is well, with my soul."*

This year, more than ever before, let's keep Christ in Christmas. Society continues its attempt to be 'politically correct' by leaving all mention of Christ out of Christmas in the stores where we shop, and in most all public places, so that non-Christians might not be offended! We must, as Christians, renew our efforts to voice our displeasure at this tragedy. Yes, tragedy is a strong word, but that is exactly what it is. Without Christ, there is no Christmas!!! There are no 'holidays' without Christ. Why would we want to wish anyone a meaningless "Happy Holidays!?"

HE is the very reason we celebrate. It is his birthday and birthdays are special. Happy Birthday Jesus!! Am I on my soapbox? You bet your sweet Christmas booties I am! Please join with me in keeping Christ in Christmas and in our hearts; not only at Christmas, but the whole year through.

God desires to give each one of us through the birth of His Son, peace through our salvation; the peace that passes all human understanding. Friend, if you don't know Him, my prayer is that you will seek Him . . . and find that peace today!

"And suddenly there was with the angel a multitude of the heavenly host praising God and saying: "Glory to God in the highest, and on earth peace, goodwill toward men!" Luke 2:13-14 (NKJV)

Christmas Is a' Comin'

December 2, 2012

Christmas time's 'a coming! Oh, how I love Christmas! Last night down at Pittman Center City Hall, Mayor Glenn set the Yule log aflame and everyone gathered round the fire to listen with rapt attention as Mayor Glenn told us the story of the **Yule Log** and how it has become a tradition and a very important part of our mountain heritage. I had the honor of reading the Christmas Story from the second chapter of the Gospel of Luke. This is a night I look forward to every year as the beginning of our town's Christmas festivities.

What a lovely night, what a wonderful tradition! Sparks from the fire were jetting toward the sky like shooting stars while the flames danced to a song of their own. Children eyes shone with wonder as the firelight lit up their faces in the fire's golden glow. And oh, that wonderful atmosphere of peace, good will toward men was everywhere. Friends greeting friends, carols being sung and everyone relaxed and enjoying this special moment in time. Plenty of delicious hot cider warmed us up . . . and there were cookies, and Santa Clause came for the children to sit on his knee and have their picture made as they told him their Christmas wishes with serious faces making sure he understood exactly what they wanted him to bring. If you could have seen me, you would have thought I was a child again . . . I really was, in my heart. I'll tell you a secret . . . I sat on Santa's knee and had my picture made as well . . . teehee.

Today is the first Sunday in Advent and we will light the first candle in our Advent wreath, the candle of hope, in our churches this morning as we celebrate this sacred time of waiting the coming of our Savior. He came first to a little town called Bethlehem in Judea and to a virgin named Mary. We know He is coming again and we watch and wait for his Second Coming, the day and hour of which no one knows.

"And there shall be signs in the sun, and in the moon, and in the stars; and upon the earth distress of nations, with perplexity; the sea and the waves roaring; Men's hearts failing them for fear, and for looking after those things which are coming on the earth: for the powers of heaven shall be shaken. And then shall they see the Son of man coming in a cloud with power and great

glory. And when these things begin to come to pass, then look up, and lift up your heads, for your redemption draweth nigh." Luke 21:25-28, (KJV)

As we begin this beautiful season called Christmas, with all its rich traditions and festivities, let's never lose sight of the real reason for it all . . . the birth of Jesus Christ, our Lord and Savior, on that starry night in a manger, in a stable . . . so long ago.

Mary's Thoughts
December 18, 2011

O God, as I walk along looking up at the stars in the sky, I feel your presence surrounding me. I've felt it all along these past months. It hasn't been easy for me or for Joseph. Such a sweet man; he tries to understand. We've endured a harsh and cruel time, listening to the endless whispers, the old wags won't let us be. I've been listening to their tales of the pains of birthing. Joseph is so good and kind to me; he stays by my side. Even though I know I am blameless and have great faith, my reputation has been brought into question. It hurts. I went to Elizabeth's house to hide from all the gossip but soon I realized that I must endure and I will not hide.

I have to admit I'm a little scared. God, I'm just a girl, barely a woman! I'm trying so hard to be brave. I'm still not sure I understand how all of this will come about but I have faith and I'm trusting in You to see me through.

I've been walking these last few miles as riding the donkey became almost unbearable. My swollen belly makes it hard to even walk now and I hope we soon find a place to stay. The baby is moving anxiously within me and I don't think he will wait much longer. The pains are becoming harder and very close together. Poor Joseph, his face mirrors his deep concern. Oh, look . . . there . . . aren't those lights in the distance? Maybe it's an inn!. Run, Joseph, run and see if they have a room for us. Father, help me make these last steps.

What, no room? Oh Joseph, what will we do? The baby is coming, I must lie down. There is only a stable? Quickly, we must hurry there. Empty this trough where the animals eat. Let us lay some clean hay in it and cover it with this soft blanket we brought with us. Here in Bethlehem of Judea; this is where He will be born; the land of our ancestors, the land where we came to be taxed. Holy God, this is the place You have chosen. I cry out ~ let it be!

Matthew 1:18 stated positively that Jesus was virgin-born: *"Now the birth of Jesus Christ was on this wise: When as his mother Mary was espoused to Joseph, before they came together, she was found with child of the Holy Ghost."* (KJV) Luke also emphasized the virgin birth, and in even greater detail.

John pointed to the virgin birth of Jesus by emphasis on the Lord's origin in heaven: *"In the beginning was the Word, and the Word was with*

God, and the Word was God . . . And the Word was made flesh, and dwelt among us, (and we beheld his glory, the glory as of the only begotten of the Father,) full of grace and truth." John 1: 1, 14 (KJV)

Even though *Mark* did not begin his gospel until Christ's public ministry, he opened with *"The beginning of the gospel of Jesus Christ, the Son of God;" 1:1 (KJV)*

Happy Birthday Jesus
December 25, 2011

Merry Christmas everyone! Happy Birthday Jesus!!! The true meaning of this day is found in the sharing of our gifts and graces in a world that has become hard and insensitive, uncaring and materialistic. Look around you and let the Spirit of Christmas become a part of your life; contrary to that of a politically correct society. Every day and every night is Christmas and we await the coming of new, and perhaps holy, encounters to invade our life.

Long after the songs of the angels have been sung, and the star in the sky has stopped shining, the real work of Christmas begins: we look for the lost, we attempt to heal the broken-hearted, we seek love between brothers, we feed the hungry, we help hearts to feel the music, we spread the word, and we worship Him. We are happy amid the sadness, we find hope where there was none, we anticipate, we wonder, we wait, smiling, weeping, laughing, mourning, we sing and we pray. It is a most blessed thing to let the mood of Christmas enter into our hearts today.

Here we are Father, your Children, each of us with our own individual needs and desires. The constant clutching for that moment of intimacy with you, the light that will overcome the darkness in our lives, the gentle laying on the altar the burdens we are no longer able to bear, the way we say we will give it all to you . . . yet, before we leave, we pick them up and drag them away with us once again. Why Father, can we not trust you more? Why, Father, do we not believe? Why do we continue to disappoint you . . . as well as ourselves?

God of our hearts and lives, hear us as we ask you to accept us, poor and meek as we are, calling on you for help, for encouragement, for enlightenment. Let your Spirit of Christmas permeate our souls today. Let that same Spirit take up permanent residence not only for today but for all the days to come.

We thirst for your blessings, let them pour down upon us like rain from heaven; soothing, comforting, reassuring, and full of peace. Father we know and learn from our **past**, we rejoice in our **present**, and we anticipate with awe the **future** you set before us. Let us be messengers of your peace as we share the tidings of great joy.

"For unto you is born this day in the city of David a Savior, which is Christ the Lord." Luke 2:11 (KJV)

White Christmas
December 26, 2010

If you have been dreaming of a white Christmas . . . wake up! And, especially, If you live in Pittman Center, you will see the world outside your window swathed in an almost foot of pristine white snow. There is no church for any of us today as the roadways are as white as our lawns; another gorgeous winter wonderland.

The beautiful fir tree in the corner of my front yard is breathtaking in its beauty. Every branch of green is adorned with a frosting of pure white, dipping low from the weight of the snow. Stark, skeletal trees are wearing capes of white and our beautiful church across the road is like a scene from your favorite Christmas card.

This very day is God's gift to us, as is every day, but today is special. This particular day in our little town comes with no need to expect visitors or to cook as we all have plenty of leftovers from Christmas dinner. We can snuggle down by the warmth of the fire and take some time to think. How long has it been since you really sat down and gave some thought to all the things you have to be thankful for? If you are like me, your days for the past few weeks have been hurried and we have been more like robots set on "go." Today is that day to "Be still, and know that I am God."

If you have just said to yourself, *"what do I have to be thankful for? Oh, woe is me."* Let me remind you grumbling gremlins, of: the air you breathe, the ability to get out of bed this morning, food to sate your hunger, clothes to keep you covered, a roof over your head, a friend to walk beside you and most importantly, the forever presence of the Lord in your life. Our salvation is a gift of God, our baptism is a gift from God, eternal life is a gift from God, and the knowledge that this is not the end, only the beginning of what He has planned for us, this is His finest gift.

When doubt enters your life, as it sometimes will, let us all remember these words from Romans: *"For God's gifts and His call are irrevocable."* Shalom my friends.

Be thankful.

Christmas Tiptoes In
December 19, 2010

This morning I'm pondering on the magic of Christmas! It came tiptoeing in quietly and gently like the first snowflakes of winter, covering the trees and hillsides of these mountains with a pristine blanket of white. The transformation into this lovely winter wonderland almost takes your breath away. I stepped out into the early dawn and filled my lungs with the frosty air. I meditated on God's great love and the magnificent beauty of his creation. I didn't linger long as the chill soon reached my bones and I sought the warmth of the fire inside.

There's an indescribable feeling that comes with Christmas as it unwraps the true gifts of the season. The eyes of little children are wide with wonder; folks we meet in passing are filled with laughter and joy and their friendliness is contagious. Glad tidings of "Merry Christmas" fill the air. We begin to focus on the real meaning of life and all its miracles. The birth of Jesus and the message it proclaimed compels us to share our gifts and graces with others.

Cherished memories from Christmases past come flooding in, reminding us of scenes from long ago. As I shared with you some years ago, I will never forget the Christmas when Granddad took me and my brother to the barn at midnight to see the cattle kneeling in their stalls. How bright the stars seemed that cold winter night and how close to heaven I felt. There were years when we gathered around the kitchen table to hear the Christmas story from Luke, read aloud from the old and well-worn family Bible. Then it was off to our grandparent's farmhouse where I still remember the smell of fresh baked bread and fried chicken. One Christmas we went to visit **Aunt Hazel and Uncle Lube Musgrove** who lived way up in the mountains in an old log house. Aunt Hazel had the best yellow cake with chocolate icing that I ever tasted. I loved the smell of smoke as it gently wafted from the chimneys into the cold air and as soon as we entered the house, that smell changed to the aroma of cedar from a tiny Christmas tree, tangy sweet oranges, peppermint sticks, and buttery popcorn.

Christmas comes with a feeling and lots of special memories. When night comes we can step outside, look up at the sky and feel again the wonder of His birth; we imagine the inn so full there was no room, the smelly stable which became sacred, the manger filled with a bed of fresh hay by an anxious father, a young mother and tiny baby, shepherds, and the animals. We listen and we hear singing from above, first soft as a whisper, words of a silent night and holy night and coming closer, the chorus grows louder as they proclaim the Holy Birth. *"Joy to the world, the Lord has come, let earth receive her King! Let every heart prepare Him room and Heaven and nature sing!"* We hear the great crescendo of Christmas declaring, *He is born, He is born! Jesus the Christ is born!*

Hope Reigns Eternal
December 5, 2010

Well good frosty morning to you! Today we take another step forward, as we enter the second Sunday of Advent. In churches all over the Christian world, the first candle "the candle of hope" will once again be lit and the second candle, "the candle of peace" will join it in the light of Christmas. We have hope because God is faithful and will keep the promises he made to us. Our hope comes from God. Peace is the calming of our hearts and lives through the grace of our Lord and Savior. We ready ourselves to welcome you, O God!

What an awesome time of watching and waiting! It's exciting as our hearts begin beating a little faster, and our steps quicken as we approach this most holy day of CHRISTmas. The day a tiny babe was placed in a manger of straw in a smelly old stable in a town called Bethlehem.

This is the season when many things stand out in stark contrast to the background of our own busy days. We ponder on little children who have never experienced Christ or Christmas. Children in refugee camps who have little more knowledge of life than the length of the hours of their long, dreary days; children in orphanages; children whose families show them so little love they are barely aware of what it means to know a tender loving touch; sick children in hospitals, many of whom have seen the beauty of the earth and will soon see it no more. Our hearts are broken and sad as we think of the children of the world.

And, we remember old folks. Those whose fires of life have become nothing more than mere coals pushed to the back of the grate; those who sit alone no longer caring to remember as memories of hard times bring no comfort; many who still keep alive that dim hope that their children will come for a visit; many who sit alone in nursing homes surrounded by those like them, huddled together for warmth and companionship. Solitary lives, waiting . . . for what?

Father, in the quietness of this early morning hour, our ponderings are sad as we think of those less fortunate. Here we are, each with our own life and world and need. We lay our life upon the altar of your mercy and grace, and we hold it there, waiting for the Holy Spirit to invade our heart

343

and soul so that we will be prepared for the living of each day, whatever may come. We breathe a silent prayer of thanks and praise in the quietness of the hour.

Yet, in each of our lives, we must always have room for the singing of angels! *"Hark the herald angels sing, glory to the new born King."*

In Clouds of Glory
December 27, 2009

I awoke to this sparkling cold morning pondering on the silence of snowfall. And how, if we listen carefully and let our minds wander, we can begin to hear the distant sound of trumpets . . . ever so softly at first, and then building and building, to the full crescendo of the triumphal blast of the angels signifying the birth of Jesus. Jesus, as a baby in a manger in a smelly old stable; Jesus, the boy-child questioning the elders in the temple; Jesus, as a young man drawing followers from *common* men; Jesus, hanging on the cross bleeding, dying for our sins; Jesus, the risen Savior walking and talking among the people; and Jesus, ascending into heaven to sit at the right hand of God as he makes intercession for *us*. And we are here, now, *waiting* for the Second Coming of our Lord and Savior in clouds of great glory! Will you be surprised when it happens?

The coming of Jesus that first Christmas night so long ago, brought with it one surprise after another. There was Mary, Joseph, the shepherds, and the officials of Jerusalem. All were surprised. Jesus came into the world in an unexpected way and with uncharacteristic impact. Many *should have been* prepared, but they were looking for a very different arrival than that which happened in Bethlehem. Everyone touched by Jesus' coming would have preferred advance notice and probably a more convenient time, but Paul wrote *"But when the fullness of the time was come, God sent forth his Son, made of a woman, made under the law, To redeem them that were under the law, that we might receive the adoption of sons." Gal. 4:4-5 (KJV))* Jesus came into the world in God's time, to fulfill God's purpose, which means that human factors and world conditions had absolutely nothing to do with it.

God's ways are not our ways. We only know in part *"For now we see through a glass darkly;" 1 Cor. 13:12a (KJV)*. Jesus still takes us by surprise. He comes unannounced. In the middle of some ordinary nothing-special kind of day we meet him and our world is never the same again. Jesus comes to us in the middle of great joy and intense sorrow. Jesus is revealed to us in the life of another person. We may meet him by a sickbed or at the death of someone we love. We never know when Jesus will come to us. That is why our journey of faith is always exciting and never dull and hopeless. We can never go so far astray that we are beyond His reach and saving touch. He goes to any length to seek us and find us. *Nothing* can keep him from coming.

May each of you welcome the surprise of Jesus' this Christmas and accept the greatest gift of love you will ever know, eternal life and a home in heaven. After all, Jesus died to give it to you. How can we let it have been in vain?

Yuletide Festivities
December 6, 2009

Time flies by so quickly! Seems it was only yesterday I was taking down the Christmas tree from last year, and here it is, time to put it up again! The sights and sounds of Christmas are all around; traditions are being put in motion once again, and I am as excited as a child. I love everything about Christmas! The old familiar carols, bells ringing out in the malls and on the streets, the sparking eyes of a child busy preparing their letter to Santa, or looking in the Christmas catalog yelling and pointing to some special toy, "Mommieeee!!! I want this for Christmas!!"

Last night, I attended the annual **Yule Log Festivities** down at the **City Hall in Pittman Center**. What a special night! An awesome tradition that I hope lives on for years and years to come. Hot chocolate flowed, along with coffee and cider. Tables were laden with oodles of Christmas cookies and candy. People were laughing and greeting old friends, children were playing, and all the while, the Yule Log burned! Sparks floated upward into the night sky and the smell of burning wood permeated the air. We munched and mingled and sang Christmas carols to the accompaniment of the keyboard played by **Suzette Huskey**. Mayor Glenn Cardwell told the story of the Yule log and what it meant to the people of Appalachia . . . with the most interesting part being there was to be *no work* during the time the Yule log burned. Naturally, the folks kept it burning as long as possible to extend their revelry.

The Yule log was cut and dragged home by horses as the people walked alongside and sang merry songs. During winter, townspeople gathered these large logs to be ridden, like a modern sled, down embankments of ice and snow. It was often decorated with evergreens and sometimes sprinkled with grain or cider before it was finally set alight. The Yule log was believed to bring beneficial powers and was kept burning for at least twelve hours and sometimes as long as twelve days, warming both the house and those who were within. When the fire of the Yule log was finally quenched, a small fragment of the wood would be saved and used to light the next year's log. The ashes that remained from the sacred Yule log were scattered over fields to bring fertility, or cast into wells to purify and sweeten the water. Such is one of the traditions of **Christ**mas still carried out, here in the mountains of East Tennessee.

Today is the Second Sunday of Advent; as we anticipate the 'coming' of Jesus as a tiny, newborn babe. *"Oh come, O come, Emmanuel and ransom captive Israel, that mourns in lonely exile here, until the son of God appears. Rejoice! Rejoice! Emmanuel shall come to thee, O Israel."*

John and Becky's Wedding

December 30, 2007

A New Year is almost upon us! Seems it was only yesterday we celebrated a new year and here it is . . . time for another one. Truly, time flies now that I have become a senior! I remember when days used to creep by, with actual minutes and hours. Now it seems as soon as I wake up, it is time to go to bed again and I haven't accomplished a thing. I just move one stack of papers to another place and try to trick myself into thinking I have made an inroad into the maze that encircles my desk.

Oh, yes! I must tell you about my son's wedding yesterday! What a perfect ending for 2007 with our family gaining another daughter and her family warmly welcoming John as another son. Needless to say, both families couldn't have been happier with this union! What a privilege for me to be able to officiate at this very special ceremony. I was only a little less nervous than the bride.

Becky was so beautiful in her white satin gown and dark curls framing her lovely face! Keeping with the Christmas theme of red and white, her matron of honor, **Carrie Marcus Hall**, was striking in her short red brocade dress. John's only attendant was his Dad, who served as his best man. Instrumental music was provided by **Jeremy Stephens** playing violin, and **Justin Hall** playing rhythm guitar. Both young men live in Nashville. Jeremy and John grew up next door to each other during most of their childhood years.

It was the end of the ceremony . . . and so far . . . I didn't think I had made a mistake or left anything out. I was ready to give myself a pat on the back and let out a deep sigh of relief . . . when John turned to me (after I had them facing the audience and had pronounced them man and wife) and whispered, *"Mom didn't you forget something?"* My mind began to race, my heart began to pound, my face must have been ashen, and for the life of me I couldn't think what I could possibly have forgotten. When John saw the stricken look on my face, he said *"Don't I get to kiss the bride?"* That brought a round of hearty laughter as John finally received permission from his mom to kiss his bride! What a spectacular day! This is the stuff that memories are made of.

Jesus graced a wedding at Cana of Galilee where he revealed his glory for the first time as he turned water into wine. Jesus was there not only because his mother had asked him to come, but to celebrate joy at God's good gift of marriage. It is in His sacrificial love that Jesus gave us the example for the love of husband and wife.

Love Came Down at Christmas

December 23, 2007

It's beginning to look a lot like Christmas, everywhere you go! We always went to my grandparents' house every Christmas Eve when I was a child. I can still remember the drive there, and me gazing up at the night sky, seeing the stars twinkling, and thinking silently *"Star light, star bright, first star I see tonight. I wish I may, I wish I might, have the wish I wish tonight."* I would wish for something special known only to me . . . not a material gift, but something far more important . . . the continued blessing of love in our home. Love has always been important to me. I love people, and I enjoy receiving love in return. When we finally arrived, my brother, **Ralph,** and I would run to the door of their big old farmhouse and scurry inside (it *used* to be very cold at Christmas, remember?). We would make a bee-line toward the fireplace where we quickly warmed our backsides. Then it was off to the feather beds where we slept fitfully until Christmas morning. When we awakened, we couldn't wait to hurry into the hallway, to be met by the fragrant smell of cedar filling the room and our gifts from Santa.

As the years passed, we grew up, married, and had children of our own and Christmas Eve's celebration moved to our parents' home. Now our families have grown so big that no single house can hold us all. We each have Christmas in our own homes for our children and grandchildren. It is hard to believe how the years have flown by . . . we have been so busy *living* . . . while they quietly slipped by.

Yesterday, **Clyde** and I had all our children and grandchildren here for Christmas brunch. There were twenty in all and we marveled at how our family has grown! There is and always has been an abundance of love in our family and we were all delighted to be together. The best gift at Christmas, or any other time, is the gift of love and our family has been blessed through the years. Loving God and loving each other . . . there's nothing like it!!

Pastor Alta Chase-Raper

As we celebrate Jesus birth, we celebrate the **Love** that came down at Christmas!

Love came down at Christmas, Love all lovely, Love divine;
Love was born at Christmas; star and angels gave the sign.
Worship we the Godhead, Love incarnate, Love divine;
Worship we our Jesus, but wherewith for sacred sign?
Love shall be our token; love be yours and love be mine;
Love to God and all men, love for plea and gift and sign.
United Methodist Hymnal #242

Lost in Christmas

December 16, 2007

Clyde came home from the hospital this past Monday afternoon, after an almost three week stay. We have now bought and paid for an entire wing at UT Hospital! Surely, they will be contacting us soon for the dedication and naming of the new wing. Ah yes, you know I'm joking.

Last night, after a very hectic week, Clyde and I went out for a nice quiet dinner. Something we both needed. When we finished eating, we were like two kids as we anxiously left the restaurant so we could see all the Christmas lights in town as they glowed and twinkled in the night. Each of us was lost in our own thoughts of Christmas past and Christmas present. There is something special when you can share the joys of the season with your sweetie. The one you have known and loved for so many years and the one who can still make your heart sing with his presence.

The Sundays of Advent focus first on *hope*, then *peace, joy*, and finally *love*, in that order. This morning we will light the third candle of Advent, the candle of "joy." We realize, feel, and experience the great joy the Christ Child's birth brought to earth. The joy of forgiveness, of salvation, of knowing we have an advocate, an intercessor, a friend, a redeemer, one who is closer than a brother and one who never leaves us alone. Hallelujah for that!!!

Jesus brought with him many gifts! He brought sight to the blind, he made the lame to walk, the deaf to hear, the dead were raised, and the Good News that the world had been longing to hear was manifest in His one extraordinary life. The best gift of all is Christ brought eternal life to all who would believe on Him. What a wonderful gift!!! If you have not accepted that gift . . . you must!

Just imagine Christ with us, Christ in us, and Christ all about us. Today let His joy fill your heart as we sing *"Joy to the World, the Lord is come. Let earth receive her king! Let every heart prepare him room, and heaven and nature sing!" ". . . Joseph, thou son of David, fear not to take unto thee Mary thy wife: for that which is conceived in her is of the Holy Ghost. And she shall bring forth a son, and thou shalt call his name Jesus: for he shall save his people from their sins." Matthew 1:20b-21 (KJV)*

Christmas Waves Its Magic Wand

December 7, 2008

Christmas in Pittman Center!!! What an exciting time of year!! Norman Vincent Peale once said *"Christmas waves a magic wand over this world, and behold, everything is softer and more beautiful."* I couldn't agree more. I begin getting ready for Christmas just as soon as Thanksgiving Dinner is over and the dishes are put away. The tree goes up that afternoon and becomes alive with crystal clear lights mingling with the green boughs as they cast a warm glow on the soft colors of the many birds nestled there. When we moved to the mountains almost nine years ago my usual Christmas tree ornaments gave way to a collection of beautiful birds that perch in its branches.

Pittman Center's Christmas Luncheon was down at City Hall on Friday. Oh, what delicious food we had . . . and lots of it; big chunks of baked ham, thick slices of turkey with dressing and gravy, veggies, salads, rolls, and we washed it all down with sweet iced tea or coffee. For dessert, there was decadent pecan pie and everyone's favorite, banana pudding! As we were leaving, **G and Vickie Webb** made us 'ooh and aah' as each of us were given a beautiful print of G's latest painting "Changing Seasons."

All of this took place in the upper floor meeting room of our historic City Hall. If you are ever passing through this area and would like to view a bit of history, stop by and ask for a tour. **Susette Huskey**, author of "The Sound of His Voice" a collection of her poetry and songs, is also the secretary of Pittman Center. She will gladly show you around. What a joyous couple of hours was had by all the employees, staff, governing body of Pittman Center, their guests, and me, their little old gray-haired Preacher Lady.

And I've saved the best for last! Last night was the Annual Lighting of the Yule Log which was outside the Pavilion at City Hall. It took me almost as long to get dressed as it took me to walk down there. First I pulled on my black tights, then black socks, then long-janes, wool pants, and boots that came up to my knees. Brrrr, it sure does get cold here in Pittman Center, (just a little dip down between the mountains). I put on my heavy winter coat with my bright red scarf wrapped around my neck. Then on with my gloves; at last I was ready to brave the cold air. I looked like that little boy in the Christmas movie, I was so bundled up. You could have tied a string around my middle and rolled me down the hill past the school to the pavilion where the festivities were held . . . lol I did manage to waddle down there just before time to begin. I had a great time and really did stay warm as a bug in a rug!!!

The night was filled with nostalgia as the yule log was set a'blaze by **Mayor Glenn Cardwell** and the sparks resembled lightning bugs as they flew up into the cold dark night. Mayor Glenn told the story of the Lighting of the Yule Log for all those who had not heard it before. We gathered under the pavilion and sang Christmas Carols, drank hot coffee, hot chocolate, or my favorite, hot mulled apple cider. There were lots of Christmas goodies to munch on and soon Santa arrived to greet all the children, let them sit on his lap and tell him what they wanted for Christmas. I came home excited, happy, and smelling like smoke, but with my heart filled with the sights and sounds of Christmas in the mountains.

God bless you and yours as you prepare for the miracle of His birth. Jesus truly is the only reason we celebrate Christmas! May the news of His birth bring the joy and contentment of the Christmas Season into your heart and home!! *"Now the God of hope fill you with all joy and peace in believing, that ye may abound in hope, through the power of the Holy Ghost."* *Romans 15:13 (KJV)*

A God of Surprises
December 9, 2007

Today is the Second Sunday of Advent and we will be lighting the Candle of Peace in all our churches. If there could be one gift we would all wish for, it would have to be the gift of peace. Peace that begins in our hearts (Jesus) and then traverses our entire being with the feeling of things being *right* and *good*. Have you experienced that peace? I truly pray that you have; there is nothing that can compare! I want to share with you a story of an unexpected gift of peace that was received by a classmate of mine from high school, **Charlyne Foster**. She has been struggling with the loss of a dear friend for the past five years. This is a portion of what she wrote:

"I was in Sevier today to put flowers on Mary Emily's grave. It worked out to be a special trip. It rained on me all the way to the cemetery. Then when I got there it stopped. Of all the trips I have made there, this was a little different. It was so peaceful there. You could not hear the traffic at all. For the first time in five years, I did feel more peaceful. The drive home it rained, but still the peaceful feeling was there. I hope my soul can be a little more at rest. Her death really put my soul in turmoil. My life has never been the same since. I hope this is a new beginning." As I read her words, I wanted to shout out loud, "What a wonderful gift God has given you!" There are so many times when we are unexpectedly surprised by God . . . truly He is a God of surprises . . . and this was a good one!

God's grace is limitless in getting us through times of difficulty and times when we are feeling alone. He is always there, waiting for us to turn toward Him. He wants us to be happy and enjoy life to the fullest! Try to let God surprise you this Christmas. Look for Him in the crispness of winter, the shake of a stranger's hand, the sparkle in a child's eyes, the touch of someone you love, the ringing of bells, the smell of spiced tea, the light from a candle, the singing of carols, and the peace in your heart. Do something good for someone else, then sit back and wait as the blessing from that act of kindness will wrap you up like a warm blanket.

My prayer for you today is that God will bless you with the gift of peace this Christmas! The pure peace that came down from Heaven was laid in a manger in Bethlehem. And the angels sang and clapped their hands . . .

All Things Work Together
December 31, 2006

Here we are on the morning of the last day of 2006!!! Can you believe it? Where has the year gone? It really is true that time flies when you're having fun. Through all the years of my life, the last six years spent in these beautiful mountains have been the happiest and most rewarding of all. God has blessed me at every breaking of dawn, every sunrise and sunset, with blessings I never dreamed possible.

There is a lot of difference in waking up dreading to go to work and waking up excited to begin the day. Most of my work experiences have been good ones with only two being not so good. One of my first jobs was political and therein I found my biggest disappointment. I began working as a deputy clerk in the Circuit Court Clerk's office of Bradley County in the early 60s. I fell in love with the job, but after four years my very good boss, **Clay King**, was not reelected. Being young and naïve, especially in the field of politics, when I was asked by the newly elected Clerk (who had no experience in the court system) to stay and train his girls, I thought it was an honor and an affirmation of my worth. Wrong! After only a few months when he and all the girls were trained I was told that (*his political party*) had said he had to get rid of me. They said he just couldn't have a (*the other party*) working for him, *it was bad for his image*. It was then I realized truth and politics do not always go together.

A rival insurance agency lured me away from the agency where I had worked for 22 years and had become Vice President. Promises were made regarding my future if I joined their agency. I accepted the offer and immediately knew it was a mistake. I was miserable in their fine establishment when I discovered they cared nothing for the *people* who brought them their business, only the amount of their money was important.

All things worked together to bring me to where I am today! God allowed me to accept His calling on my life after nineteen years! He was there all along waiting for me to get my priorities in order. My new Boss is perfect in every way. He keeps His promises, is kind, good, understanding, sympathetic, compassionate, forgiving, loving, and He wants only the best for me. He provides all the life insurance and fire insurance I could possibly ever need and it is free! The rewards and bonuses are the best and I can't wait to make 2007, our best year ever!! And may you and yours enjoy great joy, perfect peace, good health, and love beyond measure in the coming New Year!

"And we know that all things work together for good to those that love God, to them who are the called according to his purpose." Romans 8:28 (KJV)

A Gift of Toilet Paper
December 24, 2006

And so in Bethlehem, a tiny village where King David was born and grew up a thousand years before . . . another child was born. *"But thou, O Bethlehem Ephratah, though thou be little among the thousands of Judah, yet out of thee shall he come forth unto me that is to be ruler in Israel; whose goings forth have been from of old, from everlasting." Micah 5:2 (KJV)* God came in Jesus Christ and he came with such depth of love it is hard to imagine. He embodies perfect peace, *shalom.*

As Mary held her newborn son, she must have felt a mixture of emotions knowing that she held the Savior of the world in her arms as she experienced the indescribable joy of motherhood. How she must have loved her little boy; yet as she held him she knew he belonged to the world. But for that one extraordinary night he belonged to her. The joy of Christmas was in her arms.

Christmas comes in many different ways to many different people. This morning, I'm thinking of last night and the joy our family felt as we visited the **Crossville Mission Bible Training Center. MBTC** is a faith-based ministry housing 35-75 residents plus staff as it serves as a Christian in-house rehabilitation center. My **youngest son** is in their treatment program. His addiction was (is) to a prescription drug known as *adderall.* He is doing great and will soon know more about the Bible than I do. All of the residents attend counseling and in-depth Bible study five hours a day in a program that lasts from eight to ten months. If you want to know more about this program, visit their website at *missionteens.com.* The Pittman Center charge chose them as their 2006 Christmas mission project.

Last night we drove a 10 foot U-Haul filled to overflowing with paper products, cleaning supplies, industrial mops, canned food, and a cash donation from each church.

I must tell you something funny *(you know me I have to get your attention)* while it also teaches us a lesson in humility and being thankful. When I called the mission to make an appointment to deliver our love offering, I was asked to give them an idea of how much and what I would be bringing so they could prepare storage space. I was going to run down the entire list of items but I only got out the first one "480 rolls of toilet paper" when the young woman responded "Praise God!" Folks how long has it been since you saw a whole group of people get excited over a supply of toilet paper? I hope this causes you to ponder deeply as you open your own gifts Christmas morning.

May you all have a blessed and peaceful Christmas with perfect shalom!

When I Die

When I die
I will dance
Just above the horizon
With everything
Patched and mended
Where nothing hurts
Anymore.
Where memories
Break through the clouds
To the beat of the thunder
And the shine of lightning
To be destroyed forever.
Where blue jays wing
Pirouettes with sparrows
And rainbows ring
My wrists and head
Healing.
And otters will rise up
Leaping and somersaulting
All around me.
Ocean waves will clap wildly
While I bow
And the mountains bow
And I blow kisses
And give God permission
To draw the final curtain.

*Penned by a dear friend, **Connie Wright***
and given to me on January 4, 1994;
a gift of words I will always cherish.